The
Sustainability
Revolutionists

HEROES AND HOPE FOR OUR PLANET'S FUTURE

LUCIA ATHENS

Foreword by Betty Sue Flowers

throughline
press

Printed in the United States.

Cover and book design by Asya Blue Design.

ISBN 979-8-9861048-0-5 Paperback
ISBN 979-8-9861048-2-9 Hardcover
ISBN 979-8-9861048-1-2 Ebook

*For Lance Hosey, a voice for the sustainability revolution
that was quieted too soon.*

*And for my darling Bill, who can always be counted on
to dance at the revolution.*

Acknowledgments

I owe a huge debt of gratitude to my editor, Ron Seybold, who was a tireless cheerleader for this book and who drove many inspired creative decisions. Much appreciation to Asya Blue, whose graphic designs helped to make this book sing. Thank you also to the Rockefeller Foundation, which provided a residency where this book began.

Thank you to all the wonderful readers who gave feedback along this journey, including Jason Twill, Thor Peterson, Gina LaMotte, Martha Latta, Daryl Slusher, Susan Kaplan, Chris Fontana, Ashton Cumberbatch, and Chris Castro.

Table of Contents

PART ONE: Jacques Cousteau and the Ocean Revolution

PART TWO: Anita Roddick and the Green Business Revolution

PART THREE: César Chávez and the Farmworker Revolution

Foreword

A colleague who works with climate change activists recently told me that a key problem in the community has been the high rate of burnout.

"People are discouraged about the slow rate of progress," he said.

"Yes," I said, "and the climate scientists I work with are quite cynical about the pledges of the Paris agreement being met. We need to find sources of realistic hope."

Thinking back over that conversation, I realize we need to go beyond realistic hope to galvanizing inspiration. We need heroes and stories and a sense of the guiding principles—the rules of the road—that will help get us there. And we need playfulness and joy.

"Playfulness" and "joy" are not words I've ever used in relation to a book on sustainability and our planet's future. What makes The Sustainability Revolutionists so remarkable is that by telling us stories of "heroes and hope," Lucia Athens inspires us to see solutions to the most difficult challenges as well within the realm of the possible. Determined people have succeeded before in making a real difference. Why can't we?

Athens imagines dinner conversations with some of the pioneers who've had a revolutionary impact on people, planet, or profit—the three pillars of sustainability.

The stories of these revolutionaries are not simply entertaining or inspiring. They also illustrate universal guiding principles that serve as powerful foundations for action. Understanding that living systems are interconnected, for example, changes the way we look at economic decisions that might have far-reaching effects beyond the present. Or judging economic activity through its "mission to serve" could lead to changes in consumer behavior.

Even if any one of the nine core values that Athens describes were put into practice, the world would change. Inclusive empowerment, for example, would ensure that the poorest in the world had enough energy to have a better life even as we work for a healthy planet.

Climate change seems so difficult to address in part because of its scale. But though the scale of the problem is immense, Athens reminds us that individuals do make a difference. The problem is global, the solutions are local, even personal—interconnected systems of sustainable action that emerge from individuals making decisions at every level.

Change doesn't happen automatically or straightforwardly. Perhaps even more important, revolutionary change is unpredictable. The only thing we can predict is that nothing will happen if we don't try. The gloomy cynicism that so often arises in response to the truly existential threat of climate change can lead to nihilistic apathy, an acceptance of the inevitable.

Solutions emerge when people are in action toward a goal, when they are inspired or energized enough to do something. By telling the stories of sustainability heroes, Athens helps create the hope necessary for revolution to happen. She seems to understand the need for an approach that lifts us up above the swamp of despair in which we stay stuck and do nothing. As part of its joyful mission, The Sustainability Revolutionists offers us Jack Frager's words: "If I can't dance, I don't want to be part of your revolution." If despair seems a realistic response to the climate challenges threatening our planet's future, then this book leads us beyond everyday realism to extend an invitation to the revolution.

— Betty Sue Flowers
Co-author, *Presence: Human Purpose and the Field of the Future*
PBS Series Consultant, *Moyers: Joseph Campbell and the Power of Myth*

Our Moment of Change

We now find ourselves in an era defined by a heroic struggle for our planetary future. This book is for you if, like thousands of others, you have realized that sustainability's moment has finally come. The signals are disturbing and undeniable. Our global biodiversity crisis now threatens a million species with extinction at a rapidly accelerating pace. Widespread climate disasters, including wildfires, floods, and droughts tell us our planetary support systems are careening toward collapse, leaving Earth uninhabitable. Outcries against the meaningless deaths of Blacks, often at the hands of whites in positions of power, have brought the racism crisis into clear focus.

One of our biggest challenges is that there are still many among us who are left out of the story. Sustainability is an integrative and inclusive concept, offering up solutions that address and balance environmental, social, and economic needs. Hope is also one of sustainability's critical components. We can't afford to put our heads in the sand, but there is good news to be found if one knows where to look. Part of the purpose of this book is to deliver a greater sense of optimism about our ability to achieve a sustainable future.

This is a book for optimists, but it is also a book for those who have lost their sense of optimism about the future, needing a healthy shot in the arm. If you are already a part of the sustainability revolution, I hope this book will speed you on your way. If not, I enlist you to lock arms with so many others in bringing sustainability to every corner of the planet, into every heart and mind.

I first learned about sustainability from my father, who was the chairman of the Sierra Club chapter of San Antonio, the city where I grew up. He often took us hiking and camping. He was the sustainability hero of my childhood, leading a fight against building a major freeway that would eventually cut its way past nearby urban parks and the city's zoo. I watched and learned from him about how to speak up and get involved. But this book doesn't tell his story. I'll leave that for another day.

This book explores the complex topic of sustainability. It isn't just about environmental concerns, although those are at the core. It's equally about social justice issues. It's equally about economic issues. Given the breadth and scope of the various and equally important ramifications to be considered, how do we make sense of all of it? We must listen to the voices of those with power, as well as those who lack it. We must take into consideration causes and effects that may never have occurred to us before. As we gather all of these voices together to be heard, how do we prevent it all from just becoming noise?

A useful metaphor for what sustainability needs now is a bigger dinner table. Sustainability is a rich topic, with something for everyone, no matter their politics, background, or vocation. There is a saying that advises us that "When you have more than you need, build a bigger table, not a higher fence." Gathering around that great big table is the metaphor for this book's story. Sustainability must set a very large table to make sure there is a place for everyone. The bigger the table, the better our chances at succeeding. Sustainability can feed the body of our planet and the soul of our existence. We must be sure to make room for both the head and the heart at the table.

As humans who are a part of something we call civilization, we have a responsibility to engage with the world around us, to engage in good work to make it better. This is a book about revolutionists, people who are by definition activists; they *act* to create the change they want to see. Revolutionists don't sit around waiting for change to happen. They are rarely spectators. They ascribe to the aphorism "No one is coming. It's up to us."

On an emotional level, this book hopes to open our hearts, with the potential to lead to a transformation of consciousness. As a more practical matter, this book is intended to deepen our shared intellectual understanding of sustainability's core concepts. Such a foundation could support better collaboration for those struggling to work across the aisle, or a negotiating table, with people of different viewpoints. The values articulated here seek to establish a common conceptual framework for tackling our many challenges, a sort of sustainability decoder ring.

My Imaginary Dinner Party: Setting the Table

As we roll up our sleeves to make sustainability less of a dream and more of a reality, we begin with the idea of a dinner party. There, we can feed ourselves, nourished by the words and experiences of a few key revolutionists around the dinner table.

Have you ever played the imaginary dinner party game? In this game, you get to choose anyone, living or dead, to invite to your table. Who would you choose? I remember the Christmas my 7-year-old nephew included Einstein, Van Gogh, and Beethoven on his guest list. A scientist, a painter, and a composer. Now there's a gathering of distinctive viewpoints. That was the year I realized my nephew, in spite of his years, might already have been the wisest person at our table.

A good dinner party is not about picking the people who are most like you. It's about variety. Choosing guests with differing backgrounds and viewpoints creates a lively mix, one more likely to result in a memorable evening filled with the sound of "a-ha." If we surround ourselves only with people just like us, we are unlikely to grow or learn anything new. Sustainability relies on both. It's the tension between different viewpoints and approaches that generates energy, the chance to stretch ourselves and discover new potentiality.

In her fascinating book *The Art of Gathering: How We Meet and Why It Matters*, Priya Parker says, "We gather to solve problems we can't solve on our own. We gather because we need one another." If sitting alone in my home office during the pandemic taught me one thing, it's that I need other people. Sustainability is a problem that can't be solved in isolation. We need to connect with others, to share our dreams, kick the tires on our ideas, and build our collective muscle.

In my imagined dinner gathering, I have invited three of my sustainability heroes, people I consider my wise elders. In real life, none of us ever met. We are each from very different worlds and backgrounds. I have chosen these particular guests not only because I hold them in high regard, but also because I believe each of them embodies important sustainability wisdom that should be shared.

In addition to their other talents, I am hopeful that each guest will prove themselves to be something called a deipnosophist: a conversationalist skilled in table talk. A word we rarely encounter in common usage, Merriam-Webster included it in their 2021 "Great Big List of Beautiful Words." The etymology of the word comes from an ancient Greek play by Athenaeus entitled *The Deipnosophists*. Its dramatic events are primarily a series of lengthy discussions around a banquet table. It would be the chance of a lifetime to be able to talk to each of my heroes individually, but what magic might result if we were all gathered at the same banquet table for one evening?

Even though I wasn't entirely sure my guests would get along, I could be hopeful about the variety. Environmental sea icon Jacques Cousteau might share what it feels like to witness the wonder of our natural world, followed by the heartbreak at its degradation. We need his wisdom to dig ourselves out of the ecological mess we have created. We could all use a dose of his Pied Piper storytelling skills.

Anita Roddick, founder of retailer The Body Shop, might have advice about fearlessly rolling up sleeves to take on big institutional challenges.

We could all use a dose of her decisive sense of rebellion against outmoded traditions, as well as her courage.

César Chávez, renowned disciple of labor equity, would most certainly bring balance to the group, injecting his quiet wisdom and compassion when we needed it most. We could all use a dose of his clarity and patience.

As we can already see from the need to consult such varied viewpoints, sustainability will require us to hold many potentially conflicting ideas at once, and thus to find a form of balanced synthesis. This is no easy task. Take the dinner party I have planned, and the seemingly simple decision of whether to serve fish. Cousteau might want to focus on whether the fish was a species experiencing overfishing. Roddick might want to focus on whether humane methods were used in the way the fish was caught. And Chávez would be likely to focus on the livelihood of the fisherman. But if everyone is hungry, how may we address their needs equitably, considering sustainability's rubric? These challenges force us to consult people from outside our comfort zone, from entirely different viewpoints than our own. At first, we might not even appear to share the same values. Often, if we dig deeper, we may find that we have more in common than appears on the surface. But this requires patience, and good listening skills.

Sustainability needs this diversity of perspectives to form the deep well of wisdom needed now. Diverse viewpoints must be brought to the table. For this dinner party gathering, we have balanced gender with half the party being men, the other half women. We have cultural and ethnic diversity, with both European and North American perspectives, although admittedly we don't have all continents represented. We have a person of color in Chavez's Latino heritage. We also have a working-class perspective from both Chávez and Roddick. Sustainability will require a sort of hive-mind of creative problem-solving, pulling in every possible perspective and source of wisdom, from every corner of our planet. As Einstein said, "We cannot solve our problems with the same thinking we used when we created them."

If the evening is a success, our group's collective wisdom will be hard to ignore. I can hardly wait for my guests to arrive.

LIGHTING THE CANDLES

It is a perfect summer evening for a gathering. I have greeted each guest warmly at the door, showing them where to put their things and welcoming them into my home.

I have arranged the places with all my favorite dishes, wineglasses, and napkins. The food, the flowers, the lighting, the music—I have thought through each detail carefully. This is a special occasion, a gathering that I am hoping will last for hours into the night. In honor of my guests, I have mapped out a ten-course meal, far more elaborate than anything I would serve on a typical day.

I often eat very simply. Once you realize how tasty and satisfying eating beans can be, it becomes a lot easier to eat less meat. But on this night, I can't imagine serving a hero such as César Chávez a plate of beans. I hope my guests will realize that the fanciness of the meal they are about to eat is an indicator how much I revere their presence at my dinner table.

Now that everyone has been introduced, we have all settled into our seats at the table. As the host, it's now up to me to set the tone for the evening. I rise from my seat, taking in the unique presence of each of these amazing humans. I speak unhurriedly, savoring the moment that has finally arrived.

"Thank you all for coming. It is such a privilege to be your host. This evening is about something I have come to call the Sustainability Revolution. Each of you has been invited tonight because of your revolutionary efforts toward our bright future here on planet Earth."

I've chosen my next words carefully. I want to prepare my guests for what is about to happen. "You are my heroes. I have a dream of honoring what you have achieved, of finding a way to share your wisdom into the future. I agree to guide you through this evening, to serve you delicious food and keep the wine flowing."

Cousteau leaned forward. "All these accolades can make one a bit nervous, Lucia. But now that you have mentioned the wine, I'm sure I'll be able to relax sufficiently." He chuckled to himself as he glanced around the table.

I continued on, ensuring that I was able to finish making my point before the conversation veered too far into our personalities. "Good to hear, my friend. For each of your parts, I'm asking you to tell us stories that share who you are and what you believe. I'm asking you to bring all of yourself to the table, your successes as well as your failures. We must share every lesson learned on this journey, so we can help others joining the revolution."

Anita seems the most eager, bouncing in her chair, full of energy. She pushes back her trademark lustrous mane of wild brown hair. "Revolution is my middle name. Of course, I'm in! I've been looking forward to this evening for as long as I can remember."

César speaks next. He has always been a man of few and carefully chosen words. His ability to make every person he speaks with feel like they are the most important in the world is key to the farmworker revolution he helped lead. He speaks slowly, with conviction, gazing levelly into my eyes and then into the face of each person in the room in turn. "Muchas gracias for the invitation. It is indeed an honor to be included in this group. I promise to bring you my best."

Next it is Cousteau's turn. He pats my hand conspiratorially, smiling in that totally disarming way he has, eyes twinkling. His youthful charm has not faded, even in my imagination. "Mes amis, how could we possibly refuse such a delightful request from our host? It is with gusto that I join in. However, I feel it my duty to point out, the sooner the wine gets to flowing, the better the stories will be."

The group laughs, and everyone relaxes a bit. Relieved that I had remembered to open the wine earlier so it could breathe, I begin pouring the deep ruby Bordeaux into the crystal glasses. "I trust that this French vintage meets with your approval, Jacques."

I hope I have set the table for a successful evening. It is time to begin our banquet.

Introduction

Yes, finally the tables are starting to turn.
Talkin' 'bout a revolution.

— **Tracy Chapman**, singer, songwriter

THREE REVOLUTIONISTS
AT THE BANQUET TABLE

Sustainability is a journey, one that is often circuitous, surprising, and filled with challenges. This book will take you on an unforgettable trip, full of stories about faraway places and inspiring people. In her book of sustainability stories *Believers*, Lisa Wells notes, "One of the ways we humans organize and make sense of our experience is through the telling of stories." Through exploring each of the stories within this book, you can experience sustainability as a grand adventure, full of opportunities for change and redemption. At the same time, my heroes of sustainability in action can empower us to think about the topic in new and expansive ways. Each one serves as the archetypal hero of a key area we need to understand. Their sustainability adventure stories can inspire us. They can show us how the fight for sustainability can show up in the real world. Archetypal heroes provide inspiration for us as leaders today.

Why is it important for us to look back on the journeys of these revolutionists? Revolutionists are special people. They are the change-makers, the ones who kick ass and take names, who don't take no for an answer, and who march to the beat of a different drummer. They are the antithesis of the status quo. For anyone who likes to stay comfortable, revolutionists can be the enemy. For those who know things can be better but aren't comfortable leading the way, they are the swimmer who breaks a wake in the current for others to follow.

Revolutions tend to be messy endeavors with winners and losers, but without them we'd be forever stuck in the past, chained to realities that no longer serve us. Revolutionary ideas took us out of the Dark Ages into the Renaissance, and then into the Age of Enlightenment. Without revolutionist thinking, there would be no modern understanding of astronomy, no scientific method, no human rights, no electric vehicles, no constitutional democracy, and no wage equity.

Revolutionists light lamps in the dim days and dark nights when we can't see the way forward. They can point us toward innovations and critical forks in the road. Today we find ourselves poised to break the bonds of a Dark Age of fossil fuels, striving toward an enlightened Renewable Energy Age. A lot of us might not like the way things are, but revolutionists don't just sit around complaining about it. They stand up and do something about it.

The actions of the three central figures in this book were considered ground-breaking in their times. The revolutions they spawned pave the way for our sustainability work today. Some of their ideas that seemed revolutionary now appear to be common sense, based on what we have learned.

Shifting our world from its current unsustainable path will require a revolution of hearts, minds, and bodies. It will require change on virtually every front of society. It will take people from every corner of the planet, at every level, from the grassroots to those in power, to be a part of the change. Revolutionists believe that wild and wise changes are possible. A wide-scale sustainability revolution isn't likely to happen overnight, but every revolutionary act along the arc of sustainability is an act in the right direction. Together, we can get there. Arriving at that future we dream of together, ensuring that no one is left behind, requires us to build upon the wisdom of the Three Pillars of Sustainability.

UNDERSTANDING THE THREE PILLARS OF SUSTAINABILITY

Sustainability is founded upon a widely recognized framework that comprises three key areas: Environmental, Economic, and Social. (Some prefer to use Planet, Profit, and People as an alliterative mnemonic device.) This holy trinity for sustainability practitioners is often referred to as the Three Pillars.

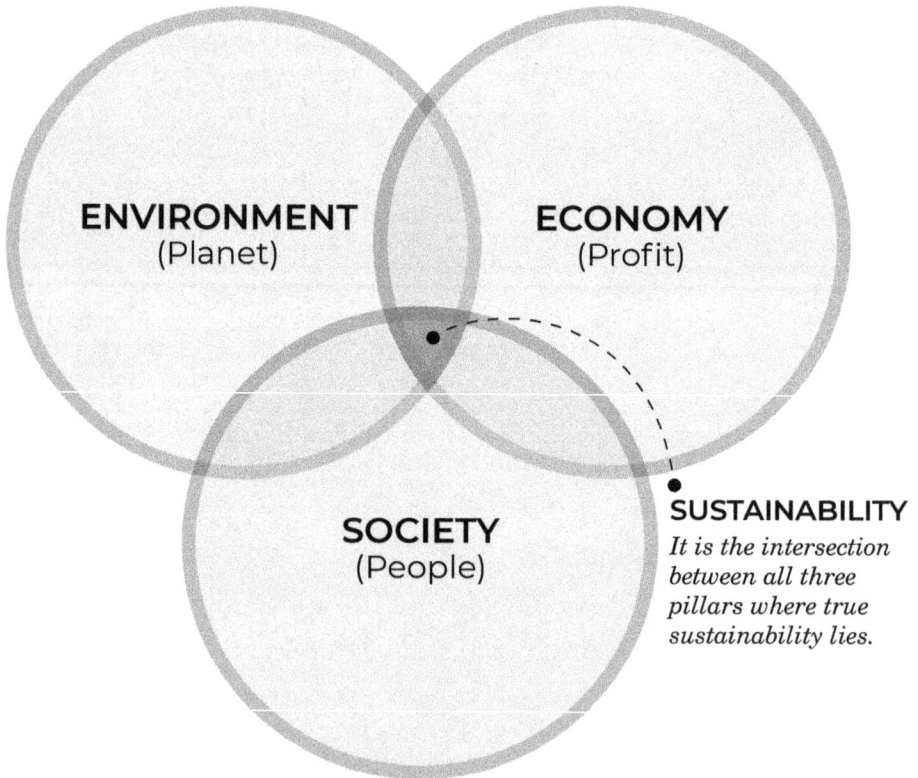

ENVIRONMENT
(Planet)

ECONOMY
(Profit)

SOCIETY
(People)

SUSTAINABILITY
It is the intersection between all three pillars where true sustainability lies.

The Three Pillars of Sustainability

The Three Pillars of Sustainability provide the basic wire frame model upon which to hang any sustainability solution. They provide a foundational framework for different ways of seeing, valuing, and measuring the world. They also represent the essential organizing concept of this book.

The Three Pillars are not a new idea. The widely recognized framework was endorsed in 2005 by the United Nations. This book does not attempt to offer a comprehensive history of the concept of the Three Pillars or the origins of the concept of sustainability. For readers seeking such a genealogy of the movement, I suggest Jeremy Caradonna's excellent book *Sustainability: A History.*

Most people tend to be oriented primarily toward only one of the Three Pillars, the pillar most comfortable to them. This occurs for a variety of reasons including life experience, education, or livelihood. Such frames for seeing the world can influence our perceptions, and people tend to make judgments based on their perceptions.

In messy, complex, real-world situations, we often find ourselves around a negotiating table, trying to muddle through the most sustainable approach to a problem. Take an example of a proposal to build a new roadway. One stakeholder may advocate for solutions that help to deliver on environmental attributes: a parkway lined with trees. Another stakeholder may promote economically-based solutions: a higher-speed roadway designed to move traffic quickly and efficiently. A third preaches solutions that prioritize community and social concerns: adding bike lanes and sidewalks to create choices and better health outcomes for people trying to get from point A to point B. While everyone may think they are championing the cause of sustainability, this diverse group of individuals simply doesn't want the same thing; they don't understand one another because they are motivated by a highly contrasting set of values.

Each of the Three Pillars is critical to sustainability in its own right. But it is the intersection between all three where true sustainability lies. While making strides in only one or two of the Three Pillars represents good progress, our best future lies only through interconnected solutions that address all three simultaneously. This simultaneous understanding is a significant challenge. Driven by a sense of urgency, we often dive into sustainability problem-solving without taking the time to fully understand the perspectives of diverse collaborators.

If we can't first empathize with the Core Values that motivate behaviors and opinions of people who are not like us, sustainability is not going to get very far. This book can be a tool to establish a fuller understanding of the meaning of sustainability, based upon the underlying values of the Pillars. Once this occurs, we can unlock new sustainability solutions, based upon better collaboration among people across a wide variety of disciplines and viewpoints. This is the only way transformational change will happen.

A ROADMAP TO THIS BOOK

This is literary nonfiction. This is not a book of solutions. There are many books that offer that. This is a book offering a way to think about and frame the solutions you might come up with. It is about learning to fish, rather than being served a fish. This is a book of real-life sustainability adventure stories, intended to entertain and delight you. The vehicle of imagination and literary nonfiction storytelling is used to make events come alive for the reader, weaving imagined details into fact. Therefore, most of the stories are re-imaginations of true events. Even though many of the minor details are imagined, each story is based on events that really happened, grounded upon facts and research.

There are three major heroes. There are three major Parts to the book, a Part tied to each of my three central revolutionists in the sustainability movement. These three protagonists are influential change agents who walked the earth in fairly recent history. Of course, there are many heroes to choose from. I hope this book will encourage readers to find their own sustainability heroes and learn their stories.

If you are wondering what led me to choose the major heroes, here are a few of the criteria I used in making my selections. First, I wanted each of the three revolutionists to have made a major contribution through their life's work, work that continues to resonate today. Second, I wanted them to be fairly well known and familiar to a very broad audience. Third, I wanted the heroes to have lived in the fairly recent past to make them more relatable to the modern reader. I have selected individuals who are no longer alive—which means their legacy is well documented and fairly well established.

These heroes deliver a healthy dose of humanity in our study of sustainability. Their stories demonstrate a set of values-in-action informing the lives they lived. Like all humans, these three heroes are flawed individuals. Each made mistakes along their own journey, which also led to their being transformed by their experiences. By holding them up as examples, I am not implying that these people are perfect. My intent is to focus on the best in them, and what we can learn about sustainability based on their experiences, good as well as bad. Their experiences established a legacy which is ours to continue, if we so choose.

Each Pillar is matched with Three Core Values. For the Three Pillars of Sustainability, I have developed an original framework, based on my own professional experience, of three Core Values associated with each Pillar. I consider those three Core Values to be essential to that Pillar. In order to bring each Core Value alive, a story about the associated revolutionist is used to illustrate the concept. Within that story section, there is a short essay that is set aside graphically, providing a distillation and overview of that Core Value concept. Many of the ideas captured within the Core Value essays are not original to me. However, over my years of working in the field, I have synthesized the ideas into a unified theory of sustainability.

Each Core Value also includes a story about one in a pantheon of nine contemporary heroes. These are people carrying on the important work of sustainability throughout today's world, from Australia's Great Barrier Reef to Puerto Rico's vibrant neighborhoods. These are referred to as Modern-day Revolutionists in the chapter headings. Contemporary stories remind us that there are sustainability heroes we may have never heard of, doing work just around the corner. They bring the perspective of each Core Value right up to date.

Diagrams provide guideposts. Each Part and each Chapter begins with a diagram. These diagrams form a visual roadmap intended to guide the reader through the wire frame structure of the book. The diagrams provide the reader a map of where they are among Three Pillars, and the associated Core Values.

The Imaginary Dinner Party continues throughout the book. Along the way, we'll refresh ourselves at the Imaginary Dinner Party in brief vignettes at the beginning of each Chapter. It's a long evening of a ten-course dinner, so each of these interludes is referred to as courses in the dinner party. After all, we will want to savor such a unique gathering. We can pause to refresh and enjoy ourselves along this journey. Sustainability isn't always a burdensome slog. There can be dancing at the revolution. There should be joy and revelry, too. This is a journey that can be filled with delight.

A note on my own history and appropriation. Let's be perfectly clear. I am a white cisgender American woman. Even though my Italian and Greek immigrant ancestors experienced discrimination after they arrived in this country, that has not been my experience. I grew up in a major American city, as part of the middle class. I never had to worry about having enough to eat, losing my home, being subjected to police brutality, or feeling safe in my neighborhood. I went to high school with mostly white people. Later I could afford college and home ownership. I have had access to incredible opportunities, including the opportunity to acquire wealth. I was born into a life of privilege, and I still live a life full of those advantages.

I have chosen the stories that are included in this book based on a desire to celebrate these journeys, and to learn from them. I have attempted to do so respectfully, and have done research to ensure that I'm sharing stores based on facts. However, there's no getting around it; these stories, for the most part, are not my own. The tales are mostly about people I have never even met. I hope that others will receive the stories in the spirit in which they are intended, as admired icons. They are offered up with respect, as beacons of hope for a better, more just, more sustainable world for us all.

PART ONE

The Environmental Pillar of Sustainability in Action

JACQUES COUSTEAU AND THE OCEAN REVOLUTION

CHAPTER ONE

Who was Jacques Cousteau?

"The happiness of the bee and the dolphin is to exist.
For man, it is to know that and to wonder at it."

— Jacques Cousteau

THREE SUSTAINABILITY PILLARS

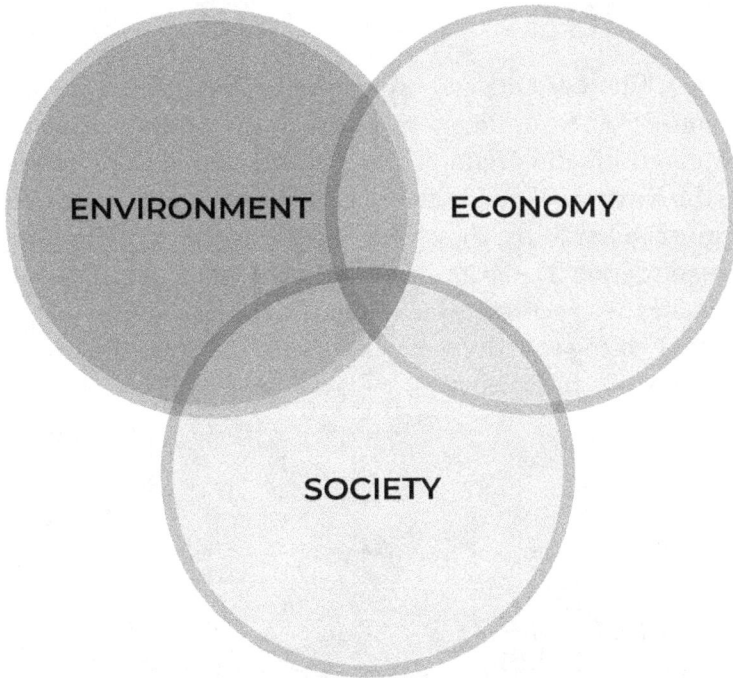

The Three Pillars of Sustainability,
Emphasizing the Environment Pillar

The **Environmental** Pillar is the focus of Part One. Environmental revolutionist Jacques Cousteau serves as the primary hero of this set of sustainability adventure stories.

INTRODUCING THREE ENVIRONMENTAL SUSTAINABILITY CORE VALUES

The stories in Chapter One will provide some background on the revolutionist Jacques Cousteau. Chapters Two, Three, and Four present a series of stories about his life organized around the three Core Values which underpin the Environmental Pillar of sustainability. These Core Values are **Interconnected Systems**, **Biophilic Stewardship**, and **The Long View**.

As we explore the life of Cousteau, his personal and professional journey will illustrate these essential values. Each Core Value story will conclude by highlighting a modern-day hero who continues the work to bring this essential value to fruition.

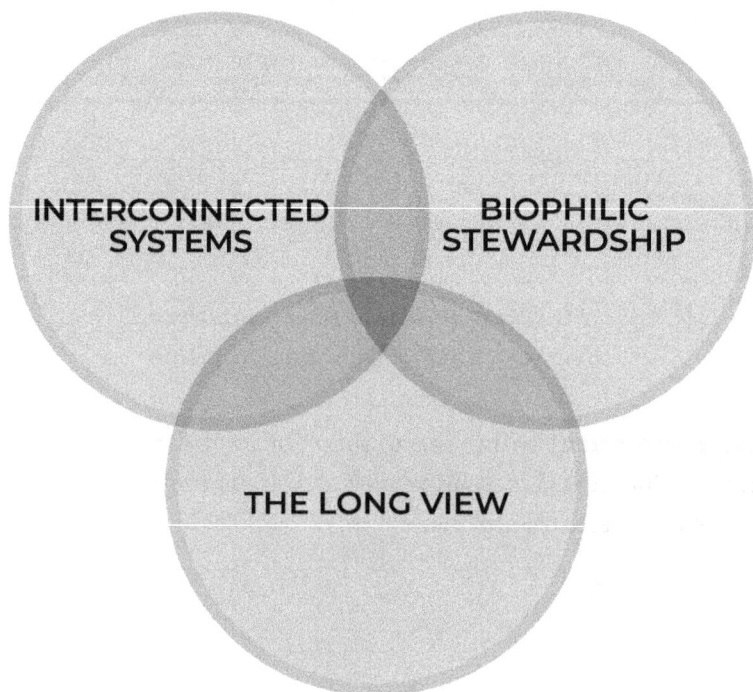

INTERCONNECTED SYSTEMS

BIOPHILIC STEWARDSHIP

THE LONG VIEW

Three Core Values of the Environmental Pillar

AN INTRODUCTION TO AN ENVIRONMENTAL REVOLUTIONIST

Jacques Yves Cousteau, born in 1910, was one of the most recognized people of the late 1960s and early 1970s, a charismatic voice for the environment and the world's oceans. During his life he played many roles: explorer, inventor, author, documentary filmmaker, war spy, and celebrity. An early experimenter in underwater diving and cinematography, he later perfected diving and camera equipment that made these hobbies widely available to amateurs. Cousteau won three Oscars for producing and directing mesmerizing, innovative films. His most famous role by far was as the star of his films, the captain of his ship *Calypso*. His research vessel's voyages spanned hundreds of thousands of miles and gathered millions of feet of documentary film footage. Cousteau's talent for storytelling was his greatest gift.

Cousteau was a man who allowed himself to be transformed by life's experiences. Within his own adulthood, he became witness to terrible human-inflicted changes wreaked upon the oceans he loved. But as a young and naive man, with little means to finance his explorer's dreams, he took on lucrative commissions to explore for oil in the Persian Gulf, something no self-respecting environmentalist would do today. Rather than being tempted to become a part of the fossil fuel industry, Cousteau instead chose to devote his life to sharing his love for the underwater world—and then later, preaching the need to stop degrading it.

He was not afraid to admit his own mistakes. During one early expedition, his crew brutally killed a shark in vengeance against the shark's attack on a baby whale. He refused to air the episode years later when asked. Looking back, he admitted that he didn't know any better at the time, and that this behavior would be unacceptable today. As an environmental revolutionist, he saw, ahead of his time, that human misbehavior was destroying the planetary systems upon which we depend. He made it his personal mission to act upon what he told others: "We have to do something."

The *Calypso* origin story echoes that of the plowshare beaten from the sword: The ship was originally a WW II minesweeper. Patron Joel Guinness (of Guinness beer) bought the vessel for Cousteau and sold it to him for a dollar. The cannons, guns, and mine-sweeping gear were promptly removed to make way for mini-submarines, a helicopter pad, a science lab, and a sub-surface observation chamber created by modifying the hull.[1] Christening the ship *Calypso* was an homage to the mythological Greek sea nymph,[2] daughter of the sea god Oceanus, who kept Odysseus company in an island cave in Homer's tales. Cousteau's outspoken lyricism, combined with his media acumen, made him a highly successful evangelist, able to engage and inspire millions about the beauty and fragility of nature—a true Revolutionary. At his funeral mass, then-president Jacques Chirac of France called him "a poet of an inaccessible reality."

Cousteau traveled the world telling tales of "the water planet." At the time, people weren't really talking about sustainability. They were just beginning to awaken to a new concern for the fate of the environment. Able to enrapture countless school children as well as adults with his charm and obvious delight in nature, he produced more than 120 television documentaries and dozens of books. Between 1966 and 1975, ABC ran thirty-six episodes of *The Undersea World of Jacques Cousteau*, reaching ten to twelve million people per episode and winning seventeen Emmys over the program's lifetime.[3] Often accompanied by his sons Jean-Michel and Phillipe, Jacques swam with giant turtles off Europa Island in Madagascar, frolicked with whales and flying fish, explored shipwrecks and sunken treasure, and braved sharks in underwater caves. It is easy to see from photographs of Cousteau posing with presidents, princesses, and movie stars that he enjoyed celebrity life. Treated like royalty by many, he considered his celebrity mostly a means to an end: enrolling more people in his love affair with the ocean.

Early on, Cousteau merely wanted to explore the oceans and share their beauty. As time went by, he witnessed the vibrant ocean world begin to decay, and thus he also became an evangelist for ocean conservation. Cousteau's greatest passions were exploring the diversity of aquatic life and protecting those natural assets for future generations, leading him to become a sort of Pied Piper of the sea. We can all become storytellers, gathering our tribe around the proverbial home fires to share stories about the heroes in our own lives and the lessons they can teach us. I have had the honor of getting to know Jacques' granddaughter, Alexandra Cousteau. She has inherited her grandfather's skill as an inspirational storyteller, as well as his vocation as a protector of the oceans.

Our environmental revolutionist's story reads like pulp fiction. Named Chevalier of the Legion of Honor for posing as an Italian officer on behalf of the French Resistance, in broad daylight he waltzed into the Toulon waterfront headquarters of Mussolini, took photos of military maps, and strolled out unnoticed. Over decades of diving exploits, he narrowly escaped many brushes with death, including the deadly rapture of the deep narcosis, navigating through dangerous submerged caves, and conducting underwater mine sweeping. Jacques possessed the gift of silver-tongued persuasion, whether convincing French naval authorities to approve his diving exploits, enrolling Louis Malle to assist him in film-making, or cajoling National Geographic Society executives to underwrite yet another research voyage. Using the magic of television, he brought the wonders of the underwater world into the living rooms of families, including my own, who crowded around their television sets anxious to join in each exotic adventure with the crew.

The gorgeous footage featured in *The Undersea World of Jacques Cousteau* was augmented by alluring narration, alternating between the haunting *Twilight Zone* voice of Rod Serling, or Captain Cousteau's mellifluous, heavily French-accented tones. Through the naturalistic style of the shooting, viewers felt an intimate sense of participation and connection with each excursion, as though they had been magically transported to the deck of the *Calypso* for a new adventure each week.

This journalistic style may not sound revolutionary today, but it represents some of the first reality TV. The audience shared in the dive experience as well as the camaraderie of the crew as they gathered around their galley table each night to drink wine, play musical instruments, and review the day's discoveries. It felt as though a curtain had somehow been magically pulled back on the world under the ocean, plus the life of the captain who loved it so much. Jacques always presided over the happenings wearing his signature red knit watchman's cap and gentle sense of authority. All this served to reveal the wonders of the ocean to a broad public audience. Perhaps for the first time, they could see the underwater world as a wondrous and magical playground, instead of a dark and dangerous place to be feared and avoided.

Renowned environmentalist Bill McKibben notes, "Cousteau arrived on the American scene at the first great ecological moment—when *Silent Spring* and David Brower and the burning Cuyahoga River and the first Earth Day were all combined to make us aware that the planet was fragile ... Cousteau divided his career, therefore, between two tasks, equally necessary: getting people to marvel at the beauty of the oceans, and then pointing out how we were destroying them."[4]

But Cousteau, like most human heroes, was far from perfect. It was a different era, to be sure, without our current-day sensitivities to how we impact the environment. This man had no scientific training or credentials, resulting in some of his early expeditions mishandling wildlife and delicate ecological systems. And while I don't mean to excuse these blunders, Cousteau learned from his mistakes. He eventually embraced more ethical treatment of animals, as well as collaboration with credentialed wildlife biologists and ocean scientists. It's important to note here that anyone, from any background, any level of education, can become a part of the sustainability movement. There are countless challenges to tackle. We can work toward sustainability at every scale, from household to boardroom solutions.

In our sustainability journey, we will likely experience many setbacks and disappointments. It is advisable to reserve judgment on such failures, because the pathway to success is also paved with setbacks. As the saying goes, it's okay to fail; just make sure you are failing forward, learning from your mistakes.

NEW WAYS OF SEEING AND BREATHING

Cousteau evolved to become a man in love with life itself, possessing a near-mystical reverence for nature. He wrote in *The Ocean World* about the Earth as "the only planet in the solar system to be endowed with appreciable quantities of liquid water. Life, born in water, must be at least as rare as water in the universe, and as such must be revered, under any of its forms, as a miracle . . . Our 'liquid future' depends upon the foresight, the care, and the love with which we will manage our only water supply: the Oceans."[5] This was likely not a viewpoint he held as a young man. Just where and how did this way of seeing the world begin?

Cousteau first learned to snorkel off the coast of the little fishing village of Le Mourillon. Now absorbed by the city of Toulon, the village sits mid-way between Marseilles and Saint-Tropez on the Southern coast of France. The French fleet have used this strategic location over the centuries as a shipyard, arsenal, and naval dockyards. Protected coves, shallow waters, and a gentle sweep of bay provide an ideal mooring and defensive position. Many shipwrights and French naval officers called the village home.

This is a place where history was often made. The hulking Fort Saint-Louis still looms over the western bay, a reminder of the days of Turkish and Barbary pirate landings. The shipyard was significantly expanded by Cardinal Richelieu as he sought to expand France's naval power. Later, it would provide the setting for a momentous change in Cousteau's life that no one could have predicted. The events leading up to that moment, however, appeared far from fortuitous.

An energetic young man of 23, he had just graduated from the French naval academy in pursuit of his ambition to become a pilot for the l'Aéronavale—and pilots have a need for speed. Just before receiving his wings, he drove his father's Salmson sports car headlong on a dark mountain road as the headlights suddenly shorted out. While lucky to be alive, the resulting accident broke both arms, one of which was so seriously injured, doctors wanted to amputate. He refused. Recovery was excruciatingly slow. Painkillers were the only pathway to sleep. One disappointment followed another. New orders arrived telling him to report to the French naval destroyer *Condorcet* to train as an ensign gunnery officer. His dreams of becoming an air force pilot were over. In hindsight, this was one of several blessings in disguise. Within three years, every man in Cousteau's flying class would perish in the war with Germany.[6]

The events surrounding Cousteau's first snorkeling excursion might have gone something like this. The basic facts are based on Cousteau's own accounts. Some of the story details are imagined with literary license.

The year was 1936. The *Condorcet's* bow glistened in the moonlight of her secure moorage. The ample stars above her deck were beginning to magically align, preparing to transform Cousteau's apparent mishap into a fortuitous kismet. Already aboard the ship was a deceptively shy superior officer, Philippe Tailliez. A physically strapping man, his visage resembled that of Picasso's —a large prominent Mediterranean nose, huge expressive eyes, a frequent wide-mouthed grin. Both Tailliez and Cousteau struggled with minor handicaps. Tailliez spoke with a stammer that disinclined him to shipboard banter, while Cousteau suffered a lack of physical stamina that embarrassed him as he tried to keep up with his fellow enlistees. The pair quickly bonded over their common frailties to form a decades-long friendship, one cemented by a shared passion for the sea.

Spearfishing was not a part of the traditional naval training program. However, the long-limbed, athletic Tailliez was well-regarded at this sport, which was all the rage along the Riviera of the 1930s. Always looking for ways to improve his diving prowess, he wrapped metal saw blade pieces between twin slabs of rubber and strapped them to his feet with pieces of twine to form flippers. He crafted a dive mask and snorkel from aviator glasses and garden hose tubes, then created spear guns from curtain rods and inner tubes. At the time, no one used the term DIY to describe such things; people just made do with what they had at hand. His contraptions sustained the generous catch he often gave away to the villagers.[7]

The two men seated in the galley were tucking into deep enamelware bowls of bouillabaisse. The cook's delectable shipboard cuisine often provided reason for celebration among the hungry crew. The dish was redolent with garlic and generous hunks of branzino that Tailliez had speared the previous day.

The older man spoke in an earnest, though hushed, voice as he struggled to hide his stammer. "Mon ami, you should swim with me. It will help regain your former force." He glanced around to see who might be listening, but the rest of the crew seemed occupied devouring their soup. "I will be spear-fishing again tomorrow afternoon when the tide is low. Join me. You can practice your strokes while I hunt for our next le dejeuner."

Cousteau reached for another hunk of baguette, considering the offer in a moment as brief as it might take for a sports car to slip off a steep road. With a quick jut of the chin, he responded in the affirmative. "Porquois pas," he said; why not?

The two began sharing an aquatic routine whenever they could get away from the ship. The inviting Mediterranean waters, combined with Cousteau's growing trust in his superior officer, provided welcome relaxation from the rigors of navy life. Cousteau would later describe how the experience of being in the sea created for him a sense of weightlessness and "being kissed all over." The crescent-shaped Mourillon beaches provided their favorite off-duty playground, with the Bay Mistral and the Plage de la Source being the loveliest. They avoided the area on weekends when families and French ingenues in revealing bathing costumes distracted them and scared away the fish. But in the early dawn hours, or the time approaching dusk, the beach was a place where even the most distracted man could gather his thoughts. Bands of turquoise and deeper ultramarine often appeared to spread off into infinity, beckoning the swimmers with a welcoming embrace.

One day, Tailliez's thoughts are drifting toward spearing a lobster dinner which they might enjoy later on the beach, accompanied by the bottle of rosé stashed in his dive bag. Cousteau is already in the water, practicing the steady crawl stroke that he is convinced will eventually strengthen his injured arms. On a whim, Tailliez beckons the younger man to give his contraptions a try. Holding out the mask and snorkel, he teases, "Allons, pourquoi pas?"

At first, Cousteau shrugs him off. He isn't here to play around. This is serious training for his naval career. But Tailliez isn't giving in, his raised eyebrows signaling a hopefulness. Cousteau doesn't want to disappoint him. At last, he allows his friend to help him strap on the odd gear.

He later wrote of that day, "Sometimes we are lucky enough to know that our lives have been changed, to discard the old, embrace the new, and run headlong into an immutable course. It happened to me at Le Mourillon on that summer's day, when my eyes were opened on the sea."[8] In the pursuit of sustainability, we must often dive headlong into unfamiliar places that may at first feel odd or even intimidating. If we approach such challenges with courage and curiosity, each day becomes an adventure, a chance to learn something new. If we can bring along an ally, so much the better.

Together the two swimmers plunge in, Tailliez staying nearby to show his friend how to hold his head just below the surface with the makeshift snorkel delivering air. At first Cousteau feels disoriented, anchored only by the acutely odd rasp of his breath through the snorkel tube. As he grows accustomed to this new way to inhale, the rhythm of his breathing slows, and he is able to relax. The view through the aviator glass lenses delivers a glimpse altogether unfamiliar. What had been fuzzy blobs in the water come into focus with highly textured rock outcrops distinctly protruding from the pale ivory sand. Small brightly colored fish dart between green and silver algae forests.

The revelation of an entire world he had never known existed comes initially as a shock. Abruptly, he stands up in the shallow water to check on his more familiar reality. Glancing to the shore, he sees people walking along the path, a trolley car, light poles. Eagerly, he plunges into the water again to witness lovely diamond patterns of light dancing across the sandy bottom, undulating in a gorgeous fractal dance. Guided by his friend, he ventures farther from the shore, where he can clearly pick out details more than 20 feet below the surface. The sudden clear visuals below the surface serve to shift Cousteau's entire world.

Brad Matsend writes in his biography *Jacques Cousteau: The Sea King,* "Bright constellations of red, orange, and lavender starfish decorated every surface to which they could cling against the surge of the sea. In the crevices of rock piles and eroded boulders, he picked out the dark purple spines of urchins. Swarms of fish were weightless and agile, with repertoires of acrobatic stunts and bursts of speed. Lumbering groupers hovered like dirigibles. Schools of synchronized mackerel flashed in the sunlight as though commanded by an invisible choreographer."[9]

Like a compass shifting to find its corrected magnetic north, Cousteau re-oriented himself that day, never looking back. He quickly deduces that everything he sees is magnified through the makeshift mask, as though a film is being created before his eyes using a telephoto lens. His sense of wonder regarding the underwater world, comparing the groupers he swam among to dirigibles, would never flag for the next sixty-plus years of his life. Along with Tailliez, and their friend Frederic Dumas whom they would recruit a brief time later, the three soon became inseparable in their passion for discovering new ways to dive. They were fondly referred to as the Three Musketeers of the Sea, or Les Mousque-Mers. Using an ancient pearl diving technique, also called free diving, they dived deeper and deeper by simply holding their breath. But they wanted to stay under for longer than apnea would allow. The Mousque-Mers experimented with on-deck tanks of pressurized oxygen, connected to the diver's face mask below the boat by a long hose.

They quickly discovered that breathing pure oxygen at depth was life-threatening. Building on the inventions of others and finally partnering with the brilliant engineer Emile Gagnan, in 1946 they patented the Aqua Lung.[10] With this new technology, a demand valve regulates pressure as the diver descends, shutting off the flow while the diver exhales, supplying air only when the diver inhales.

Death and unknown dangers confronted the young Mousque-Mers divers on their hundreds of experiments. They learned how the human body can survive challenges such as narcosis and pressure equalization. It was difficult to find tanks that could withstand pressure at depth. The young men also experimented extensively with the tanks to manage the correct flow of oxygen, seeking the amount the human body could assimilate.

Much of what they learned became the foundation of modern diving rules of thumb now taken for granted. The principle of the Cousteau-Gagnan regulator remains unchanged, according to *The Human, the Orchid, and the Octopus*. "The four prototypes that Cousteau originally produced have proliferated into untold millions of the device popularly known as SCUBA (Self-Contained Underwater Breathing Apparatus), with an estimated forty thousand neophyte divers certified worldwide each month."[11] Without those inventions and the tireless experimentation, we might never have had the opportunity to see the world under the sea—or for so many people around the globe to care so deeply for the oceans.

Sometimes new technologies propel sustainability forward. Sometimes, it is sheer passion and human will. If a young man with a shattered arm and a ruined piloting career could do all of this, what might be possible for each one of us? Who among us might free ourselves of troubles in order to be the heroes we dream of? The depths and challenges confronting sustainability lie at every turn, yet we can approach them with courage, keeping hope alive for a brighter future.

CHAPTER TWO

Interconnected Systems

*When we try to pull one thing in the universe,
we find it hitched to everything else.*

— **John Muir**, Scottish-American
mountaineer, naturalist and environmental preservation advocate

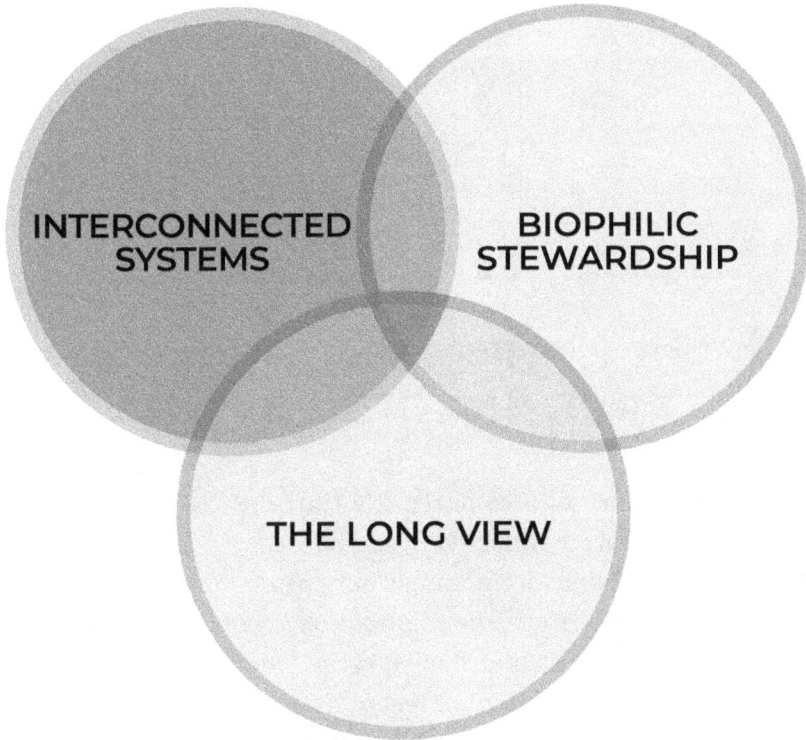

Interconnected Systems, The First Core Value
of the Environmental Pillar

FIRST COURSE: A COURSE IN INTERCONNECTED SYSTEMS

Back at my imaginary dinner party, it's time for the first course to be served: a lesson in Interconnected Systems.

My guests are nibbling on the simple antipasto I have prepared. True to my Greek and Italian heritage, the kalamata olives and marinated artichoke hearts I have included are some of my favorite foods. Cousteau has decided to ask me some questions about the rest of the evening's repast that I have already laid out upon the sideboard. "Where did you get this beautiful fish, *mon cherie*?" he says, pointing to the poached filets resting atop a platter of lemon slices. He smirks. "Have you been fishing recently?"

Luckily, I was ready for these kinds of questions. Every decision a cook makes about ingredients can feel fraught once sustainability is part of the considerations. However, it can be pretty gratifying to figure out the right answers. I had agonized over what to serve this evening, and in the end decided fish would be okay as long as it was a careful selection with sustainability in mind. "This is wild, line-caught Alaska salmon. It just came into season. The fish monger I bought it from knows the fisherman that caught this salmon personally."

"What a fine thing, to know the fisherman. Bravo!"

"The shop owner explained to me that this particular fisherman works for a family business that has been in operation for over fifty years.

Everything is done with care. According to their story, the fisherman kisses each salmon after they catch it, as a way of giving thanks."

This bit of information seemed to impress even César. "Acknowledging the work of others, even those we may never meet, is a way of practicing respect. It is an excellent habit."

Still a bit nervous about these choices, I go on. "I eat salmon only for special occasions. I know how many challenges the wild fish populations face now."

Jacques warmed to the talk of fish species. "Salmon is part of our natural world's complex interconnected web. One of our *Calypso* expeditions visited the wilds of Kodiak Island in Alaska. We were there to study the red sockeye." He slipped into his storyteller voice, as by habit. "Imagine the salmon swimming past waterfalls and hungry bears, fighting after four years at sea to get upstream, back to their spawning grounds. It is one of the most courageous journeys I have ever witnessed."

Anita jumped in. "Marvelous! I think I remember that episode."

"My television stardom," he said with chuckle. In that 1970 episode of *The Undersea World of Jacques Cousteau*, he cautioned about the dangers of overfishing using nets. His ecological warnings were prescient, I thought as I regarded the fish on my fork, because today we struggle with the massive collapse of salmon runs in our richly interconnected world.

TELLING STORIES OF THE UNSEEN, INTERCONNECTED WORLD

Since his teenage years, Cousteau had a natural talent for telling stories using film. He started out making home movies of family weddings and short humorous dramas using his friends as the actors. He found that being behind the camera gave him a unique ability to observe the world while at the same time attracting attention and admiration. Cousteau experimented with inventing ways to protect precious camera equipment while underwater. His first device used a Beaulieu 8mm camera, mounted on a handmade bracket inside a gallon-sized fruit jar. He would go on to produce *Sixty Feet Down* in 1942, the first underwater movie. It's a sportsman's film. He borrowed a hand-crank editing console from a navy photo lab to finish a simple tale about a fruitful spearfishing venture, followed by a beach barbecue.

Fourteen years and many dives later, Cousteau produced *The Silent World*, an 86-minute documentary using a young and unknown Louis Malle as the cinematographer. The film won an Oscar for best documentary. Malle would go on to a luminous filmmaking career in French cinema as well as Hollywood, including *My Dinner with Andre* and the autobiographical *Au revoir les enfants*.

Up until this moment, few people had seen life under the sea. The Oscar acclaim paved the way for Cousteau to gain funding for many future ventures, including a pivotal 1966 commission from ABC Television which would allow him to launch what would become his most famous and beloved program, *The Undersea World of Jacques Cousteau*. The episode "Savage World of the Coral Jungle," filmed on location at an atoll in the Indian Ocean, played out the story that follows.

The story takes place in an atoll, a ring-shaped coral reef that can partially or completely enclose a lagoon. It is essentially the remains of an extinct volcano, formed over periods of thousands of years. Such atolls form a ring around warm, shallow waters where sea life thrives —a veritable playground for divers, if they are lucky enough to find a way in. For sailors trying to get somewhere fast, such tropical doldrums provide little wind. But for divers, the calm waters of the tropics afford the opportunity to explore paradise undisturbed by strong currents or gusts.

The following descriptions are based on facts and footage recorded by the film crew. I will wave my literary wand here to bring us all closer.

The *Calypso* is underway just off the northern tip of Madagascar, east of Mozambique and southwest of the Seychelles Islands. The marine chronometer shows the remote location as somewhere near longitude 47 degrees east, latitude 10 degrees south. Captain Cousteau has charted a course to explore the coral reef jungles of a nearby underwater atoll. This is territory as yet undocumented, without a depth chart to assist them. If they run aground, they run the risk of being trapped for weeks.

Captain Cousteau stands on the forward deck, gazing toward the horizon as though nothing exists but himself and the sea. The unexplored atoll lies ahead, a huge, powdered donut of mystery. Pastel-blue frosting tinges the outer feathery fringe layers which stretch downward 2 miles. Nestled within, the deep turquoise filling of the inner ring promises protected waters and easy diving. But the reef is too shallow for the *Calypso* to navigate safely across it. How can they find a way in?

The *Calypso's* mini aerostat, a single-passenger balloon, is the perfect tool to send ahead of the ship in order to search out a passageway for airborne reconnaissance. It reduces the risk of running aground. Aerostats include various types of craft using buoyant lighter-than-air gases to become airborne. The obvious choice to pilot the aerostat is Jacques' second son, Phillipe. His first underwater adventure occurred when he was just four years old, diving with an "Aqua Lung" previously. Later, he earned a glider pilot license at age sixteen, becoming licensed to fly everything from seaplanes to helicopters.

The crew pulls gently on the silky white fabric of the balloon's inflatable bell, guiding its billows into place as they fill with buoyant helium gas. The balloon begins to take on a giant white jellyfish shape, in stripes of red and blue. The bold colors will make it easier to find if it becomes lost. With his father's easy grace and physicality, Phillipe quickly climbs aboard the trapeze seat tethered to the bottom of the contraption and settles his lean limbs into place. This stripped-down vessel has no gondola or navigational burner valve like those in larger pleasure balloons. The unprotected passenger has to hang on to a tiny seat and depend on the wind to plot a course.

The launch goes airborne, drifting toward the atoll. The now-shirtless father squints into the sun, his deeply lined face betraying a certain degree of worry as he watches his son drift away over the water. He knows all too well that the cameras will capture everything—every triumph and every mistake. The handheld radio is too quiet. Finally, it crackles to life with an announcement from Phillipe. He has discovered a narrow slot passage through the fringing reef. He thinks it's a navigable course. Now beaming like the sun, Captain Cousteau utters his most familiar command: "Il faut aller voir—we must go and see for ourselves." The crew springs into action. Within minutes, the *Calypso* is making way for the dangerously narrow slot. Although no one dares mention it, if they run aground the radio would not summon help soon enough. The watery depths can be a fickle mistress, reluctant to reveal their beauty's secrets. It's a tight fit, but miraculously the *Calypso* slips through. They are likely the first humans to explore this spot, but there's no way of knowing for sure.

Once safely inside the lagoon and within reach of Phillipe, they drop anchor to begin their exploration. Only a short time later, Captain Cousteau and his small dive team are shrugging on their gear: wetsuits, flippers, masks, air tanks, pressure regulators, sample collection bags, and the all-important camera gear. Two camera operators are critical—one to shoot film footage, the other to shoot still photographs with a specially designed camera, its sealed rangefinder resistant to a water depth of 50 meters. These prototype cameras would eventually be perfected by Nikon to become the go-to underwater camera for decades, dubbed the Nikonos.

The dive team scrambles aboard a miniscule Zodiac dinghy. They ferry to a spot a few hundred yards away and prepare to submerge. The anticipation just before a dive is clouded with tension. There is no margin of error for a safe dive; one tiny mistake can result in disaster. Air tank pressure dials are carefully adjusted to precise levels. A test puff ensures compressed air is flowing correctly from regulators. Everything appears to be ready—check and recheck. In the penultimate moment of the process, Cousteau perches for a brief moment on the edge of the boat, silently repeating his internal checklist. He pitches backward, away from the relative safety of the Zodiac, flipping as naturally as a playful seal, plunging head over heels into the giant teacup of the lagoon. In rapid succession, his crew of swimming seals follows him. The exploration is underway.

Within the ancient atoll, the coral metropolis is populated with a high-rise diversity of shapes and colors. Upright sea fan coral spreads its branches out like a delicate tree canopy, while tabletop coral resembles a flattened mushroom of midrise condominiums. The bustling city, crammed full of minute caves and crevices, serves as home to many diverse residents, a complex teeming with life. Coral ecosystems are often referred to as the rainforests of the ocean, equally productive places crammed with manifold flora and fauna.

The divers spook a swarm of electric blue sapphire devil fish who disappear under a deep coral overhang. Black and yellow striped Moorish idols are unperturbed, drifting calmly past, sporting crest-shaped dorsal fins that tower over their heads like elegant sporting pennants. As the humans' bubbles gently pirouette upward, the interlopers pause to take in the 360-degree marvels. Cousteau narrates. "Our first dive in a world so physically striking overwhelms our senses. We are no more explorers, but children filled in a store of surprises. We stop at random to look at the busy traffic in the crowded cities."

While our own endeavors might not always feel as dramatic as this, we are all explorers in the vast and often uncharted territory of sustainability. Often, we must create our own maps, in search of illusive answers.

CORAL — A COMPLEX ORGANISM

We will pick up the *Calypso* team's story shortly, but first let's do our own deep dive into coral biology. This will help us begin to understand the first Core Value of the Environmental Sustainability Pillar: Interconnected Systems.

A single coral reef can be described as a huge community composed of millions of tiny polyps. The reef is the only animal so large it can be seen from space. Coral reefs can live forever, their natural history going back more than 450 million years, far before the dinosaurs. These oases of life are one of the most varied and productive ecosystems on the planet, yet they cover less than 1 percent of the earth's surface. A single reef's biodiversity can comprise 465 distinct species of coral, 3,000 species of fish, countless mollusks, and multiple species of sea turtles. These underwater ecosystems provide 25 percent of critical marine habitat and marine wildlife food. Ecosystem productivity can be measured in grams of carbon per square meter, or how much the ecosystem can "fix" or convert, from inorganic carbon to organic compounds and living organisms. Surprisingly, coral reefs are far more efficient at fixing carbon than rainforests. They are also among the most productive systems at fixing nitrogen. All this is even more amazing considering that the shallow tropical seas where corals occur are the least rich in nutrients compared to other parts of the ocean.[12]

This coral productivity is possible based on a natural talent for recycling. Nothing is wasted; everything is reused somehow. Such efficiency is often referred to by recycling geeks as *closed loops*. While corals appear to be static, inanimate structures, they are actually living communities of animals, composed of thousands of distant jellyfish cousins. These tiny bucket-shaped coral polyps resemble miniature sea anemones. They are mostly a circular mouth, surrounded by small tentacles and a stomach. The polyps live inside the coral's visible structure, built up by taking in dissolved seawater minerals, mixing them with proteins, and depositing the resulting calcium carbonate mixture as a mineral skeleton. This forms the hardened structure we are most familiar with, able to grow and evolve for centuries.

The energy needed to perform coral's construction work comes from a symbiotic partnership with a single-celled plant called zooxanthellae, a tiny alga which lives within the coral tentacles. The algae form an agricultural micro-farm, providing a food source. The coral polyp's waste products are phosphorus and nitrogen, which the algae recycle as nutrients for their own photosynthetic process. Within the elegance of this closed loop system, waste equals food.

At night, filaments of stinging tentacles extrude themselves outward from the coral polyp body, catching tiny particles of sea creature food and plankton to supplement the coral diet. At the same time, they shelter a nursery for their symbiotic friends the algae. The elegant friendship between these organisms consists of the algae turning sunlight into food for the coral. In exchange, the coral provides them a protected place to live. This intricately linked system of resource flows and cycles is emblematic of how the sustainability's natural world often works as a vast interconnected system of nested relationships which function within a larger whole.

The vast dance of interconnections is often hidden from view, yet the continuation of their bonds is critical to survival. Symbiosis among coral polyps and algae is also referred to as mutualism, whereby two different species of organisms exist in a mutually beneficial association. Such mutualism represents interconnected templates for life, organized for harmony and balance rather than conflict and loss. Cousteau once noted, "However fragmented the world, however intense the national rivalries, it is an inexorable fact that we become more interdependent every day."

For the most part, humans appear to be locked in a paradigm that pits us against nature instead of living in harmony with her. So far in our own evolution, stories of mutualism among humanity appear to be the exception, rather than the rule. In the competition for space and resources, we often find ourselves, whether consciously or unconsciously, at war with the planetary systems that sustain us. Sustainability points to ways we can live in greater harmony with Earth's living systems of which we are a part. But in order to do this, we must first better understand the wisdom of interconnected systems.

ENVIRONMENTAL CORE VALUE 1:
INTERCONNECTED SYSTEMS
The Beauty of Patterns that Connect

Our spirituality is a oneness and an interconnectedness with all that lives and breathes, even with all that does not live or breathe.
— **Mudrooroo Nyoongah**, Australian aboriginal author

Ecology is the best place to start learning how **Interconnected Systems** work. No basic ecology course would be complete without a discussion of food webs, the interdependent webs of life that rely on cascading, interconnected systems. A hawk eats a snake, which eats a toad, which eats a grasshopper, which eats grass. While the hawk doesn't eat grass, it is still indirectly dependent on grass in order to survive. Indigenous wisdom teaches interconnectedness as key to survival. Chief Seattle of the Duwamish and Suquamish nations spoke eloquently to the spirit of the interconnection of systems. "All things are connected like the blood which unites one family. Man did not weave the web of life; he is merely a strand in it. Whatever he does to the web, he does to himself."

In mythological traditions, the concept of Mother Earth embodies the planet as a huge, interconnected family of relationships. The Gaia theory views the Earth as a single living system, a being whose organisms interact with inorganic environments. The Gaia body forms a self-regulating system that is both synergistic and complex.

Beyond mythological storytelling, earth science teaches about flow, transformation, and change. Nothing is static; there are perpetual hidden dimensions and energy flows underway constantly. Our planet's complex natural systems are governed by two powerful features: sunlight and water. Solar energy is not distributed evenly across the globe; the tilt of the earth's axis creates variations in climate from the poles to the equator. The sun also influences the global distribution of water, with 90 percent of fresh water coming from evaporated seawater. Mountains play a key role, too, in water distribution. They help concentrate moisture formed on one side of a mountain, forming a drier rain shadow area on the other.[13] This interactive dance is part of a complex system called the water cycle. Like many interconnected systems, the cycle's patterns flow from a chain of linked resources.

Interconnection represents an essential underpinning of sustainability: Almost anything you can think of is connected to something else. Nothing in our complex world exists in isolation. Everything is part of a grand interplay of causes and effects, interdependencies, and resource flows.

One way to unpack complex linked patterns is through systems thinking. Systems show up everywhere—in planetary weather patterns, living organisms, mechanical designs, and even within political or corporate organizations. But what defines a system? A system is a collection of parts which interact with each other to function as a whole. You can't reduce a system by looking at individual parts in isolation. A system only makes sense through understanding the relationships between and among its individual elements. Systems thinking gives rise to the expression, "The whole is greater than the sum of the parts."

Sustainability finds its voice on multiple levels. It shows up in scientific, philosophical, mythological, and spiritual discourse. The Buddhist philosopher Thich Nhat Hanh refers to our highly connected state of affairs as "interbeing" in his book *The Heart of Understanding*. He explains how a sheet of paper is interconnected with sunshine, rainclouds, soil minerals to help the forest grow, the logger who cuts the tree to provide the fiber for a mill, and more. Sustainability sees such complex interrelationships as a central tenet. Nothing is as simple as it seems on the surface. We can peel back each mundane experience we have to reveal an unseen world of relationships.

Many systems are non-linear and incredibly complex, taking on webbed, divergent structures which can be difficult to trace. Because of all this circuitous complexity, system disruptions can be amplified in unpredictable ways. Sometimes interconnected impacts are surprisingly far-removed from the original source of the change factor.

This phenomenon is known by some as the butterfly effect. MIT meteorologist Edward Lorenz suggested that a storm on one side of the globe could have its roots in the flapping of a butterfly's wings tens of thousands of miles away.[14] The butterfly effect suggests that even small changes can eventually result in massive impact elsewhere within a sensitive system.

At Yellowstone National Park, the interconnectedness of ecological systems enables wolves to change rivers. Re-introduction of native wolves in 1995 created a series of unexpected cascading changes in the park. Elk love to browse on aspen tree seedlings, which reduces the numbers of mature trees. The presence of just one pack of wolves hunting for food reduced the number of elk within the same area. When wolves are present, aspens are allowed to mature into thick groves. Aspens are also very attractive to beavers. As the aspen increase, so do beaver populations. Beaver dams and ponds in the rivers help to slow water flows and increase fish populations. The increase in tree habitat also supports more songbirds in the park.[15]

The existence of collective behaviors within systems might show up as a river that has emergent properties far beyond those of a single water molecule. A forest behaves differently than its individual trees.[16] In an ancient example of interconnected systems, cooperation and information sharing make interconnected tree communities more resilient.

Yale ecologist Suzanne Simard discovered trees communicating with one another via vast, networked lattice systems of soil fungi. Fungal filigrees assist trees by transferring nutrients, sending warning signals about environmental threats and searching for kin. Simard compares these fungi systems to neural networks in the human brain, describing forests as a cooperative system. In these complex symbiotic relationships, different tree species grow together, sometimes competing with one another, but also cooperating by sending nutrients and carbon back and forth as needed through the fungal networks. Since the fungi rely on trees for critical nutrients provided by photosynthesis, they become assistants in order to ensure a secure food source.

In the kinship networks of the trees, Simard refers to the "forest wisdom" of "mother trees," the biggest, oldest, and most highly connected through extensive root systems and carbon processing. Mother trees are also able to recognize their own offspring and favor them among the broader community.[17] This sustains the forest as a kinship community.

Our modern lifestyles often break down tribal and family interconnections, leading to feelings of separation that contribute to depression and social dysfunction. Embracing the sustenance of interconnected systems can help eliminate our sense of separation. We realize, whether by magic or science, we are a part of something much larger. In today's work of sustainability, we can take our cues from complex patterns and systems in all their myriad forms. Our work can lay a foundation for health, resilience, and prosperity if we learn to lean toward these harmonious interconnections.

Meanwhile, back on the coral jungle dive, a symphony of underwater music accompanies the proceedings. A resonant hum is created by myriads of fish, shrimp, and other creatures grunting, groaning, and crackling as they go about their business. Curious as to the sources of this background tinnitus, the dive team slowly descends to a reef area where they can hear larger crunching noises. A bright turquoise parrot fish is munching tiny bits of coral as it forages for algae. The crushed coral excretions of these fish form up to 85 percent of the region's white sand beaches. Past the busy parrot fish lies a gorgeous array of sea anemones, flowers of the undersea world. The anemones are rooted to crevices among the coral, their long spaghetti tube tentacles undulating in the currents. While these *Calypso* divers aren't sure just which of the over 4,000 species of sea anemones these particular creatures represent, they do know that they are part of a unique group of carnivorous fish traps. The traps have poisonous tentacles that can deliver a lethal neurotoxin to any fish unlucky enough to wander into the trap.

The story of the sea anemone and the clown fish is another example of nature's mutualism. Their lives are closely entwined in an interconnected and highly complex dance, a system organized for mutual benefit. The only creature immune to the poisonous stings of the sea anemone is the bright orange clown fish. The clown fish, whose white stripes encircling its head resemble a huge ornamental ruff, lives much of its life within the protective zone of a single anemone. They are underwater roommates. The clown fish leaves the anemone to forage, returning to feed the anemone bits of food. At other times, the clown fish cleans house, removing debris from among the tentacles. The clown fish lays its eggs within the anemone, using the stinging tentacles as protection for its offspring. Without the anemone, the clown fish cannot survive.

As the exploratory observer, Cousteau chronicled interactions among living organisms, capturing footage of things never before seen before by most humans. The far-flung places he explored were connected around one central theme: water. Whether in the Pacific Ocean, the Amazon River, or the frozen Arctic, Cousteau revealed watery wonders to the public that took their breath away.

Along the way, he delivered healthy doses of interconnected systems thinking. "Our water planet—too few are able to sense the serum coursing in their veins. Too few are aware that I am the sea, and the sea is me," he says on The Water Planet episode of *The Odyssey of the Cousteau Team*. "Every living thing: eagles, roses, whales, butterflies, trees, fishes, corn, turtles, amoebas, and even man himself, all are mainly composed of organized water, no matter what the form of water: clouds, snow, dew, rivers, lakes, or glaciers, there is only one source of life sustaining water—the sea. On no other planet in our entire solar system is there another great sea, ripe with the vital elements of the universe. The earth is the only water planet."

TODAY'S INTERCONNECTED CORAL SYSTEMS CRISIS

The first terrestrial species emerged from the ocean 430 million years ago. Today, the oceans control our climate, our weather, and even the oxygen we breathe. Our origin and our fate are tied to the oceans. Coral, often referred to as the nurseries of the sea, is defined as a keystone species. In architecture, a keystone is a centrally located building stone at the summit of an arch that serves to lock together the structure. If the keystone is removed, the arch falls apart. Many other organisms depend upon coral. Without them, the entire ecosystem would collapse.

Up to one billion people rely on coral ecosystems as a source of food and economic livelihood, supporting fishing and tourism industries to the tune of as much as $375 billion US dollars annually.[18] Ten percent of the world population depends on fisheries, with fish providing 15 percent of the animal protein intake of 4.3 billion Earth inhabitants.[19] Coral medicinal extracts have also been used to develop treatments for cancer, arthritis, heart disease, and asthma. Since coral provide shelter to about one-quarter of all marine species, their loss would result in mass underwater homelessness.

In addition, coral reefs sustain humans and their property. Reefs create breakwaters which help to buffer human shoreline settlements from waves, hurricanes, and rising sea levels, protecting against property damage, erosion, and human catastrophe. When hurricanes Irma and Maria ravaged the Florida coast in 2017, the reef absorbed damage from turbulent waters, taking the brunt of the force to shield coastal communities. Much of the damage in the Florida Keys occurred underwater, damaging the coral reef that runs 360 miles from Florida to the Dry Tortugas. "We should be thanking the coral reefs," said Dave Vaughan, executive director of Sarasota's Mote Marine Laboratory & Aquarium International Center for Coral Reef Research. "They broke the waves, and if they hadn't, our homes would not have survived."[20]

But coral is in trouble. Coral bleaching is a stressing phenomenon caused by global warming and the rising temperatures of the oceans. Oceanic heat waves are increasing water temperature by 1 to 2 degrees. This can cause coral polyps to become dangerously overheated, somewhat similar to how a human succumbs to a fever. Overheating causes the zooxanthellae algae to stop producing food. Once food production stops, the coral evict their freeloading algae roommates as a form of stress response. The algae give the coral their unique colors; once they are gone the remaining coral structures turn a ghostly white skeletal ruin. Without the algae to feed them, coral stops growing and begins to starve. If the bleaching conditions continue, the coral will eventually die.

All the world's warm water ocean areas and their corals are being impacted by coral bleaching. Since the 1980s, 94 percent of all coral reefs surveyed have experienced a severe bleaching incident. These incidents once occurred every twenty-five to thirty years. Anthropogenic climate change, or change caused by human activities dating back to the Industrial Age, has accelerated incidents to now recur every five to six years. Scientists watch in horror as the loss of life unfolds, sometimes within a period of months. In the past, they observed that if a fast-growing coral had about ten years between bleaching incidents, recovery was possible. With the incidence of such events increasing by a factor of five, these complex ecosystems appear unable to recover.[21]

Many scientists are giving up hope of large-scale recovery. Reef watcher Mark Eakin says, "It is clear already that we're going to lose most of the world's coral reefs." Add the stressors of pollution, overfishing, and overdevelopment, and it is now estimated that 90 percent of the world's coral reefs will disappear in the next thirty-five years.[22]

Coral researchers have called for an all-hands-on-deck crisis response. There are many ideas in the mix, including genetically modifying climate change-resistant species of algae, geo-engineering carbon dioxide removal from the environment, and field-based coral fertilization. Successful fertilization is a tricky cross between science and the magic of a full moon.

MODERN-DAY REVOLUTIONISTS: GROWING NEW CORAL REEFS

Growing reefs is a form of underwater colonization which no doubt would have made Cousteau smile. Yet he might have had a hard time imagining being a nursemaid to coral sperm donors. Just what conditions allow this to occur? It goes something like this. Let me apply some literary flair for this account, inspired by news stories and real events, as reported by Vice News.

On the night of a full moon, a lot of crazy behavior starts going on. In Austin, the locals gather at their beloved Barton Springs pool to howl. For corals, the lunar orb makes them want to mate. The full moon is the signal for an all-out coral orgy. The reason is that coral is hermaphroditic. Each polyp is both male and female, producing both sperm and eggs, which they eject into the water all at once. Each individual is dependent on other corals doing the same thing at the same time in order for cross-fertilization to occur. This is why they have evolved to behave in unison. During these times of spawning, the ocean surrounding the corals serves as a huge watery womb where swimming sperm struggle to make contact with free-floating eggs. It's a mating ritual within a massive game of chance.

Sustainability can triumph when heroes work together. One scientific group is performing day-to-day heroic acts on behalf of coral. The coral experts aboard the research ship *Secore* have gone sex mad. All they think about is sex—when the coral will be ready for it, how to snare ejected eggs and sperm, and how quickly these can be rushed back to the laboratory. *Secore*'s goal is to increase coral vitality and genetic diversity. On a particularly full-orbed night, the scientists gather hungrily in the crystal waters off the coast of Curacao. The full moon has helped them narrow their hunt for spawning brain corals down to a single magical night. Since divers can stay underwater for only limited amount of time, they need a way to pinpoint the exact moment when corals will begin mating. Butterfly fish are the answer. Somehow, these fish have evolved to know when coral are about to spawn. Excited at the opportunity for a tasty feast, they gather eagerly around the coral, wildly fluttering and dancing. This is the signal for the *Secore* egg gatherers, who swoop in with large tubular plastic bags which look like giant condoms. The condoms are carefully tented over the coral brains as they eject their precious egg and sperm nodules into the sacks.

Back on deck, the *Secore* team resembles a group of proud parents after a toddler dance recital. But there is no time to gloat. Next, they must rush their precious cargo back to the laboratory for controlled egg fertilization. In nature, the fertilization rate is around 2 percent, but the *Secore* is able to increase the rate to over 90 percent. Once fertilized in the lab, the eggs are attached to objects which resemble oversized children's jacks. These tetrapods are the vehicles used to deliver fertilized coral eggs back to the ocean in new underwater nurseries. The fertilized tetrapods will next be "planted" in identified locations where corals are struggling to survive. Some call this "assisted evolution."

Since 2018, *Secore* has been carrying out its mission across the US Virgin Islands, the Bahamas, Mexico, Guam, and Curacao. They experiment with many types of corals, including the ecologically significant and endangered mountainous star coral. In order to upscale their efforts economically, they focus on training an army of volunteers to adopt their methods using simple, inexpensive materials readily available at any hardware store. This enables their Johnny Appleseed activists to disburse hundreds of thousands of embryonic coral colonists per year. In addition, they are working with the California Academy of Sciences and the Autodesk Foundation on a project which increases the viability of repopulation efforts. They utilize 3-D printing to produce ceramic tetrapods in a variety of shapes and sizes.

In the massive shift toward sustainability that is needed, we must enlist every tool at our disposal and enroll every collaborator we can find. Ancient instincts and modern-day technology can join together. We will all need to roll up our sleeves to be a part of the change we want to see. No contribution will be too large or too small.

More Good News for Coral

It's a brave new world for coral, with further reasons for hope. Motivated by tourism and fishing impacts, forward-thinking governments are taking action. The Belize Barrier Reef, called the most remarkable reef in the West Indies by Charles Darwin, was placed on UNESCO's endangered list in 2009. Galvanized by the 2010 Deepwater Horizon oil well explosion which dumped 4.9 million barrels of oil, Belize became the first country in the world to put a moratorium on offshore oil exploration and drilling. They also implemented a mangrove protection program.[23] Protection efforts have succeeded in this country where nature tourism is fundamental to the economy. UNESCO removed the site from their endangered world heritage site list in 2018. Janelle Chanona, Belize's country director for international nonprofit Oceana noted that "What happens to the reef, happens to us. We cannot shoot the Golden Goose."[24]

Here's Hope: In other glimmers of hope for the future of sustainability, Hawaii signed the world's first ban on sunscreens that contain oxybenzone and octinoxate, which act as endocrine disruptors to juvenile coral.[25] Such developments signal that governments are increasingly taking on a stewardship role for the ocean's coral nurseries.

The rule of law continues to evolve in service to Biophilic Stewardship. In 2010, Belize's Supreme Court ruled that the Mesoamerican Reef off their coast is a living being, with protected rights. A cargo ship crashed into the reef, the largest in the Atlantic, estimated to be 225 million years old, home to more than five hundred fish species. The damage was described as injury to a living organism, different than to a non-living environment. The Court stated, "It's difficult to comprehend (the reef) within the concept of 'property' as that word is ordinarily understood." The shipping company was fined more than $5 million US dollars in injuries. [26]

Climate change remains one of the biggest threats to coral survival. It will require a massive reorientation toward stewarding the ocean's ecosystems if there is to be hope for the future we share with the sea.

CHAPTER THREE

Biophilic Stewardship

People protect what they love.

— **Jacques Yves Cousteau**

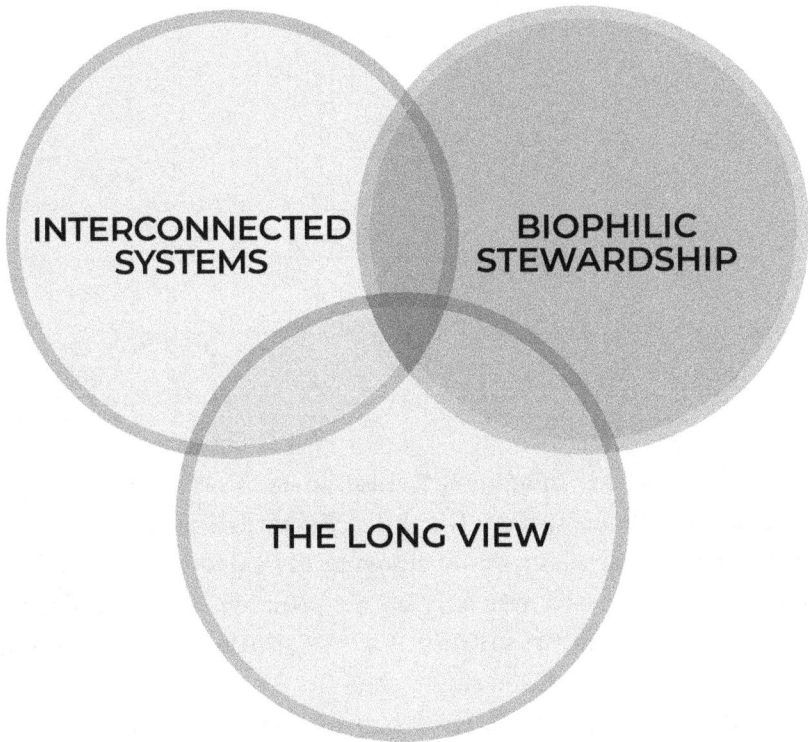

Biophilic Stewardship, The Second Core Value
of the Environmental Pillar

SECOND COURSE: A COURSE IN BIOPHILIC STEWARDSHIP

Meanwhile, back at my imaginary dinner party, it's time for the second course to be served: a course in Biophilic Stewardship.

César in particular seems to be enjoying my salad of fresh herbs, lettuce, and radishes, dressed with only the simplest lemon juice and olive oil.

"Lucia, these greens are so fresh. As a vegetarian, I have eaten a lot of salads in my day, but this is really good."

The comment threw me off. He'd spent years focused on lettuce boycotts in an attempt to secure better farmworker conditions. I recovered quickly, explaining that we are eating locally, about as local as you can get. "Thank you for noticing. I grew the salad ingredients in my garden, just a few steps from here. Would you care for a tour? We could stretch our legs before taking on the next course."

As soon as the salad is gone, we move outside to take in the evening air. I have worked hard to build this garden up over the years, tilling in yards of compost, removing invasive plants, and patiently learning each little micro-climate of the yard. I have found that it takes at least a year of seasonal changes to learn a piece of land, studying where the shadows and sunlight show up and just what wants to grow where. Gardening is an exercise in patience, which I know Chávez understands well.

Anita is ahead of us as we stroll the garden path. She suddenly shrieks with childlike delight. "Come and see! It looks like a hummingbird."

The evening's fragrant night blooms have attracted a hummingbird hawk moth. These nocturnal moths have a flight pattern similar to that of a hummingbird. We have been honored by a special visitation. "What a rare and fine thing for us to get to see! They have long snouts like hummingbirds for drinking up nectar. This makes them important pollinators."

"Beyond the bees and moths," Anita says. "I can see how much love you've put into your garden. Your little sign here says it's a Certified Wildlife Habitat."

"It's a small bit of habitat, yes," I say with as humble a tone as I can manage. "But hopefully an important piece of a larger puzzle."

"I must see if there is a program like that in the UK when I get home. We must all do what we can to steward the planet, starting with what's right in front of us."

My pride is hard to miss. I experience an inner glow, knowing that I am part of a diverse community of winged creatures, as well as caterpillars who will later become butterflies. I am stewarding a wondrous little corner of the earth that I call home.

Our garden stroll is coming to an end. My urban homestead lot is tiny, so a tour can only take so long. The white, crushed gravel pathways reflect our way through the dark, back into the welcoming arms of my cottage.

A CALL TO TESTIFY

In the previous section, we learned about coral systems and their need for protection from human-induced climate change. This is only one of the many threats the ocean faces. Luckily, elected officials are increasingly realizing their solemn responsibility to be defenders of the planet. But this wasn't always the case. The following scenes dramatize Cousteau's appearance at the 1971 International Conference on Ocean Pollution in Washington DC. The basic facts are all based on video accounts, photographs, and official transcripts. I will light the literary imagination candle to illuminate the story.

The call comes in the middle of a sweltering Paris afternoon. Jacques and his wife, Simone, are napping in an unusual moment together at their pied-á-terre. Simone had been spending even more time shipboard than Cousteau in 1971. Jacques faced a constant need to fundraise or speak in public. Simone's devotion to the *Calypso* had become legendary. Her nickname was La Bergère: The Shepherdess. In the early days, she had helped finance their expeditions by selling her family jewels. Simone doesn't get enough credit for what Cousteau was able to achieve. She was the woman behind the man.

On this afternoon, the lunch smells linger in the sun-dappled air above a table littered with breadcrumbs and half-drunk glasses of rosé. The August holiday when every Parisian deserts the city is sadly over, evidenced by traffic noises drifting up from the street. The blaring telephone, an antidote to sleep, causes Cousteau to fumble with the heavy receiver, his mind as thick and sticky as the honey he smeared on his baguette only an hour earlier. The voice coming in above the rotary dial is melodic, a woman speaking English. "Hello? I have US Senator Ernest F. Hollings on the line for Jacques Cousteau. Is Monsieur Cousteau available?"

The time is just after breakfast in Washington. The senator is still wearing the same rumpled suit from the previous day. He'd barely had time to down some scalding coffee and a Danish before asking his secretary to phone. Anxious to speak with Cousteau, he is laser-focused on issuing invitations posthaste. Hollings is hoping to add gravitas to the Commerce Subcommittee hearings he is chairing in the nation's capital within the month, a critical steppingstone toward passage of a bill called the Ocean Dumping Act to stop polluters. The chairman is looking to bring several well-known international guests to the sessions.

Cousteau was an obvious choice. The other invitees were formidable in their own right. Thor Heyerdahl, the *Kon Tiki* pilot who had sailed a double-hulled Polynesian canoe across the Pacific Ocean using traditional navigation, was on the agenda. Astronaut Scott Carpenter, SEALAB veteran and the second American to orbit the earth, had also been invited.

Sometimes a call can have the same urgency as a command from the deck of the *Calypso*, communicating perils ahead requiring a change of course. It isn't difficult to convince Cousteau to come to Washington so he can tell US lawmakers why we must stop using the oceans as a dumping ground. Once Hollings has secured Cousteau's participation, his secretary comes back on the line to provide the coordinates for Cousteau's appearance state-side.

101 Constitution Avenue Northeast is a DC address to be reckoned with. Directly south lies the forbidding US Supreme Court. A bit farther west, the US Capitol looms. Some people still remember the dilapidated housing that had previously occupied this site, considered by many to be an unsightly backdrop for the nation's capital. "Slum's Row" was demolished after the Senate acquired the land in 1948, rendering five hundred people homeless.[27] Today, such neighborhood displacement and gentrification would be met with a huge sustainability outcry. For years after the New Senate Office Building opened, it was commonly referred to as the "New SOB"[28] until the Senate renamed it the Dirksen Building after a popular Illinois Republican.

Cousteau arrives at the correct coordinates promptly at 9:45 a.m. Miraculously, he had managed to get a good night's sleep at his hotel after a long and bumpy flight. Merde, what an awful trip it had been. Shrugging off the memory, he strides briskly across the broad sidewalk. Without a single Paris-style sidewalk café in sight, he muses to himself that these Americans could be making better use of all this sprawling space. As he approaches the edifice, a frieze of bronze relief panels parades above him. One depicts a well-muscled shipyard worker guiding a massive piece of cargo into place using ropes and pulleys. This must be the right place to discuss matters of ocean commerce. Cousteau hurries on, not wishing to be late for his performance.

The hearing room is an imposing affair. Walnut-paneled walls rise to meet a high ceiling, carved in gleaming white. Ceremonial bronze light fixtures resembling ancient Greek oil lamps flank the walls. Deep crimson leather seats stand in perfectly lined rows, most already occupied. The setting evokes the stateliness of a Perry Mason–style courtroom. Indeed, humanity's moral and ethical beliefs are soon to be on trial. Alongside this scene of democratic order, imagine for a moment the contrasting dystopian ecological reality of the 1960s.

At the time, automobiles spewed uncontrolled carbon dioxide and hydrocarbons into the atmosphere, creating massive smog and respiratory death. It was considered normal to use the ocean as a giant garbage dump. Just about anything could legally be thrown in: radioactive waste, chemicals, laboratory refuse, munitions, as well as every castoff of a consumer culture. Photographers of the day, hired by the EPA, captured images of heavy oil slicks surrounding the Statue of Liberty in New York Harbor, as well as children playing in the shadow of smelter stacks spewing arsenic and lead residue down upon their Hot Wheel toys.[29] It was a time, to quote renowned biologist Edward O. Wilson from his book *Half Earth*, that "unfortunately married swift technological progress with the worst of human nature."

But things were beginning to change as the sleeping giant of public opinion was waking up, outraged that something had gone terribly wrong. In the spring of 1970, the first Earth Day was celebrated by an estimated twenty million Americans across the country. In the previous year, Richard

Nixon's newly minted presidency ushered in the start of what would later be referred to as the Environmental Decade. Government was beginning to take baby steps into a new stewardship role, using protective legislation to turn a tide of behavior that had ignored responsibility for its impact on life on Earth. Nixon would sign a groundbreaking National Environmental Policy into law that created requirements for the first Environmental Impact Statements. He launched the Environmental Protection Agency, sending dozens of sweeping environmental reform bills to Congress during his terms.

Cousteau's congressional scene is related to one of those bills, legislation proposed to fulfill America's role as a signatory in an international ocean stewardship treaty known as the London Convention. According to the EPA, the London Convention was eventually replaced with a modernized treaty called the London Protocol, but the US never became a party to the later agreement. Commonly referred to as the Ocean Dumping Act, the bill had already been passed by the House. Senator Hollings, Chair of the Commerce Subcommittee on Oceans and Atmosphere, was hoping to move on to passage in the Senate once the hearings were complete. The 1971 hearings were held on October 18 and November 8 before the Commerce Subcommittee on Oceans and Atmosphere. The following account is pulled from the official transcripts of those sessions.

It is a full house with an all-star cast. Every committee seat at the wide arc of the dais is filled. The audience includes numerous members of the press as well as the diplomatic corps. Chairman Hollings is pleased at the media turnout. "Gentlemen, we are convinced that a crisis is at hand, a crisis that not only concerns the quality of pollutants that we are putting into the world's oceans and the devastating effects, but also a crisis of inattention, incomprehension, and inactivity. Appropriate solutions to ocean pollution can be found . . . but where can the people's attention?" The senator pauses for dramatic impact. As the whispers of shuffling papers evaporate, he continues. "If the world's great oceans die, then man will die. We are fortunate to have with us today men eminently qualified to discuss the problem of ocean pollution from a broad viewpoint. Captain Jacques Cousteau has traveled all the way from France to be with us. His contributions to oceanography and marine exploration are probably better known than any during our time."

Swathed in a dark suit and narrow blue-and red-striped tie, Cousteau probably would have preferred to be aboard the *Calypso* wearing a dive suit. Whenever he was far from the ocean, he could feel its presence tugging at him like a phantom limb. After placing a crisply-typed statement on the heavy oak tabletop in front of him, it would quickly become clear he didn't need it. His words would emerge as naturally as the beating of his heart, which pumped his own private ocean of bodily fluid. He had once been gratified to learn that human blood is remarkably similar in its saltiness to the waters of his beloved sea.[30]

He leans in toward the bulbous microphones. Even without the trademark red knit cap, his face is recognizable to millions. The TV cameras prepare to eat him up. "Mr. Chairman, I am greatly honored to have been invited to appear here today to talk about the element to which I have devoted my life, the sea. My role in this gigantic enterprise is only that of a witness who has a unique quality of experience in underwater searching for more than thirty years, with the same companions most of the time."

Some of the older senators are already starting to feel a bit wistful about spending their lives trapped within air-conditioned rooms like this, their daring exploits limited to the occasional filibuster, their childhood dreams of becoming heroes or movie stars vanished among dust motes enshrined in manilla folders.

Cousteau is a hero to many, testifying to share the alarming trends he had been witnessing. The ocean's vitality was waning, prompting him to launch water quality surveys from the Mediterranean to the Caribbean, the Amazon to the Mississippi. "Everywhere around the world the coral reefs are disappearing at a very great rate. The water system has to remain alive if we are to remain alive on this earth. There is only one type of pollution because every single thing, every chemical whether in the air or on land, will end up in the ocean. Unfortunately, the authorities are so overwhelmed by day-to-day problems that problems that involve the coming generation are often put under the pile."

Shifting uncomfortably in their seats, a few of the senators are whispering to one another as they glance about to ensure the cameras are not focused on them. The chairman decides it is time to chime in. "As we meet, the destruction of the oceans continues. Not only does it continue, it accelerates. This conference is dedicated to putting people on the alert. What we lack is a sense of environment priorities. What, sir, would you say the priorities should be?"

The captain continues fluidly. "I want to talk to you today about four critical areas where I feel we must act." For the first time, he picked up the typed pages to ensure he made each point clearly. "First of all, funding for research is a critical need and an area in which resources are severely lacking. Second, one of the best remedies, in addition to ocean research, is educating the public, and I will speak more about that in a moment. Third, producers of pollution must be persuaded and required to include the cost of cleaning up the environment in the costs of their products. And fourth, we must establish drastic national and international legislation."

Cousteau adjusts his glasses, looking up into the assembled faces. The press, jumping into action, creates a blast zone of camera flashbulbs. Unlike *Calypso's* camera crew, most often gingerly attempting to avoid scaring off the wildlife, these photographers assume their subject wouldn't flee. Over the years of his fame, Cousteau had become accustomed to media attention. Unfazed, he navigates onward, staring at a horizon only he could see, the bobbing heads of the media seals left in his wake reminiscent of the actual seals that would bob behind his ship.

"Television is the best education tool which we can use to great advantage. But there is another one which is even better—it is the children themselves . . . A teenager today is the educator of the American family. He comes back from school with his head filled with new facts, and the family speaks together in the evening about pollution and the environment."

Senator Ted Stevens of Alaska, who had been personally gratified by Cousteau's previous visit to his state and the resulting *Undersea World* episode entitled "The Tragedy of the Red Salmon," is eager to find a way into this channel, to engage with this man who understands the value of the wilderness that characterizes Stevens' beloved home. "Captain Cousteau, you mentioned that you have been back to some places that you have been twenty years ago. And that in certain instances, you found specific implications of increased pollution in terms of your activities. Could you tell us any one in particular that sticks in your mind?"

Cousteau could have kissed the man on both cheeks for such a perfect setup. He began explaining his experiences diving off the coast of France in 1946, where he had documented countless damsel fish and abundant massive grouper. When he returned to these same waters three decades later, he witnessed a ghostly desert bereft of life. Similarly, along the California coast, he had witnessed the devastation of sea kelp, a keystone species within a balanced ecosystem. Sea otters love to eat sea urchins, but as sea otter populations declined, sea urchin populations rose, allowing them to eat up the kelp forests.

Too much negative news can cause people to stop listening. As sustainability evangelists, we have to balance the gloomy with the hopeful, in order to keep people engaged enough to take action. Noticing the mood in the room shifting slightly, Cousteau decides to take a different tack. "Each time man has protected a species, a turnback has occurred. Nature is ready to respond to any kind of action we take with spectacular speed and efficiency. I name quickly the gray whale, the sea otter. Each time man has officially protected an animal, even if it was near extinction, it came back. So, there is hope." Cousteau's Mona Lisa smile hints that there are many more eyewitness tales to be told, if his audience only had the time to listen.

Age has a way of creating a sense of urgency when one knows that time is running out. Jean-Michel, his oldest son, would later explain of his father, "There was a passion, an advocacy, a purpose, where there had once merely been abandon and wonder and the pure pleasure of discovery. Suddenly, the future was now all he could think about."[31]

In this twilight chapter of his life, our environmental revolutionist became an even more outspoken advocate against water pollution, over-fishing, and nuclear testing. Cousteau became increasingly concerned as the years went by, making his message more urgent. Unfortunately, this caused ABC to drop his programs, as they felt the tone becoming too dark.[32] In spite of this, Cousteau continued to spread his messages around the world with a voice that could not be quieted. His eloquent pleas for stewardship of the fragile natural environments that he loved so much reached thousands upon thousands of ardent ocean disciples.

How can each of us be that voice for sustainability? Opportunities abound to speak up, whether it's the next time you are standing in a grocery checkout line, organizing with neighbors, sending letters to elected officials, or running for public office yourself.

Next, we will look more closely at the second Environmental Core Value, which revolves around caring for Earth's complex living systems.

ENVIRONMENTAL CORE VALUE 2:

BIOPHILIC STEWARDSHIP
Protecting what we love

Everything depends on our ability to sustainably inhabit this earth, and true sustainability will require us all to change our way of thinking on how we take from the earth and how we give back.

— **Deb Haaland**, US Secretary of the Interior,
Member of the Pueblo of Laguna, and first Native American
to serve as a US cabinet secretary

The word stewardship has roots in the Middle Ages. In those days, serving in the role of a steward meant protecting a kingdom and its subjects while those in charge were absent. It often occurred in the case of a boy king, when someone was appointed to govern on their behalf until the lad was mature enough to take up the mantle of governance. Wise governance through stewardship implies a responsibility to be accountable for the well-being of a larger whole.[33] It requires self-interest to be set aside for the greater good. The moral obligation to care for others over whom we have power is a universal human value. The more power we have over someone—young or old, weak or poor, oppressed or unempowered—the more responsibility we have to act with benevolence and ethics to protect their welfare.

Today's cult of individualism and self-interest may seem counter to such responsibilities. Selfish thinking, as well as our belief in human exceptionalism, is based upon the false belief that we are separate and alone, that we can exist independently from the rest of the planet and its processes. This belief also leads us to the assumption that we bear neither individual nor collective responsibility for the welfare of those beyond our own doorstep.

In the twelfth century, St. Francis of Assisi expressed an idea of kinship with the entire solar system, referencing "Brother Sun, Sister Moon." Many cultures see the world from such a unified, universal perspective. Tikkun Olam, a popular Jewish practice, is translated from the ancient Hebrew as "world repair." It signals a responsibility to repair the world's ills through social action in pursuit of justice. Tikkun Olam aims to fix problems, as well as improving on existing conditions. The concept embraces both the human collective and the natural world. Pope Francis speaks of our responsibility to the human and natural community in his renowned encyclical "Laudato Si: On Care for Our Common Home."

The Pope could well be preaching the gospel of sustainability. "Because all creatures are connected, each must be cherished with love and respect," Francis says, "for all of us as living creatures are dependent on one another. Greater attention must be given to the needs of the poor, the weak, and the vulnerable, in a debate often dominated by more powerful interests. A fragile world, entrusted by God to human care, challenges us to devise intelligent ways of directing, developing and limiting our power."

We can frame planetary stewardship best within the confines of the ecological systems of the biosphere. The biosphere represents the boundaries of all life as we know it—all plants, animals, fungi, and microbes, from the outer reaches of our atmosphere to the deepest core of the oceans. Life within the biosphere is fragile and depends on a narrow range of life-giving resources. If these resources are removed, the result is most certainly death. In survival training, these conditions are often described as the Rule of Threes: You can live for three minutes without air; three hours without shelter or proper clothing in freezing cold; three days without water; and three weeks without food. Each species has its own resource-based survival needs. Responsible biosphere stewardship cares for all forms of life, as well as the resources upon which this life depends.

We often take for granted life's hospitability in the slender range of the sun's habitable zone within which we live, a narrow ribbon of conditions that is neither too hot nor too cold. This unique set of conditions is often referred to as the Goldilocks Zone. Appreciating our existence within such rare circumstances can lead to moments of awe and reverence.

Ownership of the planet and her resources is a myth; they are merely on loan to us. As we recognize our fundamental affiliation with all living things, we lay the foundation for an essential love of life. Renowned biologist Edward O. Wilson is Western culture's father of the concept of biodiversity, generally defined as the variety and variability of living organisms and the ecological complexes within which they reside. Of course, such world views have been understood and embraced by indigenous cultures long before Wilson provided us this language. Wilson notes in his book *Half-Earth*, "The biosphere does not belong to us; we belong to it. Will we continue to degrade the planet to satisfy our own immediate needs—or will we find a way to halt the mass extinction for the sake of future generations?"

Patterns within nature are not only practical. They can also provide more deeply satisfying experiences. Biophilia is an instinctive desire for humans to reconnect with nature, an innate bond with all living things. Spending time in nature is a balm to the spirit, lowers stress levels, and can help children improve their test scores. Renowned sustainability designer Bill Browning notes that biophilia "helps explain why crackling fires and crashing waves captivate us; why a view to nature can enhance our creativity; why shadows and heights instill fascination and fear; and why gardening and strolling through a park have restorative healing effects." Biophilic elements have genuine benefits for human performance metrics such as productivity, emotional well-being, stress, learning, and creativity. Browning says profound health and economic benefits flow from implementing biophilic design into workplaces, healthcare facilities, schools and neighborhoods.

Biophilic stewardship requires us to become trustees of Earth's species and all her living systems. But how can we be good stewards of something we barely understand? The more that we learn every day about the world around us, the more we realize what we don't know. The discovery of new species is far from over, with 18,000 new ones being discovered each year. Wilson says it's entirely possible that only 20 percent of Earth's biodiverse species have been discovered so far. At the same time, the rate of extinction due to human activity is as much as one thousand times greater than it was before humans dominated the planet. Wilson, once again in *Half-Earth*, says that when species disappear at our hands, "we throw away part of Earth's history. We erase twigs and even whole branches of life's family tree . . . we close the book on scientific knowledge important to an unknown degree but is now forever lost . . . These vanishing remnants of Earth's biodiversity test the reach and quality of human morality."[34]

We can succeed as stewards. One of the great biophilic stewardship success stories is the ongoing repair of the ozone hole. Thirty years ago, we listened to scientists about the aerosols in hairspray and refrigerants. The aerosols' chlorofluorocarbons (CFCs) are vicious greenhouse gases that cause catalytic reactions in the stratosphere. These aerosols were eating a giant gash in Earth's protective ozone layer and thinning the atmosphere over the Antarctic.

Such atmospheric thinning contributes to global climate disruption and allows cancer-causing ultraviolet radiation to penetrate the earth's surface. The Montreal Protocol that phased out CFCs was adopted just two years after these discoveries were announced. The protocol caused emissions to decrease by 90 percent. Without this decisive responsive action, unchecked CFC use would have quadrupled skin cancer cases.[35] A 2018 study using NASA Aura satellite data confirmed that the CFC ban led directly to the repair of the ozone hole.[36] The Montreal Protocol proved we can act as wise biophilic stewards—and even succeed in reversing environmental damage if we act decisively, responsibly, and swiftly.

The journey of biophilic stewardship is essentially one of caring combined with optimism. We must maintain vigilance now and into the future. We must not give up. In *Moral Ground*, the late Stephen Hawking provided words of both encouragement and warning. "The earth is in much more danger from human action than from natural disasters," he said. "This is not a prediction of doom but a wake-up call. We have to recognize the dangers and control them. I am an optimist, and I believe we can."

TODAY'S PLASTIC OCEANS

The conference on Ocean Pollution that Hollings had assembled would go on for two long days of speeches, captured via transcript and media hubbub. Cousteau's opening testimony became a common reference point for the rest of the proceedings. Thor Heyerdahl regaled the senators with tales of his voyages across the Pacific from South America to Polynesia on a primitive boat built of balsa wood. He spoke eloquently of the sea as an interconnected system. "The salt sea is a common human heritage . . . There are few things as elusive as the concept of territorial waters. What others dump at sea will come to your shores, and what you dump at home will travel abroad irrespective of national legislation." In his conference testimony, Barry Commoner, who had been instrumental in achieving the Nuclear Test Ban treaty ten years earlier, noted "It is the Congress and the President who translate abstract science into relevance."

The eloquent voices of explorers, scientists, and political activists including Cousteau helped awaken the Federal government to its stewardship responsibility. It would take another year for the final bill to be signed into law by Nixon in October 1972, the first prohibition by law on using the ocean as a garbage dump. The bill authorized the creation of the Regional Marine Research Program and the National Coastal Monitoring System. It also enabled creation of marine sanctuaries for a wide variety of purposes, including research, education, conservation, and species protection. International guidelines are now in place to assist national authorities with monitoring ocean dumping prohibitions.

While we have come a long way with protocols and regulations prohibiting the deliberate dumping of waste into the ocean, massive amounts of waste are still reaching the ocean each day—not by design, but by accident. One of the next frontiers for stewarding the ocean lies in transforming our relationship with one of today's most common materials: plastic. The ubiquitous stuff is likely to be an enduring marker for future archaeologists who might excavate our remains on land and sea.

The biggest problem is single-use plastics such as disposable straws and water bottles intended for short-term use. Once we are done with these "disposables," they can stick around for generations in what some refer to as Matter Out Of Place, or MOOP. The amount of plastic that humans have manufactured into existence from fossil fuels boggles the mind: 8,300 million metric tons since 1950, or the weight equivalent of over 6,000 Brooklyn Bridges. The majority of this has become waste, and our use is accelerating rapidly.

In the past thirteen years we've manufactured as much plastic as in the preceding fifty. We have been told for years that as long as we recycled plastic, we didn't need to worry about it. But that's no longer true. Of the waste plastics created since 1950, 79 percent is sitting in landfills or litter, and 12 percent has been incinerated. Only 9 percent has been recycled.[37] Plastic's durability is both a blessing and a curse. There is no such thing as "away" with plastics. With the collapse in the Asian plastics commodity markets, we are beginning to realize that we must find new ways to address the life cycle of plastics.

The world's biggest trash dump is not in India, China, or Brazil. It is in the middle of the ocean, and it is mostly plastic. The Great Pacific Trash Vortex covers a surface area twice the size of Texas, roughly 1.6 million square kilometers. Contrary to popular myth, it is not a solid island, but rather a massive floating blob of chunky bouillabaisse plastic soup. You can't walk around on it. If you try to put a net through it, you will capture mostly small gobs of plastic confetti and a few larger chunks. These plastics are less dense than water, meaning they won't sink but instead float near the water's surface.

The trash blob doesn't stay in one spot. It wanders around as a huge leash-less stray beast, reminiscent of the polluted "Stink" river monster in Hayao Miyazaki's film *Spirited Away*. This leviathan's territorial range is defined by two gyres, the sea's massive circulating currents. The range is determined by the West Pacific gyre off the coast of Japan and the Philippines, and the East Pacific gyre off the coast of California and

Northern Mexico. Gyres are formed by the earth's wind patterns and planetary rotational forces.

There are five major ocean gyres which help to circulate ocean water around the planet. There are also five unplanned plastic "garbage patches." Once the debris enters the gyre, it joins other debris, forming floating garbage islands that tend to stay together in convergence zones that allow debris to enter, but not to leave. These zones are also commonly referred to as ocean doldrums, which occur because there is very little wind. Sailors tend to avoid these areas, centered around the thirtieth parallel north and south. Ahab's *Pequod* crew got stuck in one, requiring them to row their whaling ship out of the doldrum.

Some marine debris is accidentally lost from cargo ships, such as the five shipping containers of Nike sneakers that were lost in a Pacific storm in 1990—resulting in people in Washington and Oregon collecting the shoes and holding swap meets to find matched pairs. Discarded fishing nets and fishery waste, which can take 600 years to break down, account for 46 percent of the trash in the Pacific garbage patch.[38] Much of the rest of the plastic waste finds its way ocean-bound by being swept or tossed into rivers and streams, where it finally makes its way to the sea. Between 1 and 2.5 million tons of plastic enter the sea each year from rivers.[39]

By 2050, there will be as much plastic in the ocean by weight as there are fish. Leatherback sea turtles, a species which has been around since the dinosaurs, choke on plastic bags, mistaking them for jellyfish. In June of 2018, a pilot whale found struggling off the coast of Thailand was later found to have ingested eighty plastic shopping bags, 17 pounds of plastic waste in all, causing it to starve. Rescue attempts failed and the whale died.

The horrors of sea pollution have only enlarged since Cousteau's campaigns. Endangered humpback whales are often spotted tangled in rope and other marine debris. This plastic marine waste can include discarded fishing nets, known as ghost nets. Over an eight-year period, the National Marine Fisheries Service recovered 870 ghost nets from Washington State alone. These nets contained 32,000 marine mammals.[40]

Once in the ocean, flip flops, plastic toys and water bottles can eventually break down into tiny particles called microplastics. The cosmetics industry also uses tiny beads of plastic that make their way into wastewater, a practice that is luckily beginning to change. Sea life often end up ingesting microplastics. Sea turtles and fish mistake little white plastic nodules for fish eggs. Microplastics can also act as tiny sponges, absorbing harmful pollutants as well as leaching them out. As the seaborne plastics photodegrade, they can also leach out the environmental toxin PCB. These toxins then enter the food chain. Humans can ingest microplastic beads lodged in the guts and muscle tissues of shellfish and fish. PCBs tend to migrate their chemicals into fatty tissues, where they persist.

Microplastic particles disturb marine food webs by blocking sunlight from reaching algae and plankton below the surface. These autotrophic food producers provide important nutrient sources at the base of the entire marine food chain. Next up the chain are fish and turtles, followed by apex predators such as tuna, sharks and whales.[41] In her fascinating book *Plastic: A Toxic Love Story*, Susan Freinkel documents the consequences of PCB migration in the Arctic ecosystem, where they have risen up through the food chain in the Inuit diet of the fatty meat of seals, whales and bears. The Inuit have some of the world's highest levels of PCBs in their blood and breast milk.

Even if we invested in cleaning up these giant garbage patches—it would take sixty-seven ships a year to clean up less than 1 percent of the North Pacific Ocean—new ocean-bound plastics would keep forming garbage patches.[42] Almost nine million tons of plastic are sent into the oceans each year by China, and another three million tons by Indonesia.[43] The better solution aims at addressing the source of the problem, rather than applying a band-aid after the damage has already been done. We must keep plastics out of the ocean in the first place.

Here's Hope: In his popular 2017 program *Blue Planet II*, environmental revolutionist David Attenborough delivered an ocean plastics plea, one which was met with a swift response. Within four months the EU proposed new rules for plastics, including a ban on single-use items and a mandatory 90 percent recycling rate for all the rest. Queen Elizabeth announced a disposable plastics ban at all royal properties, London milkmen returned to glass bottles, and Prime Minister Theresa May announced a sweeping plan to eliminate all avoidable plastic waste within twenty-five years.

At the international level, the United Nations, France, and the United States have begun forging an ambitious global treaty to reduce plastic ocean pollution. Similar to the Paris climate accords, it would include binding and non-binding elements and call for national plastics action plans.[44]

BIOPHILIC STEWARDSHIP FOR PLASTIC ACTION TODAY

Elsewhere, the forces of Biophilic Stewardship are at work among creative entrepreneurs, finding new ways to prevent ocean-bound plastics from ever becoming part of a garbage patch. Instead, stewards are mining these wastes to create new livelihoods for people near the sea. Such entrepreneurial stewards give us reasons for hope.

A group of biosphere stewardship heroes are hard at work among an archipelago of forty small islands, which form the bewitching Danajon Bank in the Camotes Sea of the central Philippines. A rare double reef formation, one of only six in the world, protects the delicate ecosystem from tsunamis. Legend has it that the area gets its name from a stingray, once abundant here. What remains are sea fans and sponges, endangered mushroom and bubble corals, mythical seahorses and exotic seagrass beds. Abundant mangrove swamps serve as a massive carbon sink, tempering floods. The swamps are also an important flyover site for birds migrating south to Australia. Functions such as flood control, carbon sequestration, and habitat provision are sometimes referred to as ecosystem services. In addition, the area provides ecotourism income from divers and amateur underwater photographers who frequent the area. These proceeds supplement the income of local peoples who rely on a daily seafood diet from subsistence fishing.

Following Cousteau's use of gorgeous photos of the natural world to inspire stewardship action, *National Geographic* captured the wonders of the Danajon Bank using photographs by Michael Ready, associate fellow at the International League of Conservation Photographers. His imagery sets the scene for our next story of sustainability revolutionists in action. Let's imagine the end of a typical day there.

The Danajon Bank Sea turns purple at dusk, alternating textural stripes of flat water and slow rippling currents. These seem to form the theater backdrop for a picture book fairy tale. Islands shaped like pointy gnome hats peak above the surface. Divers who are lucky enough to spot a family of cavorting tiger-tail seahorses may learn that the yellow males are the ones to give birth, once they have mated for life. Their relatives, the dragonface pipefish, get their name from their impossibly long pink snouts. Their prehistoric ribbon-like bodies appear ornamented with white black and tangerine Magic Marker squiggles.

Along the island shoreline, moored silhouettes of fishing canoe double-outriggers lie low in the water, mimicking the flat horizon. After a hard day of work, even the boats get to rest. The aerial drift of tree frog and cricket song suggests their day is just beginning. The exhausted fishermen who fish the reef have gone ashore, anxious to begin devouring shrimp fritters downed with cold Red Horse beers. If it's a Friday, they might join in the local version of Karaoke, Videoke. If they didn't catch many fish today, an increasingly frequent occurrence, they might eventually drink a few too many. These reefs are some of the most degraded in the world, their decline crashing down since the 1950s due to fishing with sodium cyanide or dynamite, the aquarium fish trade, sedimentation from development runoff, or more recently, plastic waste.

Degrading the reefs means that the total fish catch per day has decreased by a factor of ten since the 1940s.[45] The once abundant reefs are damaged underwater graveyards where the fairytale princess has been cast under an evil spell. Seahorses—said to have the head of a horse, the snout of an aardvark, the pouch of a kangaroo, and the tail of a monkey—are experts at changing color to camouflage themselves from predators. Unfortunately, this has not shielded them from fishing using blast explosives and trapping. The horses are prized for sale in the aquarium trade and in Chinese traditional medicine. They are currently listed as a vulnerable species, one stop before the endangered list. Such decimation travels up the food chain, as large predator fish and sharks no longer frequent this area, finding small-fry to eat.

Since the 1980s, inexpensive monofilament fishing nets have become a favorite fisherman's tool. Unfortunately, these relatively inexpensive nets are easily damaged beyond repair, and thus often discarded. Sometimes discarded plastic nets are burned to dispose of them, releasing a plume of toxic fumes. Many of the nets end up piled high on beaches or lost at sea, left to sink to the bottom or drift away. Discarded or lost floating nets, often nearly invisible, become ghost nets, silent killers leaving death in their wake, continuing to purposelessly ensnare fish. These nets they may drift out into the Pacific to get swept into the Kuroshio current that makes up part of the North Pacific Ocean gyre. If this occurs, they will likely end up trapped forever, to swirl around as part of the Great Pacific Garbage Vortex. It is believed that China, Indonesia, the Philippines, Thailand and Vietnam contribute up to 60 percent of global marine debris.[46]

But this doesn't have to happen. There is another way to think about how we do things, using entrepreneurial creativity, combined with a stewardship mindset. The Cebu, Leyte, and Bohol islanders living in this remote area of Southeast Asia suffer from low levels of education and little access to basic services such as healthcare and utilities that deliver potable water or garbage removal. Most of the fishers live below the poverty line, with 75 percent of their fishing grounds severely overfished. As the catch they rely on for their livelihood declines, they have been forced to move to other ways to generate income, including seaweed farming to create nori and natural thickeners for toothpaste and ice cream (carrageenan). Others have gone to work harvesting fishing monofilament nets for recycling.

Mounds of white, airy fluff are piled high in front of traditional Philippine nipa huts. These are not clouds; they are abandoned piles of fishing net. The vernacular architectural form of the hut takes its name from the nipa palm, *Nupa fruticans*, and also known as mangrove palm are cycads, which have been around for at least seventy million years. Roof panels are fabricated by hand from green nipa leaves, folded in half over bamboo frames and secured with rattan twine. Each roof section is securely tied to the pitched roof structure, the steep pitch allowing the roof to shed water quickly during seasonal monsoons. While the roof only lasts about three years, it is entirely biodegradable and can be easily replaced with locally abundant materials and simple skills. The pole frame of the structure is coconut lumber, making the entire building biodegradable and non-toxic.[47] If only the same were true of monofilament fishing nets. But luckily, this particular nipa hut is a processing barn for fishing nets that are bound for a second life, remanufactured into carpets.

The land-locked mounds of monofilament net are a favorite spot for children to have their photo taken, draped among the soft clouds of netting. But these old nets, collected and stockpiled by fishermen, won't be staying here for long. They are headed to a compacting machine that will prepare them to be baled and weighed on old-fashioned scales. Once weighed, they will be sold to a company called Net-Works, launched in 2012 by the Zoological Society of London, a conservation group, and Interface, one of the biggest and most innovative carpet manufacturers in the world. The baled, clean fishing nets are loaded onto boats and transferred to collection hubs. They will eventually be shipped to remanufacturing plants in Slovenia, to be broken down to a molecular level before being re-spun into nylon thread. This transformation allows the material to enter the global supply chain as a resource material.

This process, referred to as re-commercialization, can increase production costs by 6 percent compared to production using virgin nylon. However, the associated carbon emissions are reduced by 50 percent, relying on the alternative to original raw material sourced from petroleum.[48] There are now thirty-five communities participating in Net-Works. Together, more than 100 tons of fishing nets have been recycled, enough to encircle the globe twice.[49] The program continues its success, now collecting about 3.5 metric tons of nets each month in the Philippines, all destined for a new life as carpet.

MODERN-DAY REVOLUTIONISTS: SEA TURTLES AND FISHING NETS

The story of turning discarded fishing nets into carpet is a tale of bio-philic stewardship that can take us all the way from the Philippines to Australia. Let's take a quick look at where some of this carpet ended up in its new life of service, and how this reimagined product fits the mission of the organization's heroes who chose to install it. The basic facts are all true based on video accounts and written records, with a bit of literary license regarding story details.

The Great Barrier Reef Aquarium and Turtle Hospital of Australia is the world's largest living reef aquarium, with over 120 species of hard and soft corals on display. Located within the Great Barrier Reef Marine Park, it's a place to raise awareness about the plight of the coral reef and its many inhabitants, including sea turtles, which are often killed by ghost nets. Installing carpeting spun from recovered ghost nets provides the aquarium yet another way to tell the story of how we can participate in protecting sea turtles. Some interpretive signage helps visitors understand the unseen link between the carpet they are walking upon—material prevented from becoming a deadly ghost net—and the prosperity of sea turtles. We'll look further into such lifecycle impacts in Part Two.

More than two hundred turtles have been cared for here since 2008, and over 200,000 people have learned about them from people like Stephen Menzies, Chief Aquarium Curator.[50] Menzies has the kind of pale skin that seems destined for a sunburn, but that hasn't stopped him from his passionate work on behalf of the world outside this building's doors. His resume reads like an exotic travelogue: shark consultant in Quintana Roo along with jobs at aquariums in Valencia, Shanghai, and Barcelona. At the Turtle Hospital he helps people understand the amazing phylogenic history of the turtles. Sea turtles have a similar life span to humans; turtles can take twenty years or more to reach maturity. The sick and injured are brought here to recover. Today, one of Menzies' patients is a critically endangered hawksbill sea turtle who lost a flipper as a result of an entanglement with a fishing line.

Menzies has a way of speaking with a level-headed clarity that is difficult to ignore. He explains a ghost net is a perpetual killer that will continue to kill things and attract more animals to be killed. "Quite often they will come in with carcasses of animals entangled up in them, specifically turtles but also other animals, large sharks that come in to feed on the turtles then get trapped."[51] He knows there are many more dead turtles that he never gets to see. The sick and injured brought here are the ones he gets to meet for a brief moment in which their paths cross. Much as he loves these creatures, Stephen lives for the day he can say goodbye to them by releasing them back into the wild.

On a lovely July day at Townsville Strand beach park, the moment has arrived to release a recovered turtle. Mabel is a massive adult female *Chelonia mydas,* an endangered green sea turtle weighing in at 298 pounds.[52] This species is among the largest in the world, sometimes getting up to 700 pounds and 5 feet across. It takes six people to carry Mabel from the aquarium trailer to the beach, using a custom sling designed to keep her damp, cushioned, and immobile until it's time for the big release. Off in the distance looms Magnetic Island National Park, surrounded by numerous scattered reefs whose names read like an exotic bestiary: Tiger, Kangaroo, Centipede, Cockle, Leopard, Otter, Wallaby, Beaver. Meanwhile, a menagerie of t-shirt clad volunteers and children wait in a long receiving line perpendicular to the shore, eager to snap photos for their Instagram feed as they bid the turtle good luck on its journey.

The team un-swaddles Mabel as carefully as she would any human infant. A cheer goes up from the throng, and she's off. This isn't exactly a race of the tortoise and the hare, rather a race of sea turtles against the odds represented by ghost nets, overfishing, coral bleaching, and climate change. Mabel's progress is steady but awkward along the sand. Luckily, she seems to know exactly where she is going. Sea turtles use cues such as the brightness of the ocean horizon to find their way to water; scientists now believe that mature turtles are able to read the earth's magnetic fields. This reading helps them navigate thousands of miles to return to their original nesting grounds.[53] Two little girls in pink sun hats wave goodbye; their homing instincts pale by comparison.

The moment Mabel's nose hits the surf, she pauses, drinking in the prospect of her reunion with her native Coral Sea. She continues her diva's entrance into the liquid womb as her dinosaur head tilts out of the water, scanning the horizon. Her flippers gain purchase in the surf as she scoops herself away from the throng, never looking back. Menzies stands proud as he watches her disappear from view. "We are releasing her on this beautiful day so she can go out there and continue contributing to the gene pool."

Mabel is an undaunted survivor driven by ancient instincts, and the sea needs more like her. If all goes well, this grand dame will be back one day to lay a clutch of 200 eggs in the sand, continuing 80 million years of matriarchal evolutionary history.

CHAPTER FOUR

The Long View

Change often takes time. It rarely happens all at once.

— **John Lewis**, civil rights advocate and former
Georgia US Representative

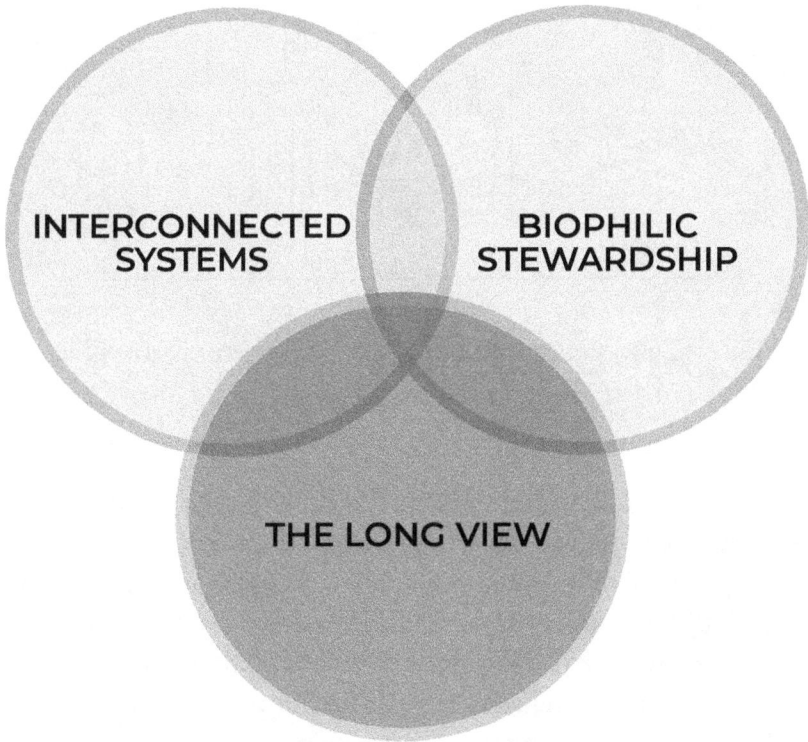

The Long View, the Third Core Value of the Environmental Pillar

THIRD COURSE: A COURSE
IN THE LONG VIEW

Back at my imaginary dinner party, it's time for the third course to be served: a course in what it means to take The Long View.

The very idea of an imaginary dinner party is founded on the idea of the Long View, with the ability to look backward across time. You can choose to invite guests who are no longer alive, in addition to those who may still be walking the earth. The timeline has no limits but your imagination.

To the delight of my guests, I have handed out tiny spoons and bowls of cool melon soup, garnished with fresh mint. The chilled soup is an unusual choice, yet perfect for the warm evening. In another unusual choice, Chávez is wearing a loose embroidered guyabera, adorned with vertical pleats and bands of embroidery. It's a departure from his typical uniform of tucked-in plain work shirt. His garment, commonly referred to as a Mexican wedding shirt, strikes me as particularly fitting. I can think of no man more wedded to his work than he.

The flavors of the soup seem to be stirring Chávez's memories long past. "I can never forget the backbreaking labor of picking melons," he says. "My bones still ache today when I think of it. One of the successes of our labor rights struggle was to ensure rest breaks and better working conditions for the pickers."

Everyone at the table has stopped eating, listening carefully in the moment. The riches of the world often appear magically at our doorsteps, without our taking the time to wonder about the potential sustainability implications—or the experiences of the people who help bring such gifts to us.

"I have often felt guilty about not spending more time with my own children because of the work I have been called to do," Chávez says. "But I think they understand. They know that if I'm successful, my work will help create a better future for them."

His wistfulness touches me. Many of us make sacrifices to protect the things we love. I wish I could tell him that his grandchildren are continuing his work today, but that might break the non-interference time travel rules governing this dinner party. This party follows the rules, including the one that precludes aliens from interfering with other civilizations. In order to prevent travelers from accidentally changing the course of history, what happens at the party, stays at the party.

Emboldened to gently lay my hand atop his, I'm suddenly aware of how much older his hands look than the rest of him. It's no doubt the result of his many years toiling in the fields. Somehow, his spirit feels young. I'm looking to lighten his mood.

"Have you ever heard the expression Pay It Forward?" I ask. "It's a form of giving where the beneficiary is a third party that the giver may never meet."

"I have never heard it called that," says Anita. "It's rather catchy. Helping others is what gives life meaning. But sometimes the results are not immediately in front of you. The positives may be felt halfway around the planet tomorrow, or by our children, years from now."

Cousteau brings the conversation home. "Some revolutionary ideas may take generations to come to fruition. I hope that my work protecting the oceans will benefit future generations of both the human and animal family, long after I'm gone."

Chávez seems to know how to make the dream a reality. "I think we could easily enroll others in the Pay It Forward concept by taking the time to sit down and explain it in person. I suggest a series of kitchen table meetings. No one is too young to grasp the idea."

AMBASSADORS FOR OUR FUTURE

Cousteau's affections were not limited to the sea. A proud family man who took joy in his sons and grandchildren, he also never lost his child-like sense of wonder. At the same time, he knew that youth presented an opportunity to become enrolled as future revolutionists for sustainability. Late in life, he launched a series of public education events with thousands showing up to hear his message.[54] Each ended with his favorite segment, when he answered questions from the youngest members of the audience.

"I believe in children. I live for children," he said, words that signaled that he somehow found a way to stay optimistic about the future in spite of the sobering deterioration of the ocean he was experiencing. At the celebration of his 75th birthday, he shared these reflections with the children, both his own and others. "Because of the hope I have for the future of mankind," he said in the documentary *Pioneer of the Sea,* "I want to join forces and forge a better world for future generations. Those first 75 years, I spent them amazed by nature, bedazzled by the exuberance of life, but worried by its fragility. For the next 75 and beyond, the spirit that inspired me must live on, and it is you that will carry further the flame of my faith."

Cousteau went on to share ideas for raising global citizens, and a proposal to spend 1 percent of all military budgets on an exchange program of children between countries. The latter was envisioned as an effective strategy for securing world peace. Today, we find that sustainability inextricably tied to achieving peace. Many modern conflicts are triggered by the fight for resources such as oil, water, or food.

At the age of 80, Cousteau launched a future generations mission to Antarctica with a group of six children aged 8 to 10 from six continents. There were three boys and three girls: Geronimo from Chile, Oko from Tanzania, Cory from the United States, Kelly from Australia, Fumiko from Japan, and Elise from France. The journey was captured in the 1990 documentary film *Lilliput in Antarctica,* a reference to Jonathan Swift's classic *Gulliver's Travels* and the mythical tiny people who inhabited the story's island. A ship dubbed the *Erebus*, a reference to their destination, was requisitioned for the voyage.

We know that connecting children more closely to nature is a good thing. Kids who spend more time outdoors are better adjusted to the stresses of the modern world and score more highly on standardized tests. However, taking young children on such a grand nature expedition was an unusual idea which the media found mesmerizing. They were on hand to capture images of hordes of children, parents and teachers in attendance at the public send-off.

Cousteau hoped the attention would be worth all the liabilities and permissions that had to be finagled to take a group of minors away from their families to a place so remote and uninhabited. His ulterior motive was inspiring stewardship of the vast and icy southern landmass of Antarctica, a place unknown to most humans. In his announcement of the venture, he called the destination "an inestimable treasure that we must preserve intact for future generations," a place that should be established as a "natural reserve, a land of peace and science."[55] We can find unlimited inspiration in connecting with the wonder of nature. We can also choose to become the leaders, revolutionists and heroes the world needs now in the sustainability journey.

Cousteau sets his course for inspiration in his captain's personal log of January 6, 1990, at the moment the expedition reaches Antarctica. "At the gate of Antarctica, the Erebus enters Admiralty Bay at reduced speed," writes Jean-Michel Cousteau in *My Father, The Captain*. "Blocks of ice are scattered in the bay. On the bridge, our six little ambassadors let out shouts of joy as two pairs of humpback whales swim about the ship, disporting themselves in a show of welcome. It is a marvelous sight. Six little faces of varying colors. Six sets of wide-open eyes. Six children, off to reclaim the continent of Antarctica in the name of all the children of the world, those of today and those of tomorrow."

Antarctica is a mysterious and vast frontier at the southern tip of planet Earth. Our last largely unspoiled wilderness holds mythic, spiritual, and scientific significance. This coldest place on Earth is also the windiest and driest, making it a desert, although not the kind of desert we usually think of. Ice shelves the size of Texas float above the ocean floor. Elsewhere, solid rock and the world's southernmost active volcano, Mount Erebus, rises more firmly about the surface. Glaciers slowly melt as massive blocks of ice calve off into the ocean to form icebergs. This fragile continent is one of the few places on Earth widely believed to have never known any native settlement due to the extreme inhospitable conditions.[56] Antarctica belongs to everyone, and to no one.

The vast 5 million square mile continent surface serves as an immense scientific laboratory. Here, the Concordia science station is used to study the effects of long space missions on astronauts, as the locale provides the closest analog for the hostile space environment.[57] In spite of the brutal living conditions, scientists of many nationalities inhabit year-round research stations and seasonal field camps across this windswept land. Some researchers dive beneath the ice surface to collect data on marine life. Others take ice core samples, research that began in the 1950s. Ice cores provide a record of past climatic conditions going back at least 800,000 years, relying on trapped air bubbles to provide a window into ancient atmospheric conditions. The bubbles are used to learn about climate stability and fluctuation over time.[58]

Let's join the *Lilliput's* expedition to see how things are going, scenes drawn from *Lilliput in Antarctica*. We will see that sometimes the way the message of sustainability is presented is just as important as the message itself. We will also see that needed essentials, fashioned from simple materials easily at-hand, lie at the heart of sustainability.

How to Build an Igloo

In an Antarctic summer, the sun never sets. Instead, it travels in a circle around you. In this Land of the Midnight Sun, Cousteau's six child ambassadors sit timidly along the icy shores of Prince George Island, bundled layer upon layer against the cold. Though none of them speak the same language, they have quickly become friends. Drawing simple pictures has provided visual storytelling about their families and lives back home. The most ambitious children have tried to learn a few words of the five languages represented by the group. Rudimentary English has become their universal tool of communication. Jacques is fluent in that language in addition to his native French, and their documentary story will also be told in English.

Their bulky, junior-sized down coats are warm enough to allow them to relax somewhat against the body's reflexive cringe against 14°F temperatures. An additional challenge to relaxation is the fact that some of the group seem to be staring into the faces of carnivorous wild animals that exceed them in size more than five-fold. The children are here to commune with elephant seals who take their name from their trunk-like inflatable snouts. Males can bulk up to 8,800 pounds, whereas this group of females weighs in at a more diminutive 2,000 pounds each. The scene brings to mind Swift's tiny Lilliputians arranged alongside the giant.

The *Lilliput* winter gear can't compare in functionality to seal blubber, which insulates the animals from extreme temperatures down to 40 degrees below zero. The blubber is a highly functional fatty substance that once brought the species to the brink of extinction due to hunting the oil-rich material for use as lamp fuel. Luckily, their numbers have bounced back due to legal protections including thirty-four country restrictions on the import and sale of seal products including fur.[59]

The sleepy harem of silvery-grey matriarchs lounges peacefully on the ice, nonchalant about the presence of humans. The extreme spirals of their cream-colored curly whiskers and dark, wideset kohl-lined eyes give them an exotic ornamented appearance. Some of the lovelies loll about clumsily on their backs, sniffing the air or scratching invisible itches. This ponderous appearance on land is misleading; their underwater swimming is agile, graceful, and powerful. Able to dive to depths of almost 5,000 feet, they can stay submerged for hours while hunting.[60] The shy seals glance toward the children occasionally. More often they look away, or close their eyes completely, dreaming of their next meal of fish or squid. A few of the children snap photos or shoot video with their camcorders, imagining how they will explain all this to their schoolmates back home.

The inter-species communion comes to an end as Cousteau arrives on the scene, announcing it is time for the ambassadors to take on an important task. His words act like a sort of incantation, bringing the children to life. They must build an igloo, something many Antarctic expeditioners undertake as part of their field training. In an emergency situation, an igloo can save your life. On the other side of the planet, the Inuit habitation of igloos was first recorded in the late sixteenth century in the Northwest Passage. The hard-packed blocks of snow used to build them serve as an excellent insulator and wind stop. While climate change and modernization have diminished the use of igloos as indigenous shelters far to the north, here they are still utilized as temporary shelters for hunting and scientific expeditions.

Learning to build an igloo, followed by spending a night under its icy dome, will be an important rite of passage for our young Antarctic ambassadors. Learning to create something you need, using only the simplest materials available from nature, is a fundamental sustainability concept. How can we live within the means of the resources in our environment? We'll dive more deeply into meeting needs within nature's limits in Chapter Four of Part Two.

The best snow for building an igloo is the kind that is laid down by the wind during a single storm, forming a deep drift of hard and dry snow perfect for cutting blocks.[61] The expedition leaders dig a circular outline for the igloo into the frozen ground plane, near a steep snow embankment formed from this perfect type of snow. The children pitch in, cutting rectangular blocks with a serrated saw. Passing the cut blocks hand to hand along a relay line, the blocks arrive at the spot for the imagined shelter. Each block is carefully tapped into place with the help of an experienced guide. The dome of the igloo slowly rises in a continuous spiral of frozen layers. Each block is beveled to improve the joint, and snow is packed into the gaps between blocks to form a seal.

Sound construction detailing is important, so the igloo doesn't collapse in the middle of the night. If done correctly, a person should be able to stand on the roof. As each spiraling layer is set in place, the dome of the sky through the roof opening begins to recede, until finally the last block closes in. From inside, the wind is silenced and the eerie blue emanations of the sun filter through 8 inches of frozen water crystals. The shelter is complete.

Cousteau has planned a ceremony for this moment, to be captured on film. One by one, the children crawl out of the igloo to join him next to the shelter. A flag is unfurled, created specially to communicate a message. With help from his *Lilliput* ambassadors, they affix the flag to the igloo, using handfuls of snow to hold it in place. Superimposed on the icy blue flimsy scrap of nylon are three images: an outline of the Antarctic continent, a child with arms flung wide, and a penguin apparently mimicking the child with its flippers broadly spread. Cousteau fondly refers to it as "the flag of tomorrow." The artwork is clumsy, but it's the message that's important.

The children gather around Cousteau, clearly under his mesmerizing spell, waiting intently for him to speak. "This is a symbol that we are taking over the Antarctic for future generations, for your children and your grandchildren. Perhaps in the name of future generations, our generation can preserve forever this distant land of life so vital to our own."

In a few hours, the children will curl up inside the igloo in their fluffy sleeping bags, attempting to sleep through a sunlit night that exists only as time on a clock. They will complete what Cousteau calls a "symbolic night in a symbolic home." Under the icy vault of their shelter, they will dream of chicken soup and infinite stars in a dark sky they have not seen for days. The next morning, they will wake up to hot chocolate and sandwiches before they depart for the next phase of their adventure. They will never forget their night in an igloo, sheltered by a creation of their own hands.

As all expeditions must, eventually the voyage of the *Lilliput* comes to an end. The children reunite with their families and home-grown playmates, beginning a new adventure of endless storytelling and junior rev-olutionist endeavors.

The resulting documentary film, *Lilliput in Antarctica*, was broadcast in France, the United States, and beyond. Cousteau distributed copies of the film to each United States Supreme Court justice, senator, and congressman. He collected millions of signatures on a petition to ban mineral exploitation of Antarctica. In June 1991, Cousteau and his son Jean-Michel met with President George H. W. Bush. The following day, the President announced that the US would join in the Protocol on Environmental Protection to the Antarctic Treaty, an agreement aimed at environmental, flora and fauna con-servation. The treaty commits the parties to the comprehensive protection of the Antarctic environment and dependent and associated ecosystems. It also designates Antarctica as "a natural reserve, devoted to peace and science." It prohibits all mining of mineral resources except for scientific purposes, as well as a requirement that "protection of the environment shall be a fundamental consideration in the planning and conduct of all activities." The Protocol was an addendum to a previous 1959 treaty, which the United States was instrumental in negotiating, that effectively eliminated territorial claims to Antarctica's expanse and the entire areas south of 60 degrees South Latitude. As of 2016, there were 37 signatory countries. A committee to over-see implementation of the treaty meets regularly, conducting its meetings in four official languages: English, French, Russian, and Spanish.

The igloo-building *Lilliput* children will grow up bearing witness to events that will make Antarctica's future uncertain. They will probably worry to find out that since their visit in 1990, scientists at the Vernasdky research station have seen an increase in air temperatures of two degrees Fahrenheit every ten years. They may be disturbed to know that the frequency of icebergs calving off the mainland is increasing at an alarming rate, accompanied by explosive cracks that can be heard for miles. They will no doubt be puzzled to hear that a flotilla of over one hundred wayward icebergs unexpectedly showed up off the coast of New Zealand, creating a tourist frenzy. And they will probably find it difficult not to be heartbroken when they find out about the breakup of a massive iceberg called B-15 which blocked emperor penguins from their food sources. The berg doubled the distance the penguins had to travel to feed their young, causing starvation for many parents and chicks.[62]

It will be difficult for the children not to imagine that many of the wonders they saw will be gone by the time their own children might enjoy them. Yet, inspired by the example set by their revolutionist guide, they will also hold out hope for a better environmental future.

Years later, Elise Otzenberger, the little girl from France, shared her adult reflections of the *Lilliput* journey and her memories of Captain Cousteau. "He was interested in what we were thinking and in what we were feeling," she said in an account in *My Father, the Captain*. "In this way, he was very different from the other adults we knew. He never treated us like children. And when he asked us what we thought, it was not to flatter us or indulge us. It was because he really valued our opinion."

Cousteau would die in 1997 at age 87, seven years after his voyage with the *Lilliput*. But his heirs and the children of the world continue to speak out to protect their birthright to the natural wonders of the world. They continue to repeat one of the captain's favorite sayings: L'avenir peut étre á nous. The future may be ours.

How can we envision the sustainability future we most desire? What stories, journeys, and tools can we use to increase our ability to imagine that future and enroll others in it?

ENVIRONMENTAL CORE VALUE 3:
THE LONG VIEW
Thinking Big about the Future

What is a legacy? It's planting seeds in a garden you never get to see.
— **Lin-Manuel Miranda**, actor, playwright, producer, singer

The Long View Core Value fits nicely alongside the environmental sciences, which include the study of astronomy, physics, geology, and climatology. All of these embrace the idea of evolutionary time scales. The entire 4.5-billion-year history of our planet is sometimes expressed as existing within deep time, or within the expanse of geologic or astronomical time. Humans are relative newcomers to the planet, having emerged only 200,000 years ago.[63]

Humanity's early history was characterized by a struggle for survival among the elements. More recently, our experience has been characterized by developments emerging from the industrial revolution, with its technological innovations and associated burning of fossil fuels and throughput of resources. The primary driver of planetary change was once considered to be geologic forces. This shifted somewhere around 1800, with the advent of the Industrial Age. Today, the largest driver of planetary change is human activity, commonly referred to as anthropogenic causes. This has led many scientists to suggest that we are now living within a geological era that should be referred to as the Anthropocene, or human, era. The Anthropocene succeeds the Holocene Era, which began after the earth's last major glacial retreat.

In today's human experience, time is often framed within the short-term. We find it difficult to focus our minds beyond the next news headline or social media post. The idea of multi-generational, epochal time is difficult to relate to as we hustle and bustle along. If we look a bit closer, we may find that our ephemeral sense of time is an illusion. Instead, we may discover that what we do now has reverberations across space and time, far into the future. As we shift our thinking to a more patient timeframe, we can weigh the legacy of various choices and their consequences, informed by the past as well as by the future. Such a measured viewpoint is called taking the Long View.

Dramatic impacts, resulting from the acceleration of human consumption and economic development since the 1950s, is often referred to as the Great Acceleration. This acceleration is characterized by global population increase, associated upticks in consumption, and an explosive increase in the use of plastics. These are unsustainable patterns. Longitudinal research data reveals undesirable trends. Systemic destabilization is occurring across multiple earth-system and socio-economic indicators. Many of these acceleration trends have shockingly happened within a single human lifetime.[64] Unbridled capitalism driven by short-term gain has created massive resource depletion, species collapse, and planetary disruption.

Sustainability requires us to look back at what we have learned, while at the same time preparing for the future. Some scientists worry about the long-term sustainability of the world food supply. Planetary disruptions caused by climate change could endanger the survival of plants we depend upon. The Svalbard Global Seed Vault, located deep within an icy mountain steel tunnel in the Norwegian Arctic, is intended as a hedge against the risks to potential disastrous unknowns. The vault was conceived as a vast repository of 13,000 years of agricultural heritage. Seeds are stored at minus 0.4°F in a facility intended to endure for a thousand years. Popularly referred to as the "Doomsday Vault," the remote high-security location holds hundreds of thousands of biodiverse seed samples, a library of plant-based genetic heritage. In 2017, one effect of climate change flooded the facility. The melting of the permafrost within which the vault is located caused the facility to flood—although the water did not reach the precious seed vaults on this occasion.[65] The future is coming at us so fast that it's increasingly difficult to plan for it.

In sharp contrast to the idea of a seed holding inestimable value a thousand years from today, much of our economy is organized around a disposable lifestyle, based on the planned obsolescence of consumer goods. Our choices are riddled with unintended consequences. The constantly turning wheel of fashion fads use advertising, based on psychological manipulation, telling us that we need to consume in order to achieve happiness. We buy vast amounts of clothing we don't need, only to discard these cheap items within a single season. A plastic beverage bottle will experience an all-too-brief useful life, followed by a 450-year timespan to decompose.

Many are fighting back, looking for ways to cut the chatter. The world-wide "slow" movement encourages social downshifting by simplifying everything from eating to travel to education to cities. Slow food focuses on locally grown food and meals prepared and enjoyed with care, the antithesis of fast food. The slow food manifesto states, "Homo Sapiens should rid ourselves of speed before it reduces us to a species in danger of extinction. May long-lasting enjoyment preserve us from the contagion of the multitude who mistake frenzy for efficiency. In the name of productivity, fast life has changed our way of being and threatens our environment and our landscapes."

Patient thoughtfulness is mandatory to the Long View. In the world of finance, the drive toward short-term windfalls and earnings is commonplace. Some investors excel financially while taking the Long View. Warren Buffet, declared by *Forbes* at one point as the richest man in the world, is known for his wildly successful investment acumen as well as his philanthropy. He aims to give away most of his wealth before he dies and was once heard to say "Someone is sitting in the shade today because someone planted a tree a long time ago."

Success is not always tied to quick wins. The ability to delay gratification is part of the executive function of our frontal lobe that allows long-term strategic goal achievement.[66] This ability is fundamental to the long-term thinking required in order to achieve sustainability. However, it may be daunting to realize that many humans are hard-wired for short term thinking. Our brains are complex organs ruled by a wide variety of cognitive functions, not all of them based on logic.

Neuropsychologists untangle why humans behave the way they do, based on genetic, environmental, situational, or biological factors. The Marshmallow Test was devised in the early 1970s as a way to understand human self-control. Preschool children were offered a variety of treats and told that if they waited to eat them, they could get even more treats. Some children with better gratification delay coping strategies did better at the test.[67] When researchers followed up with their test subjects some seventeen years later, they found that those who were able to delay gratification were also experiencing greater success in their careers and marriages. (Subsequent research has attempted to debunk the Marshmallow Test, using a larger test population and controlling for various factors such as affluence, which might explain the ability to delay gratification.)

Tapping into our executive function utilizing the Long View is needed now more than ever. We grapple with an incredible acceleration of consumer uptake and choice, data and digital sharing, technology advancement, climate and planetary disruption, and the pace of change itself. Our society is shuddering to normalize and internalize so much so fast.

But there is another way. Thinking from a Long View state of mind can be freeing. It can help to eliminate many distractions and give us permission to think bigger. When we remember that we exist within an eyeblink of deep time, we realize that our path is one of many steps in a long continuum. Even though we won't be able to do it all or save the world with a single well-informed action, our lives are still connected across time with those who will inhabit the future.

How then may we begin to future-proof our thinking for the benefit of our progeny and the planet as a whole? Rather than releasing us from culpability, living within a sense of deep time can enrich our lives. The Long View perspective sets the stage for us to achieve sustainability, by considering how our actions today will impact those who will live in a time we will never know.

THE RIGHTS OF
FUTURE GENERATIONS

As he was nearing the end of his life, Cousteau was thinking about how he could use the mediums available to him as levers for a final big push of some kind. He had lived long enough to see that the enormous price of the environmental destruction underway "will not be paid by us but by future generations, those who are not yet alive."[68] He compared the situation to the terrible hangover that follows a huge feast and the patent unfairness of passing the hangover on to our children. Cousteau mused on the fact that political and economic forces tend to think very short-term, not much past the next election or assembly of shareholders.

In the year following his youth ambassador voyage, Cousteau began to actively push forward an idea he had first conceived of in 1979, a Bill of Rights for Future Generations. He wanted the United Nations to adopt it as a missing piece within their powerful Universal Declaration of Human Rights. The initial draft fleshing out the concept was largely the work of three members of the Cousteau Society's Advisory Council.[69] The resulting document affirms that "Every person has the right to inherit an uncontaminated planet on which all forms of life may flourish . . . and to its enjoyment as the ground of human history, of culture, and of the social bonds that make each generation and individual a member of one human family."[70] We are all related, across bloodlines, and timelines, in the rich world of sustainability.

In 1993, Cousteau was successful in convincing UNESCO to join his Future Generations project. In the following year, he helped to organize a UNESCO and Cousteau Society meeting in Tenerife, Spain that assembled various human rights experts and leaders to draft the final declaration. Such declarations should be considered in the public and corporate sectors to ensure wise governance, but the same principles can also flow down to us at the personal level, informing our individual as well as our collective actions. We can craft our own personal or family sustainability mission statements and declarations.

The preamble to the UNESCO document is one of gravity. "At this point in history" it states, "the very existence of humankind and its environment are threatened." It asserts the need to establish "intergenerational solidarity" as part of the intellectual and moral responsibilities of mankind, and to "formulate behavioral guidelines for the present generation within a broad, future-oriented perspective."[71] The declaration outlines freedom of choice and future generation rights with protections in the following key areas:

- Environment including ecosystems,
  natural resources, and pollution prevention

- Human genome and biodiversity

- Cultural diversity and heritage

- War and conflict

- Right to education and equitable
  socio-economic development

- Non-discrimination

During deliberations, hope was expressed by many of the participating delegates that the declaration might inspire momentum for present generations to solve current problems such that a better world could be passed on to future generations, not just passing on the status quo. At their 1997 General Conference, in the same year of Cousteau's death, UNESCO formally adopted his beloved Bill of Rights for Future Generations.

In 2001, Kofi Annan, Secretary General of the United Nations, received Cousteau's widow Francine (his second wife), at a ceremony in which she presented thousands of signatures in support of the Bill of Rights. She was accompanied by five child ambassadors from the signatory continents. To date, more than nine million people have signed a petition in support of the Bill of Rights for Future Generations. It is easy to picture the spirit of Cousteau looking down over the ceremony, a triumphant grin beaming ear to ear.

Here's Hope: Fast forward fifteen years to Wales. In 2016, the Welsh broke new political ground by becoming the first country to appoint a Minister of Future Generations. Their Well-Being of Future Generations Act establishes a goal to "encourage public bodies to take greater account of the long-term impact of the things they do." The Act has specific requirements for the public sector to consider persistent long-term environmental, economic, and social problems.

Sophie Howe, who at the age of 21 became the first Future Generations Commissioner for Wales, was also the youngest person ever to win a popular vote to join the Welsh Council. She served on a committee entitled "Children and Young People Scrutiny." Howe manages to maintain a crisp air of no-nonsense efficiency while at the same time exuding warm openness. She appears to take in each detail in her wake while filing everything neatly away for future reference. As Minister, she defines a broad agenda with four key future generations' challenges: climate change, economic change, population change, and citizen disengagement. Minister Howe has pronounced firmly that "We have big ambitions for protecting our environment and the future generations in Wales."[72] There's no mistaking the gravity of her commitment to the Long View.

In other sustainability developments back in Antarctica, scientists use robotic explorers to document conditions beneath the ice. Researchers are finding that warming ocean temperatures, prompted by climate change, are causing an alarming melt of the ice shelves that underlie massive glaciers. Rising sea levels caused by ice melt at the poles impact people around the globe. The rise of seas is more profound for island nations near the equator. These events are happening thousands of miles apart, as we see the essence of a saying Cousteau often liked to quote, that "we are all in the same boat."

Here's Hope: The Antarctic is host to many forms of research, and the designs for new research stations are increasingly innovative. The

British Antarctic Survey has operated the Halley Research Station since 1952. Unable to stand up to harsh conditions, the survey has struggled with a series of short-lived lifespans for their research facilities. In 2005, they launched a design competition for a new station in collaboration with the Royal Institute of British Architects. The winning design by Hugh Broughton Architects provides a creative new way of thinking about architecture that can adapt to its environment. The structure sits on hydraulic stilts which allow it to be lifted up out of snow drifts. In addition, skis at the base of the stilts allow the entire structure to be relocated. These innovative models may provide new ways of thinking about the sustainability of buildings in other parts of the world. Shelter must adapt to a changing climate, including rising sea levels, flooding, and other extreme weather events.

MODERN-DAY REVOLUTIONISTS: COUSTEAU'S FAMILY LEGACY

Cousteau's inter-generational legacy is being carried out by legions of people he inspired, too countless to track. His more personal legacy continues through his grandchildren. One of these is Alexandra Cousteau, who talked with me about legacy as "not just something related to famous people who have died. It's about how we love our children and what we want to leave for them."

No stranger to a life of adventure, Alexandra joined her parents, Phillipe and Jan Cousteau, on an expedition to Easter Island at the age of 4 months. Able to swim before she could walk, her grandfather taught her to dive when she was 7. She helped gather signatures on his petition to save Antarctica at the age of 8. Alexandra's fearless advocacy as an ocean protector and revolutionist continues through her work today and her concern for future generations that will follow her. "Young people are justifiably angry," she says. "They want to live in a world with polar bears and orangutans and fish in the ocean and that should be their right." She is painfully aware that, since her grandfather explored the oceans, 50 percent of their abundance has been lost. She talks about her own dive experiences as being experiences "among ghosts."

Alexandra sports an ethereal form of beauty that would not look out of place in an Arthurian legend. A long-limbed, willowy woman, her tresses often appear untamed, as do her deeply piercing blue eyes that miss nothing. This adventuress is comfortable at the prow of ship, marching in the streets as a protester, negotiating around a conference table with ministers of state, or sitting alongside climate activist youth, listening carefully to their worries about the future.

In 2018, in honor of International Women's Day, she explored sea caves in the Playa del Carmen. Her diving companion, the 83-year-old Sylvia Earle, is a renowned ocean scientist and the first female chief scientist of the U.S. National Oceanographic and Atmospheric Administration. As a member of ocean royalty, many people refer to Earle as "Her Deepness." As something of a celebrity herself, Alexandra is at ease with such nobility, comfortable in front of a camera or a crowd. She is often invited to share her inspirational message with audiences from around the world, or to pose for photos that might end up in calendars or women's magazines.

Alexandra's minimalist wardrobe, composed of carefully edited ethical and sustainable brands, allows Alexandra to "walk the talk" of her values. One of her concerns is the impact the textile and plastic industries have on oceans, through toxic runoff and plastic pollution. "The fingerprints of fashion are all over the ocean," she says. In 2016, she hosted the *National Geographic* special *For the Love of Fashion*, which looked deeply into the sustainability implications of cotton production. The documentary visited a twice-yearly fashion show called Ethical Fashion Berlin. The models walking down the catwalk, swathed in glamorous organic cotton outfits produced by small fashion houses, were at the same time strutting the benefits of more sustainable, ethical fashion.

Alexandra and her film crew went next on location to India, one of the world's largest cotton producers, where up to six million people work in the industry. The program focused on several small-hold farmers who receive assistance to convert growing cotton to organic methods. Instead of purchasing expensive chemical pesticides and fertilizers, they make their own organic versions of these products from scratch. Fertilizer comes from cow dung. Organic pest control is achieved with a concoction of spicy peppers, garlic, ginger, and onions. These are all ingredients the growers can source from their own land, or purchase inexpensively. It's an easy sell for farmers who previously found themselves going into debt and mort-gaging their land in order to buy expensive agricultural commodities. In addition, instead of purchasing GMO cotton seed each year, they harvest seed from their own crops.

On this particular day, Alexandra is visiting cotton growers in the Indian town of Ratlam, where she wants to gain firsthand experience with the process. The pickers are all women, arrayed across the field of cotton.

They appear to be shrouded in white, an effect created by the large white picking bags encircling the form of each worker. Several sacred cows wait patiently nearby, their large curved horns painted an exotic blue. The cows will haul the cotton harvest once it fills their wooden carts. Even the cows benefit from traditional remedies to prevent pests, as they are often bathed in turmeric-infused water, prized for its anti-microbial properties.

In India, the temperatures can be brutal. One of the women, concerned that Alexandra doesn't have a head covering to protect her from the sun, offers up her own cotton head wrap. It's a beautiful piece of fabric in shades of vibrant orange and red. Alexandra accepts graciously, bowing to receive the gift. The women smile and laugh together at the communion the gesture brings. This is hard work, to be sure. But with the improved organic practices, these mothers and grandmothers don't need to worry about the pesticide contamination they would have been exposed to previously, and the potential health risks it would have represented to them and their children.

Organic cotton production currently represents less than 1 percent of global cotton production. Concerns remain regarding the veracity of claims about organic cotton production and its supply chain integrity. However, recent trends are encouraging. The global organic cotton yield, produced across 19 different countries, has been reported to have increased by 31 percent in 2019. Some of the biggest clothing companies now using organic cotton include familiar names such as H&M and Nike.[73] "At the end of this journey," Alexandra says in the special, "It's become apparent to me that the sustainable production of cotton is not only possible, but it's a necessary way forward benefitting people, communities, wildlife, soil, and water. Each item of clothing that we buy, from our socks to our t-shirts to our favorite pair of jeans, has a story. And for us to have a sustainable future, that story needs to start with each and every one of us."

Alexandra's favorite ways to spend time are either on expedition or with her children at their home in the French countryside. Having kids brought her a sustainability a-ha moment, when she realized that conservation alone isn't enough. Knowing the extent of the massive ecological devastation we have already experienced renders maintaining the status quo inadequate. "Telling [my daughter] that the 50 percent we have left is what we are going to try to sustain, which is kind-of what conservation is about, felt terribly insufficient." Instead, her philosophy and vision have shifted to the idea of restoring lost abundance by the time her daughter is the age she is now, by 2050. This vision is not mere fantasy; it's based on science.

A new partnership with world-renowned marine biologist Dr. Carlos Duarte is serving to bring viability to Alexandra's dreams. "That was a revelation for me," she explains. "Doctor Duarte helped me put a scientific foundation to this idea that we should, as a matter of principle, as a matter of moral obligation to our children, rebuild what we've destroyed in the past 50 years."[74] In a 2020 paper published in the science journal *Nature*, Duarte and his colleagues say that "Recovery rates . . . suggest that substantial recovery of the abundance, structure and function of marine life could be achieved by 2050, if major pressures—including climate change—are mitigated. Rebuilding marine life represents a doable Grand Challenge for humanity, an ethical obligation, and a smart economic objective to achieve a sustainable future. The ability of the ocean to support human wellbeing is at a crossroads."[75] The message of these sustainability revolutionists is clear: We must restore our natural and human systems in order to increase planetary health and vitality. Often referred to as "regenerative" thinking, their philosophy goes far beyond fundamental sustainability. The concept of Blue Carbon is one of the key regenerative strategies.

Blue Carbon is a key component of the Paris Climate Agreement. Blue Carbon refers to the massive amount of carbon sequestered by oceanic and coastal systems across the globe. Atmospheric carbon dioxide is the most common greenhouse gas, and carbon is naturally stored or "sequestered" within geologic or biologic systems. We don't often think of underwater forests and grasslands, yet they are significant ecosystems with the ability to store carbon. For example, coastal wetlands occupy less than 1 percent of the ocean, yet they store over 50 percent of the ocean's stored carbon. Compared to a terrestrial forest, seagrass beds can store twice the amount of carbon.[76] Blue Carbon strategies include restoration of seagrass, salt-marsh, and mangrove habitats.

In 2021, Alexandra co-founded Oceans 2050 to advance Blue Carbon recovery strategies. Oceans 2050 is conducting research focused on kelp farming across the globe. Across twelve countries, nineteen seaweed farms—some of which have been in operation for over 300 years—are contributing to data collection efforts. The goal is to assess the carbon storage capabilities of kelp farming. Thus far, kelp is grown primarily for its use in food and other products. But people like Alexandra have realized there is far more potential here. The results of the study can inform new kelp farming methodologies in order to achieve ocean-based carbon credits. Carbon credits, monetized on the global carbon market, can bring new revenue streams to kelp farmers. In addition to the benefits of greenhouse gas reductions, kelp farming can provide new job opportunities for Arctic indigenous communities such as the Inuit, Gwich'in, and Athabaskan peoples. This can allow them to co-create new practices in harmony with their cultural beliefs and traditions.

Here's Hope: Alexandra is buoyed by the work of Oceans 2050. She seems to share her grandfather's superpower for storytelling. "We can chart a course to a totally different future, a future where our children will know the lost abundance that we no longer do."[77] She hopes this will be a part of her own Long View legacy. "Legacy is not just something related to famous people who have died. It's about how we love our children and what we want to leave for them. What matters about legacy is what we do every day. This can show up as helping friends and family in need, and also the choices we make about the environment that will impact it on a daily basis. The sum total of these individually and collectively is what will define our future and what kind of world we will leave for our children."

At a commencement address at her alma mater Georgetown's class of

2016, Alexandra boldly charted a new cradle of sustainability ideals for humankind. Make no mistake, these are revolutionary ideas. "Nothing short of a total shift away from our carbon-based economy can address the planetary emergency we all face," she told graduates. "Yours is the generation that will impose a radical reconsideration of how we live in this world, how we consume resources, how we restore natural capital, how we protect the future from the excesses of the past. You will be the brave architects of this new world."

Such visionary, lengthwise thinking has the potential to energize a new generation of sustainability entrepreneurs to join in creating livelihoods with transformative global impact. These future revolutionists will be able to advance the cause in ways we only dream of today.

PART TWO

The Economic Pillar of Sustainability in Action

ANITA RODDICK AND THE GREEN BUSINESS REVOLUTION

CHAPTER ONE

Who Was Anita Roddick?

If you think you are too small to have an impact,
try sleeping in a closed room with a mosquito.

— African proverb

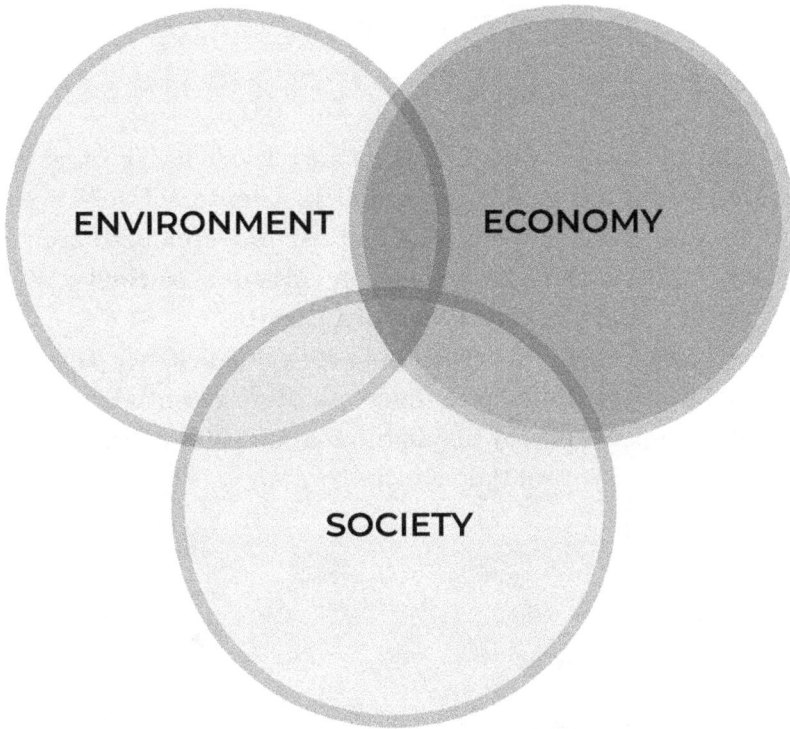

The Three Pillars of Sustainability,
Emphasizing the Economic Pillar

The **Economic** Pillar of Sustainability is the focus of Part Two. Economic revolutionist Anita Roddick serves as the primary hero of these sustainability adventure stories.

THREE ECONOMIC SUSTAINABILITY CORE VALUES

The stories in this section's Chapter One provide background on sustainability revolutionist Anita Roddick. Chapters Two, Three, and Four present a series of stories about her life, organized around the three Core Values of the Economic Pillar: **Mission to Serve**, **Ethical Transparency**, and **Creativity within Limits**.

As we explore the life experiences of Anita Roddick, her personal and professional journey will help to illustrate these essential values. Each Core Value story concludes by highlighting a current-day hero continuing the work to bring the essential value to fruition.

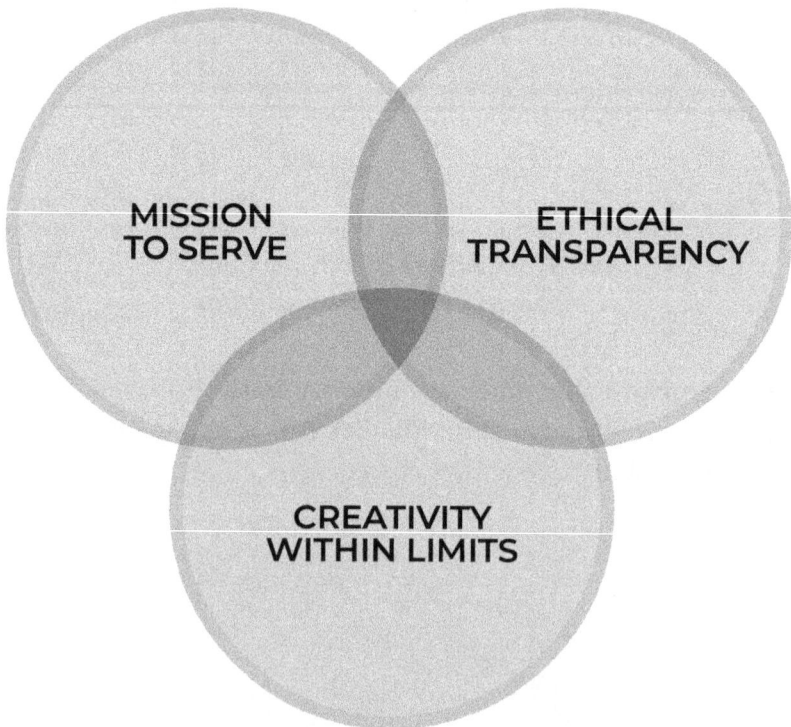

MISSION
TO SERVE

ETHICAL
TRANSPARENCY

CREATIVITY
WITHIN LIMITS

Three Core Values of the Economic Pillar

AN INTRODUCTION TO AN ECONOMIC REVOLUTIONIST

A nita Roddick was born in 1942 in Littlehampton, England, the child of immigrants. A trailblazer in the green business movement, this passionate, iconoclastic woman rarely took no for an answer. As a small business owner, she was an early leader for fair trade with indigenous peoples, and an activist for the protection of animal and human rights. She died in 2007 at age 65. Hers may not be a household name, but the company she founded, The Body Shop, is familiar to many. This retailer continues purveying beauty products inspired by nature. Many of their hundreds of outlets across the globe are located in international airports, a good fit with Anita's passion for seeing the world.

Roddick's early retail explorations helped to lay a foundation for the green business revolution. Her critics may tend to remember her mistakes more than her contributions, yet there is much to celebrate about her life. A journey that may have been naive at times was driven primarily by a passion to make the world a better place. This passion kept her always moving forward, an unquenchable light in the sustainability revolution. She provided an example for many of a woman's right to define success by her own set of rules, at a time when the Women's Liberation movement was just getting started. In her work with indigenous peoples, Roddick was often blinded by a white savior mentality, convinced that she knew best how things should be done. Yet she undoubtably meant well, retaining a youthful openness to learn new ways of doing things throughout her relatively short life.

Body Shop beauty products provided Anita opportunities to experiment. Some of the earliest forays were inspired by her travel experiences, observing indigenous women using raw plant-based ingredients on their skin or hair. In those early days, her main focus was on the sustainability sourcing of her products. Today, green businesses and corporations are expected to address sustainability to consider everything from how their products are manufactured, to lowering the carbon footprint of their operations, to embracing workplace diversity.

Roddick never wavered in her belief that environmental and social values could be brought into the business world, a novel idea for her time. "Doing well by doing good" is a common yardstick for excellence in today's commercial world, but this was not always the case. Since Roddick's days as a corporate sustainability pioneer, the green business movement has grown and matured, developing many useful benchmarking tools that serve as guideposts and tools for measuring excellence. Without these to aid her, Anita made many mistakes that can be instructive today. We can learn from her successes as well as her failures.

As a sustainability revolutionist, Roddick swept away many well-established business norms. Both a revered and a controversial figure, she inspired many and angered others. Some of the controversy had to do with her feminism at a time that women were finding their voice. Some was because the ideas she was speaking up about signaled the need to reinvent how generations of mostly male entrepreneurs and leaders had been conducting their businesses. Anita's iconoclastic lightning rod style was more confrontational than that of Cousteau, who seemed to be adept at charming people into listening to him. Anita was clear: She didn't need to be pleasing or charming in order to deserve being listened to.

Perhaps the most important lesson Anita was able to offer was that businesses can become powerful agents of social and environmental change. As the emerging feminist movement was taking shape, women were discovering their personal power, often motivated by their care for the world beyond the walls of home. Anita used her business platform to speak out on many issues. Her ideas of beauty were based on the whole person, a celebration of diversity rather than conformity to an ideal.

Social norms related to cosmetics were something she vigorously questioned, norms we still struggle with today. "The cosmetics industry today is dominated by men," she said, "who use fear to create needs women don't have, and sell them camouflage under the heading 'beauty.' Make no mistake, these men are talking to themselves, not to women. One of my greatest pleasures in running The Body Shop is the tremendous input of women, who own and run more than 90 percent of our shops. We feel the word 'beauty' is old-fashioned and ally ourselves strongly with health and lifestyle."[78]

Anita was coming into her own as an adult during the late 1960s and '70s, periods of intense social change. The counter-culture movement of the day embraced the idea that "the personal is political" as lifestyle and consumer choices were being questioned. Anita was influenced by emerging movements which shared a common theme of freedom from oppression through individual rights. Her experiments with trade collaboration in developing countries contributed to a transformational movement later known as fair trade. The basic concept of fairness—fundamental to the idea of sustainability and to fair trade—relates to the idea of Inclusive Empowerment that we'll discuss later in Part Three.

In addition, The Body Shop's early animal testing ban created ripple effects locally and internationally, resulting in a permanent ban in the UK and improved standards for many companies across the world. These achievements didn't come easily. By exploring Anita's personal experiences, we will see that the corporate journey toward sustainability continues to be a challenging work in progress, but one well worth pursuing. To begin to understand Anita, it's helpful to go back to her family's immigrant roots.

Anita's working-class parents were born in a small village in central Italy. Like many emigrants wanting to maintain ties, a group of several families from this same village settled together after they arrived in their new country. They chose the town of Littlehampton on the southern coast of England as their home. Over the years, the Perella and Perilli families operated a series of cafes, the women serving as prep cooks and chefs and the men running the business side of things. Anita's parents, Henry and Gilda Perella, were romantics. After Henry's death, Anita's mother opened a bar called the El Cubano, which attempted to evoke a Latin vibe with Spanish jukebox music, castanets, and matador decor. Gilda was the ever-present impresario wearing shimmering cocktail dresses or glamorous tunic-style pantsuits.

The wanderlust of Anita's youth sent her backpacking and vagabonding around the world at a fairly young age. She hitchhiked through Greece, spent time at a kibbutz in Israel, and worked at a newspaper library during a year in Paris. In Geneva, she got a job at the International Labor Organization Women's Rights office, conducting research on issues in the developing world. She visited Australia and Tahiti. In the Apartheid of Johannesburg, South Africa, she narrowly escaped arrest for visiting a blacks-only nightclub.

Gilda's El Cubano nightclub played an important role in Anita's life once she had returned home from her adventures in 1968. Her mother introduced Anita to a regular customer who would eventually become her husband, Gordon Roddick. He shared Anita's passion for travel.[79] They became a free-spirited, adventurous young couple. Once married, they operated a small Littlehampton hotel dubbed St. Winifred's, an eight-bedroom red brick domicile that became the couple's home. They worked hard to transform the place into a charming guest house. Summer visitors loved being lavished with handmade breakfasts and tips about beachcombing on the nearby Arun River.

The Roddick family mission statement was "Follow your bliss." This motto seems to have given Gordon permission to become restless with his life. His lifelong dream wasn't running a hotel; it was to ride horseback across South America with the wind in his hair. Such a journey might entail an absence of up to two years. Many spouses might have put their foot down, but Anita wasn't just any spouse. She declared "It blissed me out to have a partner that said 'I've got to do this. I've got to be remarkable.'" Anita was ever open-minded. She avoided labelling Gordon's ideas as either good or bad, an attitude related to the concept of nonviolent communication we'll discuss later in Part Three. She got on board with Gordon's adventure plans, but there was the practical matter of how she would manage while he was away. Their little hotel was notoriously slow in the off season, barely generating enough income for the family to survive, much less financing trips to South America. Anita came up with the idea of augmenting their income with a new business venture in nearby Brighton, focused on tourist trade. Brighton was a good fit for the health-minded business she dreamed of. Sometimes referred to as London by the Sea, or Brighton Beach, the popular weekend destination was only a one-hour train ride from London. Tuberculosis patients had once come to swim in the bracing waters and take in the healing sea air. Modern day escapees from the city still flocked there, intent on relaxing while connecting with the elements.

Anita's idea was to open a shop selling natural, health-inspired beauty products to vacationers. But the Roddicks didn't have enough cash to cover startup costs. Like many an entrepreneur, they were going to have to take out a business loan.

Let's imagine the challenges that the couple experienced securing a loan to open the first Body Shop. Anita reported the basic facts in her book *Body and Soul*. The events occurred in 1975, when the Women's Liberation movement was in full swing. However, there were varying levels of uptake depending on which corner of the world one inhabited. The story told here uses some literary license for an account inspired by real events.

NAVIGATING THE VELVET GHETTO

Off the southern coast of England, the day was warming up as Littlehampton was coming fully awake. Anita felt invigorated by the salt tang coming off the English Channel. Full of her usual buoyant energy, she made her way up High Street where many of the town's banking institutions and neat little shops were located. Anita could hardly get to the bank fast enough, but she was forced to slow her pace to accommodate her two young daughters, Samantha and Justine, aged five and seven.

They pulled up in front of the bank, a trim two-story brick façade with freshly painted white windows and overhead pediment. Justine tugged Anita's trouser leg and started to whine. "Mum, you promised we'd go to the beach. I want to look for starfish." Anita leaned down, balancing Samantha on her hip. "Yes darling, just as soon as we get our money from this nice bank. I'm sure it will be easy-peasy when they hear Mummy's brilliant ideas. If you're a good girl, we can stop to pick up some Cream Buns on our way to the beach."

As they passed under the Georgian columns flanking a deep doorway, Anita glanced down to brush off any remaining breakfast crumbs from the front of the Bob Dylan t-shirt she was wearing. It never occurred to her that she should arrive at the bank presenting herself as anyone but her authentic self. She was a fan of Dylan's rebellious ballads and poetic lyrics. She started to hum a fragment of one of her favorites, "Like a Rolling Stone."

The bank was not busy, allowing mother and daughters to navigate quickly past the velvet ghetto of female bank tellers and pantyhose-clad receptionists. In short order, they found themselves ushered in to see the loan officer. The mushroom-colored office's only adornments were a few framed scroll-lettered certificates which Anita wasn't even vaguely interested in. Instead, she thought to herself that the man barricaded on the other side of the massive oak desk could use his own trip to the beach, his oatmeal complexion badly in need of a tan.

From the discomfort of her stiffly upright guest chair, she began her pitch as the children went blessedly quiet. "My husband and I own a little hotel here. I plan to start a new business in Brighton. It's sure to be a money-maker as my shop will be an original with body care products hand-crafted using natural, organic ingredients." Anita gestured to illustrate her excitement, undeterred by the chill emanating from the desk. "I plan to import ingredients from exotic places such as Tahiti, which I'm sure the London ladies will adore."

Anita gushed on. She might as well have been speaking in dog whistle. The banker's gaze had become fixated on a rather large water spot on the ceiling. Pressing his fingertips together, suddenly he was interrupting. "I'm a very busy man Missus—what's it, Roddwick? The idea of giving you a business loan is quite impossible." The man explained it would "simply be too difficult to manage a business while caring for little rug rats. In my experience . . ."

Anita had stopped listening. Instead of a loan, she would be receiving a mansplaining lecture. The recently popular term "male chauvinist pig" was not one that she used, preferring to think of things in more poetic terms. She recalled something she had once heard about Ginger Rogers being able to do everything Fred Astaire could, but backwards while wearing heels. As the lecture droned on before her, Anita abruptly realized the man standing between her and her business dreams had risen from his chair and was wishing her good day.

Hastily gathering up her belongings, she hauled the children back out onto the street, where the sun continued to cheerfully shine as though nothing unusual had happened. The journey of the sustainability revolutionist is no stranger to setbacks and barriers. Sometimes it feels like we are taking two steps forward followed by one back, but we can choose to persevere, keeping hope alive at all times.

In spite of the fact that his manners could have used some polish, perhaps that middle-aged banker nearing his retirement couldn't entirely be blamed for buying into the dogma of the times. His perspectives were a symptom of the era.

Less than a fortnight later, Anita was sitting in the same uncomfortable chair in the same drab office. She wondered if the manager even remembered her. He had barely given her a glance along with his limp handshake. This time, she had wisely left the girls with Mum. A few other things were also different. Sitting next to her was her husband, and they were both wearing business suits. She tugged at her scratchy collar impatiently as she noticed the water spot on the ceiling appeared to have grown.

This time they had decided Gordon would do all the talking. Now it seemed she might as well not even be in the room as the two men pored over the figures and charts in the business plan that Gordon had asked a friend to help him draw up. The thing was enshrined in a red plastic folder which had been ceremoniously handed over as though it were some sort of secret handshake. Anita had to bite her tongue as the conversation turned to the fact that they would be putting up the hotel, also their home, as collateral. In short order, satisfaction with the "profit and loss" projections was expressed and the loan was approved. At times we must "play the game," as Gordon referred to this round, according to many of the rules that have been set by others. But learning to speak the language of players within the systems we are trying to change can ultimately lead to a winning proposition, if we are patient. As the adage goes, we must first learn the rules, so we can then break them properly.

Anita was understandably frustrated with the misogyny she had encountered at the bank. Why did she need a man to secure a loan? While her sex was no doubt a factor in her brusque treatment, her poor choice of the Bob Dylan t-shirt and lack of a business plan couldn't have helped much either. Being forced to bring her children with her was also less than ideal. Perhaps such experiences contributed to her decision to later open a daycare center for Body Shop employees. In any case, Anita couldn't stay mad for long, as she was feeling pretty chuffed about getting what she needed to help to realize her dreams.

Soon she was absorbed in long to-do lists for launching the business. In later years, she would not remember the bank experience kindly. "I often wonder how many fantastic ideas never came to fruition because of the lack of imagination of those people who sit behind desks in banks all over the country and who are too frightened to take a gamble."[80]

The first Body Shop opened its doors at 22 Kensington Gardens on March 27, 1976. The media covered the unique retail concept as merchandise quickly started flying off the shelves. In short order, the second Body Shop opened in Chichester, featuring a sumptuous hand-painted mural of giant six-foot-high flowers. Within two years, an additional infusion of cash invested by a family friend allowed for multiple shop locations in England and the first international shop in Belgium. Anita's entrepreneurial venture had taken flight. Suddenly it seemed that hers was a force to be reckoned with. By 2017, there were 3,000 Body Shop outlets in 66 countries.[81]

CHAPTER TWO

Mission to Serve

What counts in life is not the mere fact that we have lived.
It is what difference we have made to the lives of others.

— **Nelson Mandela,** Madiba Clan member, anti-apartheid
revolutionary, first democratically elected president of South Africa

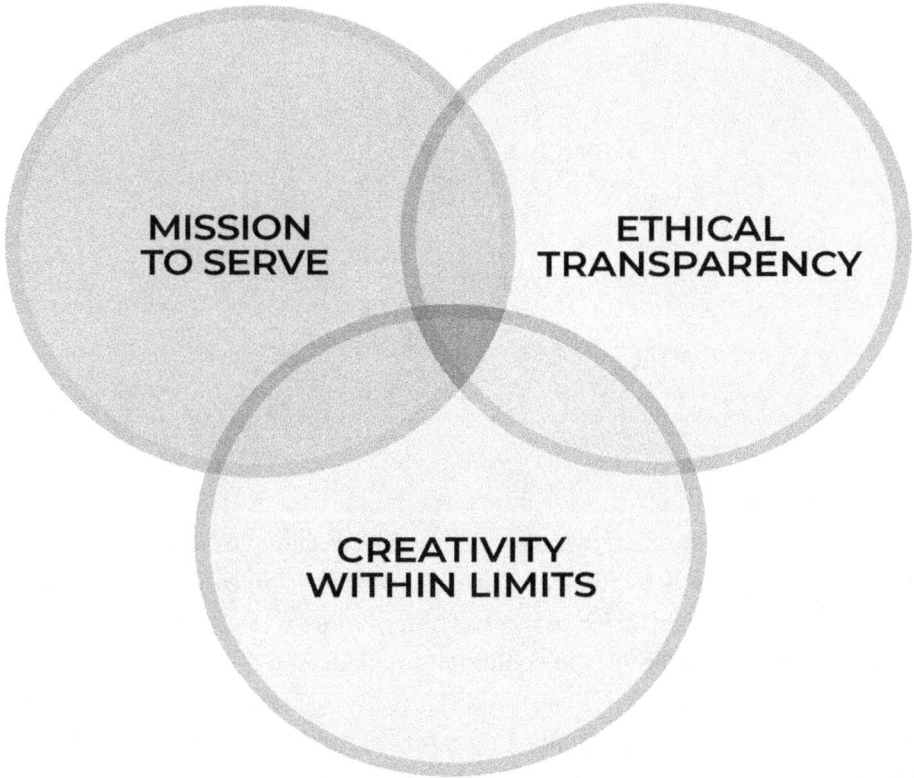

Economic Core Value One: Mission to Serve

FOURTH COURSE:
A COURSE IN THE MISSION TO SERVE

Back at my imaginary dinner party, it's time for the fourth course to be served: a course in what it means to have a Mission to Serve.

I'm serving pasta, a traditional Roman preparation called Cacio y Pepe, with black pepper and Pecorino Romano cheese. It's a simple peasant dish with few ingredients, no cookbook needed. As I busy myself with the dish in the quiet kitchen, I recognize that I have a case of hostess jitters. Perhaps it's my old friend the imposter syndrome kicking in. Who am I to pronounce what is important about sustainability, to decide whose stories get to be told? César is bringing in the dishes from the last course. At first, I think I should stop him, but then I remember that every pair of helping hands should be welcomed.

He places the crockery carefully in the sink as I acknowledge his gift of service. "I'm afraid I'm a bit nervous hosting such an august gathering."

He squeezes my hand gently, bending over it briefly in gracious acknowledgement. As though he somehow telepathically knows what I have been thinking, he says "No one expects you to have all the answers, my friend. It's okay to say 'I don't know' sometimes."

We share a smile. I feel buoyed by his words, remembering that each person is on their own personal journey, doing the best they can with what resources and abilities they have. Of course, we are going to make mistakes. We must believe in ourselves, and in one another, with love in our hearts. Feeling brave enough to return to the table, I begin serving up the next course.

Anita, like any good Italian, is delighted with being presented a plate of pasta. "Lucia, your name as well as your cooking seems to be very much in a Mediterranean tradition. It reminds me of the days of my youth, wandering around Greece and France, wondering what my life purpose was." It isn't hard to imagine her tramping around the world.

Being a good conversationalist means you can always think of something interesting to say, on almost any topic. I'm ready for this one. "Ah, you were wondering about your vocation. Did you know that the word comes from the Latin *vocare*, which means to call or give voice?" I decide this might be a useful segue into some more stories from my dinner guests. "I'm curious to hear more about the sense of purpose that each of you feel called by."

"I see the logic of the word origin," Anita says. "When you first understand who you are, and then why you are here, life begins to make sense. It's a bit like learning the words to a song that feel so right, you could have written them yourself. Our Body Shop mission is simple: to leave the world a better place than we found it."

César adjusts his napkin before he digs in. "We can choose to use our lives toward a mission. My own mission to restore the dignity of my fellow workers presented profound struggle. But I have found joy, too. If you give yourself totally to a cause, you will never go hungry and never be alone. In giving of yourself you can discover a whole new life full of meaning and love."

For a few moments, it is quiet except for the clinking of silverware. The candles flicker, as though listening for what might come next.

"My own mission has always been to protect my beloved ocean," Cousteau says, passing the wine. "Work with a purpose builds the ranks of like-minded people. Success is a lonely place if you don't build a community around it. And with all of you here tonight, how can I feel alone?"

César nods as he twirls his fork in the pasta. "Gathering around a table like this, with new friends and old, is my favorite way to live life. As I always say, if you really want to make a friend, go to someone's house and eat with him. The people who give you their food, give you their heart."

JOURNEY TO THE
HEART OF THE AMAZON

After launching her business, Anita was feeling the sweet relief of the entrepreneur whose project is greeted with initial success. Over the next thirteen years, her endeavor became profitable. Gordon's trip to Argentina proved relatively short-lived, and he returned to help run the company. Additional angel investors helped to fuel the growth of the company, along with a franchise model whereby new business allies could own their own Body Shop stores. In 1984, the company went public, and the next year, accolades arrived for her business acumen.

With the business on solid footing, there was breathing room for Anita's restless mind. Like a bee always looking for the next nectar flower, she mused on her lifelong love affair with travel and dreamt of her next exotic destination. The Body Shop's cocoa butter products had been inspired by a visit in her youth to Tahiti, where she had luxuriated in the archipelago's lush climate. Enraptured by the sensuality of the native women, she had discovered cocoa butter was the key to their lustrous skin, a tradition handed down through generations. The search for traditional, organically-based body care secrets was one of Anita's ongoing passions. If there was a women's or indigenous people's angle, so much the better. She continued looking for social causes that might align with her personal and business mission.

The deepest green endeavors are constantly on the hunt for opportunities to align what they do with the myriad aspects of sustainability. Each wrinkle in the story can present a new challenge, or a new opportunity. Such moments can often show up in unusual ways, or in places far from the home fires. In Anita's story, opportunity from the rainforest presented itself next.

Rainforests once covered 14 percent of the earth's surface, but today they make up only about 6 percent of the globe. As the rainforest is cut down, massive amounts of carbon dioxide are released into the atmosphere as organic matter decays. The thick canopy cover of the Amazon Basin helps regulate global temperature and humidity, serving as the source of much of Earth's fresh water. Local and global weather patterns are reg- ulated by the rainforest's rainfall cycle combined with transpiration, the atmospheric gas exchange through plant leaves. Fifty to 80 percent of the moisture remains within the rainforest in a closed cycle, but some ends up as rainfall in places as far away as Texas. This means cutting down rain- forests can result in not only local dry conditions, but drought situations around the world. Rainforests serve to stabilize the global climate and water supply. Yet it is estimated that 80,000 acres of tropical rainforest are destroyed daily. According to Conservation International, 1.3 billion metric tons of carbon are stored in the Kayapo rainforests alone.[82]

Anita felt a sense of urgency around her mission to make the world a better place. Always looking for new ways to make this a reality, she read stories in the British newspapers about government-sponsored dam-build- ing projects in the Brazilian rainforest. The articles included reports of rippling cultural unrest. Anita had already been curious what kind of plant-based ingredients the rich ecology of the rainforest might reveal. She was also hungry to learn first-hand what was going on.

Brazil's lush Xingu River basin is one of the most ethnically and bio- logically diverse places in the world. It is home to 25,000 indigenous resi- dents, living until recently in a largely pre-industrial world. The Amazon rainforest climate includes only two seasons: a rainy season, and a very rainy season. Some scientists refer to a process they call "flying rivers"[83] whereby each tree can "sweat" 200 gallons of water per year, enabling the forest to create its own clouds. These releases of humidity can help to form eventual rainfall, feeding ecosystem health thousands of miles beyond their own boundaries. These tropical woodlands produce 20 percent of the world's oxygen sometimes, causing many to call them the "lungs of the earth." The rainforest's biological mass in the form of trees and a biodiverse array of other plants serve as a colossal global carbon sink.

The massive Belo Monte dam project, one of the largest in the world, has been battled for decades by Brazilian environmental activists and the indigenous peoples whose way of life it will destroy. Altamira is the site of the first of many phases of dam construction. The dam will alter the flow of the Rio Xingu, destroying habitat of endangered rainforest species such as the white-cheeked spider monkey or eagle-beaked pacu fish. It will cut off navigable waters and fishing grounds that many tribes depend on for survival and transportation. One of these tribes, the Kayapo, has become impatient with the tone-deaf reception their complaints have received. But at the Altamira Gathering of tribes in 1989, things seem poised for change.

Let's imagine Anita's adventures attending the gathering, organized by the Coordination of the Indigenous Organizations of the Brazilian Amazon. The story here is based on video accounts, photographs, and written records. I imagined some of the literary details.

The Kayapo tribespeople are in full warrior regalia. Muscular arms and ankles are adorned with intricate beads, banded in primary colors. Geometric patterns play across the canvases of faces and torsos, marked with the lifeblood of the Kayapo's rich mineral earth. Most dramatic of all are the men's fine headdresses, crafted from intense yellow and blue feathers of the hyacinth macaw. These proud displays echo the habits of male birds, who fan their prowess to out-compete interlopers trying to invade their territorial habitat.

Each Kayapo warrior carries a spear or war club, as though to remind the corporate managers here that the tribe has never been conquered. Pulsating chants, somewhere between a hum and a howl, are building to a crescendo. Ten abreast, wave upon wave of warriors march down the turquoise-painted stadium steps to take their place on the vast carpet of palm leaves that have been prepared to receive them.

Anita feels colorless in comparison to this riveting display. Wearing tan cargo shorts, her skin is devoid of makeup, her attire devoid of baubles. She notices an unfamiliar speechless feeling as her pale arms prickle with goose pimples. Failing to speak up is against her nature, but she is not here in any official capacity. Sustainability revolutionists must often make up their own invitations to attend important events, sometimes barging into negotiating rooms or finding creative ways to crash stockholder meetings.

The stadium is now filled to overflowing with tribespeople. The Kayapo organizers have issued invitations to thirty-four other rainforest tribes. Over 500 strong, the collective tribal representatives in attendance vastly outnumber the white negotiators. A few international journalists are scattered about. Company men in rumpled suits occupy bare metal folding chairs around the perimeter, clearly not the main attraction. Cameras and recorders are poised to capture the action in what would later come to be known as the famed Altamira Gathering.

A sense of excitement fills the space, but the mood is also fraught with tension. The fate of these warriors' homes hangs in the balance between their own traditional ways of living and the vast sweep of Western-style progress. The World Bank has funded a massive dam project, destined to bring cheap electricity to feed industrial expansion, even as it floods 15 million acres of rainforest and displaces tens of thousands of Amazon peoples. No one has thought to ask them for permission, let alone their advice. They have flourished in harmony with this place on Earth based upon generation after generation of collaborative indigenous wisdom. The Kayapo believe their skill at living in social cooperation was originally learned by their ancestors from rainforest bees.[84]

The Brazilian government and the EletroNorte power utility claim the Belo Monte dam will bring jobs and much-needed carbon-free electricity to a growing country. On the other hand, climate change models show that river flow will drop by 30 percent within decades. Critics claim the dam will generate far less energy than claimed, then pave the way for at least three other massive dam projects in the same region, all while releasing huge amounts of potent greenhouse gases into the atmosphere as submerged trees decompose. Many indigenous tribes including the Kayapo will lose their homes and fishing grounds as massive amounts of land are flooded by the dam. In a vicious cycle, more abundant cheap electricity will serve to power the voracious, destructive appetite of even more mining and industrial operations.

Many such "economic development" projects bring few long-term local jobs. They are designed primarily to pilfer the rainforest's mineral and biological resources while exporting profits to Chinese and French investors. The temporary influxes of cheap labor these investors tend to bring create social destabilization, leading to increased violent crime and sex trafficking. Dams create stagnant water which add to the human health burden, bringing malaria, Zika, and dengue fever. For indigenous peoples, these are matters of life and death.

One of the tribesmen has seen both worlds firsthand. Paulinho Paiakan holds a unique ability to understand how EletroNorte officials think. He had worked as a guide for the Brazilian government surveyors who could barely find their way through the uncharted rainforest. Helping them find their way through the maze of sometimes hostile tribes, he abruptly realized this work would bring bulldozers and paving machines, all leaving behind a wake of violent destruction. He quit his job to become a rainforest defender.[85] This gathering, a model of sustainability advocacy, was organized under his leadership. He and Anita could well have been cut from the same cloth. They are adept at leveraging their unique roles and knowledge to build the confidence of their followers. People in every corner of the world are hungry for leadership, and good leaders are hard to find.

Negotiations are in full swing back at Altamira. Company officials have not been forthcoming, and now the chiefs are angry. How will the construction impact their homes? Paulinho stands straight as his war spear as he prepares to speak. The yellow-feathered headdress surrounding his brow glows like a halo. The Kayapo arrange the feathers to radiate outwards to represent the universe. Another part of the design relates to the Kayapo origin story, symbolizing the rope the Kayapo used to descend from the sky.[86]

The strands of bright green beads adorning Paulinho's muscular neck tremble as his words boom out. "We are fighting to defend the forest because the forest is what makes us, and what makes our hearts go. Because without the forest we won't be able to breathe and our hearts will stop and we will die." His eloquence reminds Anita of Gandhi.

Jose Antonio Muniz Lopes, EletroNorte's project leader, is perpetually surrounded by his goons who stand with their arms crossed, perspiring into their button-down shirts. They are not accustomed to the lack of air conditioning. After four days of speeches, on-camera interviews, war dance displays, and pleading declarations from environmentalists and ethno-biologists, no progress has been made in the negotiations. Not even pleas against the dam the previous day by the rock star Sting have moved the needle. The Kayapo are soul-weary of this concrete world, shut off from their familiar way of life. Unmoved by all the protestations, Senhor Lopes's hairline is receding as obviously as his patience. Tensions are about to come to a head.

Suddenly a topless woman wearing long white beaded earrings emerges from the tribal throng. Her name is Tuira. She moves as swiftly and silently as a polka-dotted Amazon stingray. Propelling herself with unstoppable force toward the creaking folding tables behind which the company executives are barricaded, she thrusts her 36-inch machete toward the head of Muniz Lopes before anyone can move. The swing moves his head several inches to one side as an eerie silence overtakes the crowd. A dark shadow of collective shock scurries around the room, trying to find a place to settle. Some people seem to be looking for blood. Luckily for Lopes, Tuira has decided to use the flat edge of her blade, injuring only the senor's dignity. "You are a liar," she roars in her native tongue. "We do not need electricity. Electricity is not going to give us our food. We need our rivers to flow freely: Our future depends on it. We need our jungles for hunting and gathering. We do not need your dam."

One of the less stunned journalists was lucky enough to snap a photo of the machete slap, a photo destined to become a recognized symbol of the rainforest struggle. The photo will be reproduced over and over, serving as a rallying point for many indigenous voices, joined together in their traditional Kayapo battle cry: "Karraro." They will never give up in their battle against the salary men and their misguided dam.

A shiver thrums Anita's spine, breaking the breathless spell she has been under. Suddenly aware of the perspiration that's been pooling at the front of her t-shirt, she pats the damp area uselessly. Thinking to herself that sitting on the sidelines isn't a role she feels comfortable with, she shifts restlessly in her miserable folding chair. The corporate walls of The Body Shop offices back home don't seem terribly important right now, but maybe that could change. What Anita didn't realize was that this trip to Altamira would serve to irrevocably alter the course of events for her and Gordon and the business they owned, and for the Kayapo.

International Outcry

Before the gathering ended, Anita had made contact with Paulinho. There was so much she wanted to talk to him about. Later they would hold a clandestine meeting on the roof of her hotel. Secrecy was needed, as his life was reportedly being threatened. There were fears he would be assassinated, as Brazilian activist Chico Mendes had been the previous year.

Within days of the gathering, media pressure and public outcry against the Belo Monte dam reached a crescendo. It was widely agreed that the project violated the Universal Declaration of Human Rights. The Pope sent a telegram. The United Nations and the Organization of American States requested the cancellation of the dam project. The World Bank withdrew its funding. The project was put on hold. Sting established the Rainforest Foundation, a nonprofit that continues work today protecting indigenous peoples and fragile forests across Brazil, Guyana, Panama and Peru. Many other organizations were also mobilizing.

Protecting the rainforest was not the first sustainability-related cause Anita had jumped into. Previously, she had partnered with Greenpeace on a Save the Whales campaign, delivering consumer messaging that raised awareness regarding the use of whale sperm oil in many products including cosmetics. In spite of the effectiveness of the campaign, Anita eventually became frustrated trying to work with Greenpeace because, although they were an international organization, they had various country-based offices that had to be coordinated with in order to approve each nation-based campaign. This was far too much bureaucracy for the impatient Anita. On the plus side, the experience helped Anita discover she could leverage her customers' voices along with their buying power to serve as powerful agents of change.

One British Body Shop aficionado exclaimed, "I never knew a thing about how the ingredients in my perfume might harm whales, of all things, until The Body Shop opened up my eyes. Now I do my research on every product I buy." All these experiences helped Anita crystalize a business purpose far beyond supporting her young family. "I believe we need to measure ourselves against a different standard. We need business that respects and supports communities and families . . . that safeguards the environment . . . that encourages countries to educate their children, heal their sick, value the work of women and respect human rights. Companies have to ask themselves: 'What does profit mean? Profit for whom?' Maybe we should redefine profit. We need to measure progress by human development, not gross national product."[87] Anita was beginning to articulate her own company's mission to serve as well as greater aspirations for the corporate world writ large.

ECONOMIC SUSTAINABILITY CORE VALUE 1:

MISSION TO SERVE
Establishing a North Star

The function of freedom is to free someone else.
— **Toni Morrison**, American author, teacher and editor

What does it mean to serve the purpose of sustainability? In his foundational book *Servant Leadership*, Robert K. Greenleaf says servant leaders in the business world use a strong inner compass defined by a moral sense of right and wrong. It's their conscience that guides them. He writes about "a set of values, a sense of fairness, honesty, respect, and contribution that transcends culture." This forms a spiritual basis for our actions around sustainability and everything else.

Our world is slipping into disrepair, in part because we bought into the myth that spirituality and compassion must be kept separate from commerce. We are finally recognizing that decisions that have been made solely in the context of financial return have resulted in a myriad of complex problems we are now struggling to realign and repair. A singular focus on profit and the power that comes with it has delivered colonization, exploitation, and subjugation of the less powerful. These have not yielded the kind of world we want to live in.

Fresh practices are emerging in the business world, related to how we define mission and purpose. In 2006, the United Nations created a set of principles for responsible, mission-based investing (also known as impact investing), defining environmental, social, and governance principles. Impact investing carries an intentional desire to solve social or environmental challenges.[88] This type of investing has quickly leveraged $45 trillion in signatories' assets.[89]

The global financial crisis of 2007–2008 was caused by mindless lending practices designed to create profit at the expense of unsuspecting customers. This led to a lack of trust in banking institutions, but also seems to have put wind in the sails to its counterpoint: service mission-based investing. Helping others versus taking advantage of them, guided by community trust among partners, is the core of impact investing. The movement is on the rise. These responsible investment funds have quickly grown by 25 percent to represent over a quarter of all managed assets.[90]

It's no longer enough just to turn a profit. Behemoth financial services firm Morgan Stanley has committed to net-zero carbon emissions for their investments by 2050.[91] Impact investing is even being mandated by some governments. India now requires all companies turning a minimum level of profit to invest a percent of their returns in socially responsible activities.[92]

CVS Caremark is one of the largest healthcare brands in the US, operating clinics as well as pharmacies. In early 2014, CVS stopped selling cigarettes at its 7,700 retail pharmacies. This surprising move erased $2 billion per year in revenues.[93] CEO Larry J. Merlo said, "The sale of tobacco products is inconsistent with our purpose—helping people on their path to better health. [These] products have no place in a setting where health care is delivered." CVS wisely realized that selling products that caused cancer was inconsistent with its larger mission to serve health.

Establishing a sense of purpose is an essential sustainability Core Value, requiring us to recognize our connection to a wider world than what we see right in front of us. A service-based mission establishes a north star for our efforts, a place we fix upon as we navigate challenges. Such a north star can prevent us from getting too far off course. The sustainability journey is filled with twists and turns that can be difficult to anticipate. Service-based sustainability shows us that having a compass is ultimately more important than having a map. Our north star keeps our vision in sight as we navigate each setback and each success.

Author Stephen Covey describes finding one's mission as "changing our questions from asking what it is we want, to what is being asked of us." Altruistic, optimistic millennials are fueling this trend. Emerging young professionals expect to join organizations with a sense of purpose and some kind of social mission. A study by Rutgers University and Net Impact found that students said wealth was a less important career goal than making a difference to issues they cared about. In a competitive hiring market, a firm's commitment to social good can attract and retain the best young talent.

In her book *Manifesto for a Moral Revolution*, Jacqueline Novogratz, CEO of a global anti-poverty nonprofit, suggests a return to the basics of what we were taught as children. "What if our Golden Rule were not only 'Do unto others as you would have them do unto you' but also 'Give more to the world more than you take from it'? If enough of us pursued that path, the world of inequality, exploitation, and injustice would slowly be replaced by a world of inclusion, fairness, and dignity."

Working within the sustainability guideposts of a service-based mission allows us to contribute to making the world a better place, for our community and our descendants. Serving such a higher purpose is often thought of as a calling, a vocation versus just a job. If this alone doesn't seem reason enough, we may also find that devotion to the deeply meaningful work of sustainability makes life richer and more satisfying. Top deathbed regrets rarely include wishing to have worked more. Regrets often include things like putting dreams into action, connecting with community more, and telling others more often that they are loved. Embracing a mission to serve can satisfy many of these regrets, aligning service to others, and love, with the business of work.

MISSION TO SERVE THE RAINFOREST

A new sense of purpose accompanied Anita as she returned home from the Altamira gathering. On the long flight home, she turned over ideas about how to raise customer awareness of the need to protect the rainforests. Widespread burning of these fragile planetary lungs was being carried out to clear land for cattle ranching, palm oil, and soybean production. This was just as big a threat as building dams like Belo Monte. In the year of the Altamira gathering, 300,000 square kilometers, an area larger than the whole of Britain, had been burned.

Anita quickly responded, organizing a Body Shop campaign using disturbing photos of the rainforest in flames. The large images were splashed with slogans such as "The Future of the Planet is Going Up in Smoke" and "Stop the Burning." Using her business platform, posters went up in 450 shops, t-shirts were printed for retail staff to wear, and delivery trucks were splashed with visceral images. A buzz was building. Customers dropping into the shops were urged to make sure their banks were not funding rainforest-destroying projects. They were also asked to boycott tropical hardwoods and meat from Brazil, and to sign a petition.[94] Things could have gone the other way, and The Body Shop could have lost customers. Sometimes, sustainability leaders have to take risks, willing to live with potential negative consequences. This is bravery in service to the mission. Luckily in this case, the campaign only served to bolster the support of loyal customers. The company was able to balance the rainforest cause with the need for sales and profits.

Half a million signatures had been collected within two weeks. The petitions were piling up. It would have been easy enough to drop everything into the local post box. But Anita knew her mission would be better served by making a bold, more visible move. She decided to create a scene cribbed from the movie *Miracle on 34th Street*, wherein mail bags of letters to Santa are dumped in the middle of a courtroom where Santa is on trial. She decided to deliver the petitions in person to the Brazilian Embassy in London. The drama of the moment, championing the home of indigenous peoples, might also be heightened by the fact that the embassy offices were located in Mayfair's highly affluent West End, one of the most expensive neighborhoods in the world.

The press rose to the occasion, capturing footage of several hundred protesters on the doorstep of the Embassy, clad in campaign t-shirts, dumping huge burlap sacks of petitions at the feet of stunned diplomatic staff. Widespread news coverage followed. One of the widely published images depicted a woman with a wild mane of unbound curls, her fists held high, sitting atop a mountain of petition mail sacks stamped with the "Stop the Burning" slogan. The woman was Anita Roddick.

The Altamira gathering helped to galvanize a global movement to protect rainforests. The extent and value of this new global awareness can scarcely be counted or valued in full, and the fight is far from over. Countless nonprofits continue today, focused on the preservation of the rainforests and its peoples. Popular films such as the animated features *FernGully* and *Avatar* further raised awareness, even if they did overly romanticize the situation. In 2014, the United Nations endorsed the New York Declaration on Forests, a set of ten specific goals related to forest loss. Since that time over 190 endorsers, including 60 national and sub-national governments, 57 multi-national companies, and 16 indigenous community groups, have become involved.

Next, Brazil amended its constitution to confer full property rights to indigenous tribes, creating a situation in which economic activity couldn't be carried out on the land unless both the tribe and federal government agreed. Between 2006 and 2015, Brazil reduced its Amazon deforestation by almost two-thirds. As one might expect, research has shown that land under indigenous control is better protected. A study by researchers at Columbia University and UC San Diego found a significant decline in deforestation of territories under tribal control.

Unfortunately, the political winds have not blown in the movement's favor, and progress has proven fragile. Conservative President Jair Bolsonaro, elected in 2018, led a full-scale raid on the rainforest and her peoples. No new land has been set aside since Bolsonaro or his immediate successor were elected, and authority has been shifted away from protection-based agencies and toward pro-development groups such as the Ministry of Agriculture. In 2019, images of massive rainforest fires swept around the globe, receiving international attention and public outcry. Millions of hectares remain outside of protections, and fires are often set by farmers clearing land for agricultural purposes, who believe they have their government's support. Elected leaders deny culpability. International attempts at intervention have been soundly resisted, focusing on the nation's sovereign right to plunder their own lands while denying the rainforest's role in sequestering carbon.[95]

The forces that oppose sustainability can be relentless. In late 2019, some thirty years after Altamira arena gathering, the Belo Monte dam project was completed. This was in spite of a human rights lawsuit filed against the Brazilian government alleging failure of protection and reparation for impacted communities. Many are now calling the dam project a boondoggle, with significantly less energy than was promised being produced, driving energy prices up. This is in part due to reduced river flows—in a bit of irony, the likely result of deforestation and climate change impacts.[96] Brazilian rainforest depletion is driving massive water shortages and fires in nearby Argentina. Sixty cities along the Paraná River are dangerously low on water supplies, while shallow waters are decimating the shipping trade that Argentina relies on for over 80 percent of its agricultural exports.[97]

Here's Hope: While hydropower has been Brazil's traditional method of generating electricity, it has been estimated that wind energy alone could provide at least 20 percent of the country's energy needs. As tens of millions of Brazilians move out of poverty and increase their appetite for electricity, Brazil must satisfy their demands with an additional 6,000 MW of power production each year.[98] In windy Northeastern Brazil, wind turbines generate 36 percent of the region's electricity. Wind generating capacity is expected to double by 2024. This hopeful sign of a transition to a clean energy future holds its own promise of economic gain balanced with sustainability benefits.

MODERN-DAY REVOLUTIONISTS: THE TECHNICAL KAYAPO TODAY

The unfolding story of the Kayapo offers reason for hope, as they increasingly take control of their own destiny. By most accounts, today they are the most prosperous and powerful of all the 240 remaining indigenous tribes in Brazil. In 2014, *National Geographic* expedition reporter Chip Brown traveled deep into the rainforest, revealing self-organized tribal groups working in close collaboration. The Kayapo's home is among the largest protected tropical rainforest reserves in the world, controlled by 9,000 indigenous Kayapo tribespeople among 44 villages. Just as vast portions of their native lands are still intact, so are their kinship systems, ceremonies, language, and knowledge of the forest with which they survive. As they find new pathways to self-empowerment, they move away from the cliché of the white savior. Sustainability often requires us to explore new ways of meeting our needs, sometimes using emerging technologies unfamiliar to us. Other pathways may require us to question assumptions regarding what the problem is, inviting the possibility that we were solving the wrong problem all along.

Modernization brings its own challenges. While many Kayapo still follow a largely subsistence way of life, conveniences are making an appearance. As they abandon hunting and fishing, they may turn to unhealthy purchased foods associated with obesity. They may use technology such as television, cell phones, and video recording devices. The appropriate use of technology is generally a good thing, but at the same time, we have seen how overreliance on social and other media can lead to isolation and an unhealthy, sedentary lifestyle.

Brown sees technology as contributing to a unique evolution, one that transcends the idea of static preservation. "From shotguns and motorized aluminum boats to Facebook pages, the Kayapo have shown a canny ability to adopt technologies and practices of the cash-based society at their borders without compromising the essence of their culture."[99]

Better mapping and record-making of ancestral rainforest lands, residents, and their activities is proving to be a crucial preservation strategy, based on the advantages of adopting new technologies. After the Altamira Gathering, the Rainforest Foundation made great strides in recording and demarcating the boundaries of tribal lands in order to legally protect them from development and squatting. This led to significant progress during the 1990s with the mapping and boundary-setting of 200 different tribal lands in the Amazon and other rainforest lands.

From an industry perspective, state-of-the-art remote data sensing can help to avoid products produced at the expense of the rainforest. Satellite-based supply chain mapping combined with customs, shipping, and storage records can now provide a record of rainforest destruction tied to soy, palm oil, and beef production. However, much work remains to be done to achieve widespread industry participation in such supply chain disclosure.

Creating and compiling data empowers the Kayapo to use technology as a defensive weapon. Chip Brown's journal of his visit, accompanied by Martin Schoeller's photographs, tells the story.

Kiabieti Metuktire is making waves with a new and unexpected vocation for a rainforest native—he is the tribe's first native videographer. His red-tasseled armbands, bare chest, and black body paint feel oddly incongruous with the huge headphones that are snug against his ears. He ignores the rambunctious protesters assembled nearby. As he listens intently to his camera's audio levels, making sure everything is just right, his brow wrinkles even further with concentration.

Kiabieti's powerful images capture political demonstrations, protest marches, traditional tribal dances, and free-spirited Kayapo children. "I always say video is our bow. It's our weapon. With a film, it shows everything that has happened. My way of thinking is, I want to make videos in our villages to register our lives, then send them to others outside to watch. We don't want strangers arriving here, filming us and never giving us the images. The technology of the whites is now ours to use and arm ourselves."[100]

The day's protest is picking up steam, and Kiabieti is using every tool in his war chest to capture the moment. A white drone whirring like a maddened insect flings itself up and over the village, guided by his steady hand. The warriors below have collected into a perfect arc that mimics the sweep of the palm-roofed huts and the river beyond. Greenery and a few taller trees are markers in the distance, providing gorgeous cinematic contrast to the flat red dirt below. Kiabieti visualizes the perfect geometry this aerial shot will create. The massive spears are much taller than the men carrying them. They march in lockstep, with an unhurried choreography, chanting and pumping their war spears into the sky in unison.

The warriors are a formidable sight, even from 40 feet up. Satisfied with his footage, he guides the drone gently back to Earth. Children run to greet the returning camera with curious stares or toothy grins, hoping to be in the shot so they can watch themselves later when he shares the footage on the village monitor. Finding the right balance between selected modern conveniences and traditional ways of living sparks a temptation to fetishize indigenous lifestyles.

"The first film I made was about Belo Monte," Kiabieti says. "Now when we enter the forest, accompanying officials who survey our lands, we hear about ranchers who are invading our lands. We say, let's go there and film. We also register the GPS location. The film goes to the President of the Republic and to the Ministry of the Environment for them to see that something is really happening here."

The rights of all peoples to tell their own stories, and to own those stories, has become increasingly recognized as a part of equity and empowerment. In the next chapter, we will see how this became an issue between the Kayapo and the Roddicks with the commercialization of photographs without the tribe's permission. Chip Brown must take a different approach in order to earn and maintain the trust of the tribe. Journalists across the world use the documentary tools at hand to hold their government accountable. They know that pictures can sometimes be more powerful than words, and that they can use the tools of technology to help protect themselves. At the same time, Kiabieti and other indigenous correspondents are creating a record of a fragile way of life.

There are many avenues and tools to provide agency to those who need it most. The various forms these tools may take can surprise us, or show up in unexpected places. Those who wield the tools must have the freedom to make their own choices about how they are used.

CHAPTER THREE

Ethical Transparency

We are choosing our memories—whether we took action, whether we stood by, whether we told ourselves it was just a job, whether we held onto comforts we knew came with extreme costs.

— **Tara Houska**, member of the Couchiching First Nation, attorney, and climate justice advocate

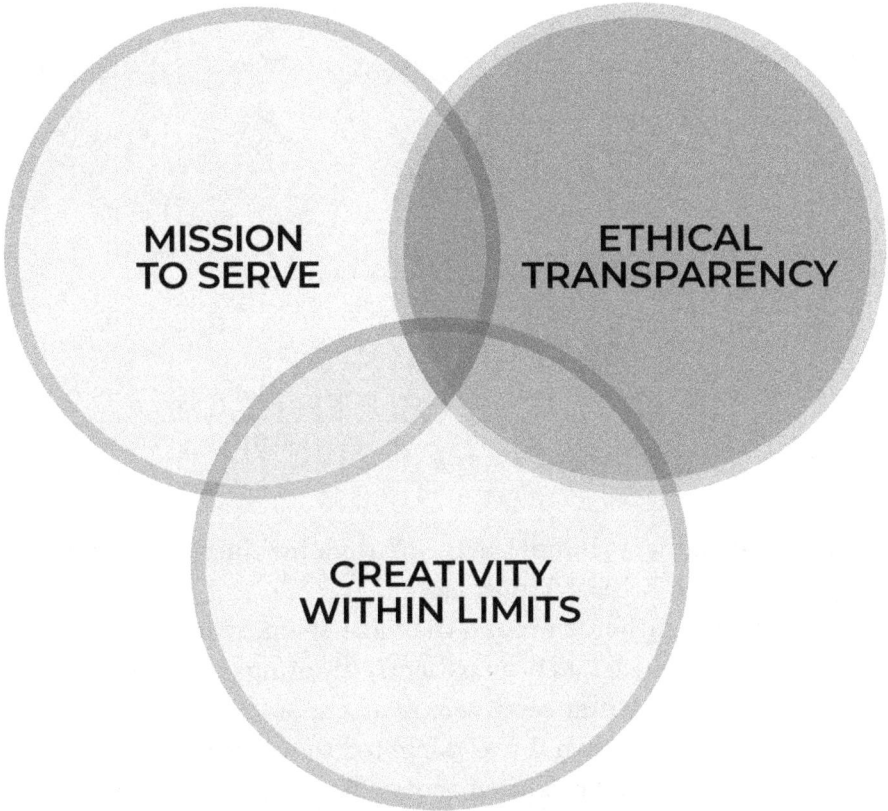

Economic Core Values Two: Ethical Transparency

FIFTH COURSE: A COURSE IN ETHICAL TRANSPARENCY

Back at my imaginary dinner party, it's time for the fifth course to be served: a course in Ethical Transparency.

The group has gathered around the table again, ready to dig into the poached fish dish which had been patiently awaiting us on the sideboard. I had decided to serve it at room temperature, alongside grilled asparagus spears from my garden. I was delighted that this was the first year the asparagus patch had produced enough for several meals. Sometimes sustainability requires patience.

César is skipping the fish and focusing on the vegetable. With so many courses to enjoy, I know he won't be going hungry. As everyone begins eating, the ever-curious Anita pipes up. "I hope you will tell us where you found this lovely table, Lucia. I'm noticing the gorgeous wood grain."

I was proud to say the table aligned with my sustainability values. When I first moved into this house, I knew the tiny table that I had before wouldn't be big enough for the kind of gatherings I dreamt of hosting. "I heard a saying once about building a bigger table, not a higher wall, if you have more than you need."

César warms to the topic. "In my experience, walls serve only the people on one side." He pauses as everyone nods in agreement. "But surely your table came from no ordinary market?" He is admiring the thick slab of lumber which bears the marks of a craftsman's hand-hewn attentions.

"Imagine my delight when I found this one at a big box retailer, of all places. The product information told me all about the table's origin. The wood came from plantations where the trees are grown using stringent environmental and social standards."

Jacques leaned in eagerly. "Voila! What you're saying is that a simple product label told you the table's story."

"Exactly. This particular piece was created by families of Indonesian craftsmen. Sometimes I daydream about the glade where the original tree grew, and the loving hands crafting the teak from a log into a solid piece of furniture."

Anita feels called to explain how these kinds of stories make her heart sing. "My favorite product story comes from Ghana. In spite of the harsh harmattan dry winds that always seem to be blowing there, the Jisonayili women have the most luminous skin I have ever seen."

I was curious. "What is their secret, Anita?"

"The women make a cream from the fruit of their native karite trees. We eventually made it one of Body Shop's top sellers. Now everyone calls it shea butter. We did business with a women's trade cooperative, who used shea butter proceeds to build a maternity clinic in their village."

Now it was all making sense to me. "I never leave home without a tub of it stashed in my handbag. My hands are always a mess from all of the gardening. I'll always think of this story when I use it."

EARLY EXPLORATIONS IN FAIR TRADE

Back at the Altamira Gathering in Brazil, Anita struck up an alliance with a young Brazilian scientist conducting research on rainforest medicinal plants and pharmacological ingredients. The two women agreed to continue sharing information on potential rainforest ingredients for beauty products. Anita was seeking low-impact opportunities that might deliver an economic return, which could then be used as a hedge against other far more destructive interventions.

In the late 1980s, the idea of fair trade was not well developed. There were few, if any, models to follow. But the idea of blazing her own trail didn't faze Anita in the least. If anything, it made the activist's heart beat even stronger. In the sustainability revolution, we are often the trailblazers who must creatively make it up as we go along. Anita knew it was going to take more than people signing petitions from the armchairs of their first-world lives to save the rainforest. It was going to require an economic revolution, one waged on the ground and far from home.

During their secret rooftop meeting, Paulinho Paiakan had invited Anita to visit his village. She was eager to return to the rainforest to spend time getting to know his community. She hoped that if things went well, there would be opportunity to forge a trade relationship based on mutual trust. During her ensuing visit, she would end up focusing on a natural beauty ingredient that would lead to new products and adventures in the world of Fair Trade. To begin, we need to look at the source of this ingredient.

The Brazil nut tree can live over 500 years, growing to a height of up to 200 feet. The tree's nuts are prized as a nutrient-dense food, rich in protein and unsaturated fats, plus selenium, a known cancer-fighting agent. Since the tree is part of an intricate, highly specialized ecosystem of relationships, no commercial monoculture or plantation production of Brazil nuts has ever been economically viable. The nuts grow only within their native rainforest. But why? The answer lies in the ecology of Interconnected Systems.

Brazil nut tree survival is dependent on pollination provided by one creature: the female long-tongue orchid bee. The bees feed on the orchid's blossoms to coat themselves in their intoxicating scent, attempting to make themselves attractive to desired females. Without orchid perfume, the male bees simply cannot attract the females.

The tree's large, dense blossoms feature complex coils and a heavy hooded structure, making it impossible for an ordinary bee to penetrate. Only the long tongues of the female orchid bees can get the job done during the tree's three-month bloom season.

There's another partner this ecosystem dance: the Agouti rodent. They are the only animal able to assist with Brazil nut tree propagation. The tree's Brazil nuts occur within dense fibrous globes the size of a large grapefruit. The Agouti's incredibly sharp front teeth act as chisels, enabling them to chew through the tough, fibrous outer pods to get to the rich feast within. Unable to consume all of the nuts they glean, the Agouti bury the uneaten seeds. They tend to forget where they have buried their treasures, effectively planting new trees.[101] This interconnected system enables a forest to produce many such riches, sharing them freely with the Kayapo.

Based on events as reported by Anita, as well as photographic documentation, let's use some literary imagination to tell a tale of her visit to Paulinho's village, not long after the Altamira Gathering. What the Roddicks cannot yet know is that this trip will turn a new chapter in Body Shop history. A trade agreement with the company will effectively change the course of history for the Kayapo tribe, making them one of the richest indigenous groups in Brazil.[102]

Anita and Gordon are on the last leg of the long journey from London to meet the Kayapo. Paiakan has agreed to meet them in the tiny Aukre township and guide them the rest of the way to his remote village. For this final flight, they had used some of their rainforest crusade donations to purchase a small twin-engine aircraft. The old beater was less than glamorous, but they had been assured by the pilot whose services came with it that it was a reliable ride. Anita and Gordon were traveling light.

Most of their luggage consisted of cameras, notebooks, sample collection equipment, and some Body Shop samples as gifts for their hosts.

As they fly farther inland, the scribbles of civilization eventually give way to the green tufted carpet of lush canopy. All human markers have disappeared. Gordon can't help but wonder what will happen to them if the plane breaks down and they end up stranded far out in the jungle. But he is also reassured by their guide's confidence, who appears to know exactly where he is going, following various landmarks which seemed indistinguishable to the outsiders, or "poanjos" as the Kayapo refer to them. After an hour of line-of-sight navigation, the plane drops down over a red dirt clearing, surrounded by a semi-circle of thatched huts and a larger central community hall. Paiakan proudly explains that the circular form of the village reflects the Kayapo belief that the universe is round.

As they find their way to the tiny landing strip of packed earth, the plane bumps and shudders to a stop. Once the pilot kills the engine, the rainforest falls uncharacteristically silent, and then nothing happens. The forest listens, wondering if these are friends or enemies. Eventually, the cabin door clatters open. The hot moist air hits the disembarking passengers like a warm embrace, announcing their arrival in a place where the humidity levels can often reach 88 percent. The entire village is there to greet them. The men wear western-style shorts and no shirts. The young women draped in long cross-body bands of multi-stranded beads wear little else but brilliant red face paint. Anita and Gordon have donned simple khaki shorts and t-shirts.

The villagers welcome Paiakan, hugging him as they weep tears of joy. A few of the young women approach Anita timidly. They have formed a long serpentine row, arms intertwined. Someone relieves Anita of her bags as she is guided to join the line. Secretly delighted at this immediate immersion among the females, they march her toward the village in a syncopated rhythm, singing as they go.

For the next few days, the Roddicks make the village their home, sleeping in hammocks, eating mangos and fish. Anita dances and sings and lounges among the women. She admires their physicality, natural beauty, and sense of humor. Eager to learn about the Kayapo traditional ways, the couple hears stories about the belief that their ancestors learned cooperative ways of living from colonies of bees. The couple takes long walks with the village medicine man, who explains hundreds of plant species and their healing properties, as well as how the tribe cultivates certain plant combinations and beneficial insects. Each family in the tribe is allocated a species of plant which it is their responsibility to nurture and protect. Anita is about to become enrolled in this idea as an outside volunteer, an honorary protector of the Brazil nut tree. Why do the Kayapo trust Anita? Perhaps it's her wide-eyed innocence. Perhaps it's how she and Gordon are willing to spend so much time learning about their way of life, their way of seeing the world. It's hard to know. But trust her they do.

Anita is a fast study under the tutelage of the village medicine man, quickly becoming enamored with the magical Brazil nut trees. For the Kayapo, Brazil nuts are an important food source. Anita also notices the nuts are rich in oil. She lands on the idea of Brazil nut oil as a moisturizing ingredient for shampoo and hair conditioner that could be formulated by The Body Shop. This could provide an opportunity for economic trade, supporting the tribe and sustaining the rainforest. Paulinho agrees to lead trade negotiations for the tribe to become a Body Shop supplier. It is an arduous process because the very idea of monetary gain from the mother forest is a foreign concept. There are many hours of storytelling in the central meeting house interspersed with numerous heated discussions. Convinced such an agreement could ultimately lead to more rainforest protections, Paulinho's earnest entreaties finally prevail. But will this new economic venture help to keep the rainforest intact?

In many sustainability negotiations, we must find ways to satisfy multiple needs with our solutions, appealing to competing demands. Sometimes we don't know for sure if our ideas will succeed. It's rarely a perfect cut-and-dried situation.

Anita often talked about their efforts as "trade, not aid," a reference to a 1968 United Nations Conference that concluded trade and development were the best form of assistance. Traditional aid methodologies were beginning to be seen as patronizing, top-down, out of touch with people's real needs, and unable to effect long-term change. Fair trade was seen as a way of empowering indigenous peoples, giving them the financial resources to take their fate into their own hands. With this in mind, the Roddicks created The Body Shop Community Trade program, an ingredient-sourcing initiative that connected customers with stories of far-away places and people.

Anita was understandably concerned about how the experimental venture with the Kayapo might alter their traditional way of life. "I was convinced that we had to look for ways to make the rainforest economically viable, with an internationally acceptable strategy for trade that was based on conservation and husbandry," she wrote in *Body and Soul*. "If the controlled extraction of sustainably managed plant materials could provide a permanent livelihood for the rainforest peoples, it was my view that the people themselves should decide how much change they wanted to accept."

In addition, there were many logistical challenges to be solved. The idea of building an access road runs counter to rainforest preservation, so transporting products out of this remote location was not going to be easy. An exploratory flight along the river located a series of impassable waterfalls. This dashed Anita's idea of boat transport. Air transport was the only way.

It was quickly realized it would be more profitable for the Kayapo and cost effective overall if the tribe did their own oil processing to create the value-added commodity. Brazil nut oil would yield a much higher price to the tribe than raw nuts, and it would be less costly to airlift out of the jungle. The Kayapo agreed to receive several things: a manual crushing machine that could produce oil, operational training in its use, and new huts to house the drying and processing operations. They even agreed to receive a video camera that Anita thought might be useful for them to document their way of life. What could possibly go wrong?

FAIR TRADE CHALLENGES AND PROGRESS

Unfortunately, the Roddicks had no experience with indigenous peoples or the risks of cultural interference and exploitation. They eventually fumbled the Kayapo business relationship with a series of misunderstandings and intellectual property disputes. In particular the Kayapo became angry that photographs taken of them were being used in Body Shop advertising without permission or compensation. One image eventually made it into an American Express ad, an egregious appropriation.

Perhaps some of these missteps could have been avoided if best practice standards of fair trade had been available at the time. But such tools were just beginning to materialize. Perhaps these businesspeople could have brought along a cultural anthropologist. Perhaps they could have questioned their advertiser's requests more thoroughly. Sometimes, the path of the sustainability revolutionist is one that must enter uncharted waters. Self-reflection, thinking through unintended consequences, and ensuring we have asked every possible question of ourselves and others, are some of the deeper practices we must all take up.

At around the same time Anita was launching her venture with the Kayapo, the fair trade movement was beginning to gel. But it took over 200 years for fair trade to become a well-organized global endeavor. Sally Blundell's *No-Nonsense Guide to Fair Trade* is a useful reference on the history of the movement. The first inklings of the movement emerged in the late 1700s when a campaign against slave-made products was launched by Quakers and Colonial abolitionists. This resulted in a British mass boycott of slave-grown sugar, sending market shock waves from the Americas to India.

Many faith-based trade initiatives would eventually follow, with significant leadership from American, German, and Dutch organizations. Via this grass roots movement, a wide variety of alternative trade products began emerging from Cuba, Puerto Rico, Algeria, Mozambique, Nicaragua,

157

Jordan, Bangladesh, Thailand, and Mexico. It would take until 2001 before a widely agreed-upon definition of fair trade was developed, along with ten widely recognized principles addressing complex supply chain issues, including working conditions, wages, child labor, non-discrimination, and environmental protection. These issues cover the full range of all three Sustainability Pillars.

Here's Hope: Today, the market share of the economic justice fair trade movement is growing. Established, ethical, transparent practices help ensure the success of worker collectives and farmer cooperatives, by providing guaranteed prices and thus stable sources of income. This is particularly valuable for those involved in commodities markets that are volatile, such as coffee. Support is provided for complexities including working conditions, wages, child labor, non-discrimination, and environmental protection.

According to Fair Trade Certified, this alternative market now functions in over forty-five countries with more than 1.4 million farmers and artisans, clocking sales of over $740 million since 1998. Their market share shows up most significantly in coffee, tea, sugar, coconut, cocoa, and apparel commodities. There are many powerful success stories, including coffee cooperatives such as CEPCO and UCIRI which have their own coffee shops in Mexico. In some cases, farmer cooperatives have increased decision-making roles as they own shares in alternative trade organizations such as Cafedirect and Equal Exchange. A groundbreaking multi-national coalition of nine countries in Central and South America and the Caribbean, ALBA, has forged agreements that align fair trade with small farmer empowerment and food security.[103]

Fair trade empowers small-scale farmers and artisans, allowing them access to markets and livelihoods that "support their transition from a position of vulnerability to one of strength and self-sufficiency."[104] Self-sufficiency is essential to sustainability. It can also be thought of as a way to bring the concept of inclusion to business, whereby all participants, not just a few at the top of the supply chain, deserve to prosper and benefit from any transaction.

Today's sustainability revolution offers up a wide range of protocols, standards, and rating systems to help guide efficacy and excellence. These tools are evolving as we continue to learn and grow.

ECONOMIC SUSTAINABILITY CORE VALUE 2:

ETHICAL TRANSPARENCY
Making the Invisible Visible

Social injustice and environmental injustice are fueled by the same flame: the undervaluing, commodification, and exploitation of all forms of life and natural resources.

— **Leah Thomas**, Black American environmentalist and author

How do we establish our credibility in the world of sustainability? According to Aristotle, part of the answer is related to the Greek word ethos. Ethos means character. It is the root word underlying the etymology of ethics. Our rights and responsibilities as humans are guided by ethics, which can help us know how to embody goodness.

The ethical path is not for the faint of heart. Throughout our lives, we are likely to face challenging or confusing decisions relative to right and wrong. Ethics serve as touchstones helping us decide what to do. Following a moral compass may not point us to the easiest or most obvious choice, but it is a path well worth pursuing.

An ethical livelihood requires us to be aware of the moral consequences of activities that turn a profit. Ethical businesses must operate within the law. In the business of sustainability, ethical practices cast a broader net, to address moral or ethical problems which often are not regulated by law. Ethical business issues may include paying fair wages, refusing child labor, or eliminating toxics. Managing resource extraction in a way that does not devastate the environment is a central tenet of ethical product production.

Ethical choices require organizations to take responsibility for their actions. But how do we know they are honoring their promises? We know if they are being transparent. Transparency refers to an organization's actions being observable by external parties, creating accountability. In her *Foreign Policy* journal article "The End of Secrecy," author Ann Florini says, "Simply put, transparency is the opposite of secrecy. Secrecy means deliberately hiding your actions; transparency means deliberately revealing them. Transparency is a choice, encouraged by changing attitudes about what constitutes appropriate behavior."

Recently, it has become more common for corporations to disclose the salaries of their employees, particularly for those at the top. This form of transparency has opened up many organizations to criticism regarding salary inequities. Some companies telegraph their internal transparency through their office designs, utilizing glass-enclosure conference rooms that negate the idea of secret meetings. Some are even eliminating enclosed offices for CEOs. This means there are no walls to hide behind for employees at any level. Sometimes these early steps in transparency address the optics of behavior.

Applying sustainability ethics to business behavior is often referred to with terms such as corporate citizenship or corporate social responsibility. Organizations engaged in these practices employ self-governing practices to help them target sustainability. In order to achieve transparency, data is voluntarily collected and reported to shareholders and outsiders, providing the opportunity for independent oversight. Transparent reports on business sustainability show how a company creates value in environmental and social arenas. The resulting public scrutiny can make an organization nervous; it can reveal failures and mistakes at the same that it celebrates successes.

Aristotle praised the virtues of the courageous transparent path. "Criticism is something we can avoid easily," he wrote, "by saying nothing, doing nothing, and being nothing." We build trust, both within organizations and with our customers, through accurate reporting paired with transparent disclosure. This builds confidence that the data was neither embellished nor distorted. It signals that the people in the organization are striving to be the very best versions of themselves.

When employees are equipped with knowledge, as well as an accurate picture of how well their organization is meeting its goals, workers at every level can make daily decisions to help achieve a broader corporate mission. Keith Rabois, who has helped to build companies including PayPal and LinkedIn, was interviewed by the startup team at the website First Round Review. "If you want people to make the same decisions that you would make, but in a more scalable way, you have to give them the same information you have." Good information is not only empowering, it can add meaning to jobs up and down the chain. Information sharing entrusts people with knowledge that empowers them. It can enroll people in the belief that they are part of something larger than their individual tasks. President Kennedy once visited NASA and stopped to speak to a janitor who was mopping a floor. When asked what his job was, the janitor replied, "I'm helping to send a man to the moon."[105]

For companies producing products, their commodity supply chain first turns raw materials and components into a finished product, then distributes it to customers. Here, ethical transparency must include sharing information about source materials and processes used to create products or commodities. The supply chain includes all resources, activities, organizations, and people involved in the processes, with impacts at every stage. Patagonia, an early leader in environmental sourcing, provides customers with an interactive website entitled "The Footprint Chronicles." It maps the origins of finished outdoor products, from organic cotton farms in Texas, to garment sewing factories in Jordan. At the end of the products' life, Patagonia also takes back old outerwear for recycling. They recycle fibers into new products, or repair gently worn products or jackets with a broken zipper, giving items a second life and a more extended life cycle.

The Forestry Stewardship Council (FSC) label is one of the most successful product disclosure programs to-date. The FSC label covers wood and lumber commodities through a robust system of supply chain custody certification. FSC enables informed consumer purchases of lumber, wood furnishings, and paper. FSC International works across Guatemala, Honduras, Nicaragua, Columbia, Ecuador, Peru, Chile, Brazil, Bolivia, and Argentina. Home Depot developed a preferential treatment program for FSC-certified lumber in 1999. The FSC preference resulted in the company becoming the largest supplier of certified lumber on the planet. FSC also provided brand value for Home Depot, whose loyal customers feel good about buying products that don't contribute to rainforest destruction.[106]

Occasionally a dramatic event can uncover hidden unethical practices within the supply chain. This presents an opportunity for consumer awareness via the media. One such event was the 2013 Bangladeshi Rana Plaza garment factory disaster. More than 1,100 people were killed and 2,500 injured due to unsafe working conditions. Since the disaster, more than 200 international clothing brands, including Gap and H&M, pledged to work together. The aim is to protect workers in developing countries and ensure safer factory conditions, as well as increasing transparency of the global supply chain. Cheap clothing and other products can cloak unseen costs that stand in the way of sustainability.

Tracking sustainability requires an increased awareness of broad global conditions, such as climate change. Companies with an ear to the ground on sustainability may also be better at tracking far-flung issues that could impact their business. Audrey Choi, head of Global Sustainable Finance for Morgan Stanley, says narrowly focused traditional business viewpoints attempt to see the whole wide world through a telephoto lens. According to Choi, businesses with a broader sustainability focus are using a more effective wide-angle lens—with far-reaching results and profitability.[107] In her paper "Sustainability Incorporated," Denise Nogueira, sustainability manager for Itau Inibanco, writes, "When we talk about integrated reporting we are not talking about the publication. We are talking about an integrated process of defining what's relevant and collecting that information. The importance is the process, not the report itself."

Widespread adoption of sustainable, ethical business practices is a long way from being commonplace. Unfortunately, turning a profit doesn't always align with ethical choices, although this is beginning to change. The ethical pathway requires fortitude and patience. One also needs to be comfortable with moral ambiguity, because ethics rarely deliver only one correct answer. No handy rulebook exists to steer us toward the ethical choice for every scenario. Carefully considered details for each situation must inform an ethical path forward.

We can drive organization, consumer and marketplace change with rigorous tracking and strict public reporting. We can envision a world where social and environmental impact will be integrated into the world around us by default, not as a specialized boutique process. This vision is embraced by the Global Reporting Initiative, the recognized international standards body for corporate social responsibility. Their "We Believe" statement refers to transparency as "a catalyst for change." Public interest, the vision says, can drive every decision an organization makes. These words signal the sustainability revolution.

MODERN-DAY REVOLUTIONISTS: FAIR TRADE IN THE MADRE DE DIOS

The Body Shop's fair trade program still exists today. The company states, "We choose to harness the skills of farmers, traditional artisans and rural co-ops. In exchange we offer good trading practices and a fair wage." Their ingredient list reads like a travelogue of souvenirs spanning twenty-one countries that export aloe, babassu, peppermint, shea, chamomile, honey, beeswax, cocoa, coconut, and cane sugar. There are also Brazil and Argan nuts, soya, and olives that provide rich, moisturizing oil.

Next, we'll follow the story of Brazil nut oil which The Body Shop sources today from Candela, a Peruvian nonprofit. (Despite the name, Brazil nut trees can be found throughout South American rainforests.) Candela empowers producers and communities to conserve biodiversity through trade, which serves to provide a hedge against competing unsustainable practices and income streams.

Let's imagine day-to-day operations at one of Candela's small production cooperatives, a community-based enterprise. It produces Brazil nuts using sustainability practices that protect the environment while also benefiting local peoples. I have waved the literary wand of my imagination in order to create this fictional account, inspired by facts and real events.

The Madre de Dios, translated as Mother of God, is the locale's largest river. Eventually, it will make its way to join the Amazon. The river shares its name with this particular Peruvian rainforest, a rare pristine preserve still largely untouched by gold, rubber, or lumber extraction. A Tamarindo monkey swings through the branches, high overhead. His incredibly long arms give the appearance of a Dr. Seuss character. His aerial acrobatics are hard to track, and soon the dense canopy swallows him up. On the forest floor below, a small group of Brazil nut workers gather up fallen nut pods into piles. Some call these "cannonball trees" because the orb-shaped nut pods can weigh up to five pounds. Falling pods have been known to be lethal to humans unlucky enough to be hit on the head. This is why the harvesting crews wait until after all the pods have fallen to the ground to do their work. At the base of a nearby tree, a worker uses a machete to expertly split the pods into geodes, revealing a hidden cache of riches. Everyone here knows that these jewels are the highest-value commodity their beloved rainforest produces.

Dona Justa's broad, friendly face watches carefully over the operations. She owns the harvest rights to 360 trees deep in the Madre de Dios rainforest, the most biologically diverse region in the country, as well as the least populated by humans. According to the Amazon Rainforest Conservancy, a single one of these precious trees can produce 250 pounds of nuts in a single season. The annual busy season from December to March requires that the lucrative harvest must be carried out without fail on nature's timeclock. Locals refer to these majestic trees as *Castana*. The Dona knows the growing habits of each one, as well as the best and worst habits of each of her workers, the castaneros. With no patience for carelessness, her dark eyes never miss a thing, ensuring that every last nut makes it into the large canvas bags emphatically labeled CANDELA—PERU—ORGANIC. The Dona's monitoring activities are accompanied by the patient thwap of the machete.

A sharp cry punctuating the quiet provides the Dona an unwelcome reminder of the catcalls she suffered in her youth. Luckily those experiences had been counterbalanced by the devotion of her Papa, who used to refer to her as his "precious little bird." As though on cue, a red-headed phia bird flitting through the clearing reveals itself as the responsible party for the bird call. She has always loved this species in spite of its ubiquity. If her luck holds today, she might also catch a glimpse of the rarer macaw parrot, with its brilliant azure wingspan and huge hooked beak. Luckily, it's far too late in the day to be concerned about running into a jaguar.

The men are taking a break to eat a few tamales they have brought, with their conveniently travel-ready wrapping of banana leaves. The Peruvian version of tamales use cassava or yucca flour, stuffed with chicken, black olives and spicy aji Amarillo yellow peppers. As the day grows late, the crew will throw the bulging bags of nuts over their shoulders, carrying them several miles down an unmarked narrow trail. Long, wooden banana boats will then be loaded for the trip down-river. The narrow hulls of the boats, which give them their name, are painted a cheerful turquoise. Once they arrive at the village with their haul, the harvest continues on to the processing barn. There, groups of women will hand-crack each nut using a small table-top metal device. Next, the nuts will be packed into large metal drums to be dried before the final grinding step.

These hard-working individuals power the Candela cooperative, enabling them to serve forty-seven clients across sixteen countries. Relying on over four hundred production chains like this one, Candela's combined sales of sustainably-produced products tallied over $6 million dollars in 2016.[108] The productivity of the cooperative goes hand-in-hand with the productivity of the forest. The labor-intensive hand harvesting, transporting, and processing are part of what keeps the forest and this community intact. It's a symbiotic relationship among people and nature, allowing the forest to continue to thrive, so people like the Dona can have a reliable livelihood. Her earnings have allowed her to build aquaculture fish ponds and to expand her chicken-raising operation. Once she has enough savings set aside, she plans to start a rotisserie chicken restaurant.

Peru is well-known for such micro and small enterprise economic endeavors, which comprise 98 percent of all businesses in the country. Dona Justa is in good company, as 40 percent of these are run by women.[109] Candela's work includes training in sustainable agro-forestry practices, as well as developing new market opportunities to increase the economic value of rainforest preservation. Candela is a member of the *Union for Ethical BioTrade*. Among their stated Core Values are fair and equitable benefit sharing, respect for worker rights, clarity regarding land tenure, and biodiversity conservation.

As the fair trade movement has matured, its success has also resulted in large corporate involvement. While at first blush this may seem positive, it may ultimately result in changing the rules of the game to suit big business, threatening the empowerment of smaller players. There is also growing concern that the halo effect of fair trade may be conferred to companies who don't deserve it.

Some believe fair trade is now at a crossroads as it struggles to grow from a niche market to a significant constellation of business interests. The real rub is the fact that the goals upon which fair trade was originally built—to create lasting trade partnerships based on relationships, shorter and more transparent value chains, and more equitable systems of economic exchange—seem diametrically opposed to the global economy, with its roots in traditional stock market exchange systems and endless hunger for cheap commodities. Fair trade provides an inspiring example of a business movement based on an aspirational Mission to Serve. With its growing success as well as emerging challenges, it's one to continue to study. This story also reminds us that bigger is not always better. The need to forge sustainability solutions, founded in human relationships, requires ongoing patience, trust, and care.

CHAPTER FOUR

Creativity Within Limits

Imagination is everything. It's the preview of life's coming attractions.

–Albert Einstein

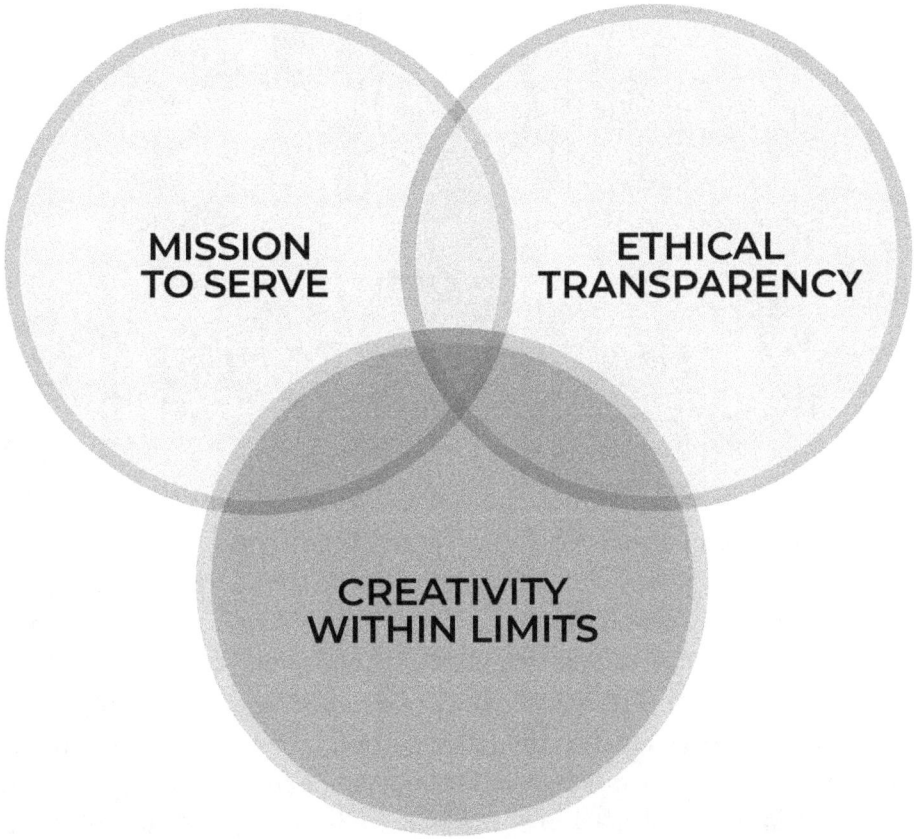

Economic Core Value Three: Creativity within Limits

SIXTH COURSE: A COURSE IN CREATIVITY WITHIN LIMITS

Back at my imaginary dinner party, it's time for the sixth course to be served: a course in exercising Creativity within Limits.

We are at the halfway point of our feast, so it's time for a palate cleanser to refresh ourselves and make space for what more is to come. I have prepared an Italian fruit granita, made with organic strawberries from the farmer's market. The ingredients are deceptively simple: fruit, sugar, lemon juice, and water. It's the freezing action that makes the magic happen. A granita is similar to sorbet, but made by hand in the freezer, instead of in a special machine. The texture is not quite as smooth as a sorbet. The grains of frozen fruit are slightly crunchy at first, and then melt lusciously away. It's a bit like eating strawberry flavored snow.

As my guests sample the frozen treat, the dining room grows quiet. As the host, I always want to make sure that the conversation includes everyone. Often the people in a group who say the least have the most important perspectives needing to be heard. I decided to ask César, my least gregarious guest, some questions to draw him out.

"César, I'd love to hear more about your experiences growing up. What was it like?"

He glances around the room, taking everything in. By most standards of living, I was a rich woman, although I thought of myself more as comfortably well off. Certainly, I lacked for nothing that I truly needed. In recent years I had become increasingly aware of my privilege as a white person with a steady job, good healthcare, and a retirement plan.

"People living off the land naturally know how to use everything they have," he says. "My family never wasted anything. We didn't call it sustainability; it was just common sense."

I didn't take César's perspective as a criticism about my own life, yet I thought there might be a way to build a bridge with my own experience. Growing up in the hippie era, my mom made her own yogurt and grew sprouts. She helped me sew a purse out of an old pair of my jeans. Later, I decorated my first apartment with printed cotton Indian bedspreads from Goodwill and candleholders repurposed from empty chianti bottles.

I wanted to find a way to connect, even as different as our lives have been. "I have never lived off the land," I said. "I never lacked for anything growing up. I'm a city kid. But in the sixties, reusing old scraps creatively was part of being hip. I think that trend is coming back. Sustainability is what the cool kids are doing now."

Cousteau seemed to find amusement in the idea, chuckling as he joined in. "How delightful for us elders, growing grey and wrinkled while we have worked in the trenches for decades. We have finally become fashionable!"

NECESSITY—THE MOTHER OF INVENTION

The Body Shop grew out of the idea of making something out of nothing. Growing up in a large Italian immigrant family, Anita no doubt absorbed the idea of creative frugality somewhat organically. Italian peasant cuisine, known as *cucina povera*, is based on the idea that no scrap of food should ever be thrown away. Italian peasants of rural Italy are well known for their ingenious transformations of humble ingredients, such as potatoes or stale bread, into gnocchi (flour or root vegetable dumplings) or panzanella (bread salad). They were masters at delivering elevated food experiences, born out of necessity. "The spirit of *la cucina povera* is about embracing constraints and discovering the delicious creativity that can spring from making do with what you've got," says Faith Durand in her Cucina Povera article at TheKitchn.com. In stark contrast, today's culture of food extravagance results in throwing away as much as one third of still edible food.

Anita concocted the first Body Shop beauty products by rolling up her sleeves in her own kitchen. She used old stock pots to stir up readily available edible ingredients. Such modest beginnings. The first results sounded good enough to eat. *Cucumber Cleansing Cream. Watermelon Sun Block. Banana Shampoo.* Eventually Anita partnered with a local herbalist to produce small quantities of the first twenty Body Shop products, using a short list of natural ingredients including cocoa butter, almond oil, and aloe vera.[110]

In 1976, Anita rented a modest storefront for the first shop, located on a Brighton street with a fair amount of walk-by traffic. But the space had an unfortunate problem: a leaky roof. There were damp, discolored patches on the walls. When it rained, water dripped down from the ceiling cornices. Ever the creative problem-solver, Anita came up with the idea of dark green wall paint to mask the moisture discoloration. (This deep green shade would later become a signature of The Body Shop brand.) *Body and Soul* tells of Anita hanging fence panels of rough-sawn larch against the painted walls. In part, she wanted to create a wholesome outdoorsy aesthetic. More importantly, she was looking for a way to intercept the leaks so they wouldn't splash down onto the products.

Another Body Shop feature was also born out of creativity driven by necessity. In order to eliminate the appearance of empty store shelves, Anita came up with the idea of offering products in five different sizes. At the time, health food stores were becoming popular, with bulk sections allowing consumers to select specific quantities for purchase. Anita allowed customers to purchase only the amount they needed, reinforcing ideas of frugality and waste minimization.

Anita liked to explain that "The idea of The Body Shop is not new. In India and the Arab world for centuries perfume has been decanted and sold in the amounts the customer wanted, and in California in the sixties you could bring your own bottle and get it filled. Greengrocers and confectioners also trade this way: you can buy as much or as little as you want. What was new was that we applied it to cosmetics . . . due to lack of money."[111]

Packaging can represent a huge cost to product producers, as well as to the environment. Formulating her first run of merchandise required more of Anita's initial budget than she had reckoned on, so she started thinking about how to reduce packaging costs. Sterile urine sample bottles were the cheapest containers she could find. Product labels were written out in her own hand. The store's refill bar offered discounted product refills to customers bringing back their empty containers. This saved the company on the cost of purchasing new containers. In the 1970s, recycling was not yet a well-established consumer concept. A frugal customer mindset brought people back over and over, reusing the same bottles, and helping to build a loyal following of those ready for an alternative to mass consumerism. Over time, The Body Shop's waste minimization strategies included the elimination of packaging entirely for some goods.

The biggest consumers of packaging are Asia, Western Europe, and North America, gobbling up paper, wood, plastic, metal, and glass packing materials. According to the World Packaging Organization, in a single year the world spent $485 billion on packaging for food, drink, healthcare, cosmetics, and other consumer goods. The fastest-growing component of the packaging industry springs from the consumption of bottled water and the increased demand for convenience-packaging of prepared foods in rigid plastic. This resource-intensive sector is ripe for creative reimagination and reinvention, informed by creativity within limits.

COMPANY GROWTH AND CHANGE

The Body Shop's immediate popularity led to rapid business expansion. By 1995 there were over 1,300 outlets retailing four hundred products in forty-five countries, including the United Arab Emirates, Singapore, Hong Kong, Greece, and Australia.

Through this period of growth, Anita continued her activist agenda focused on transforming suppliers, employees, and customers. Given the company's iconoclastic reputation, it came as a shock to cadres of loyal customers when the Roddicks sold the business in 2006 to L'Oréal, the number one cosmetics company in the world, for $1.1 billion.[112] The sale was seen by critics as both a literal and philosophical sell-out. Ever the maverick, Anita defended the decision as well as the new owner. "I believe they are honorable and the work they do is honorable," she said of L'Oréal, "especially the work they do on sourcing ingredients."[113]

The Creativity within Limits storyline now follows a thread within L'Oréal's sustainability journey.

According to the website Cosmetics Technology, L'Oréal is the world's largest cosmetics company, representing over $33 billion in annual revenues. The parent company's holdings include Maybelline New York, Lancôme, Kiehl's, and Garnier. Many consumers are surprised to learn that L'Oréal has an aggressive corporate sustainability agenda. Their environmental and supply chain goals align with the United Nations Sustainable Development target areas and include metrics for product sourcing, production, packaging, impacts to biodiversity, carbon emissions, water use, and deforestation. L'Oréal refers to their fair trade product sourcing as "Solidarity Sourcing."

In 2001, the company joined the World Business Council for Sustainable Development, closely followed in 2002 by membership in the United Nations Global Compact on sustainable development. In 2012 they hired Alexandra Palt as Chief Sustainability Officer. She reports directly to the COO, a strong indicator of the level of importance that sustainability plays within the organization. As part of its organizational change strategy, L'Oréal includes sustainability performance targets in the bonus system for all its country and brand executives, further signaling a belief in doing well by doing good.

The nonprofit Ethisphere Foundation included L'Oréal on their list of the world's most ethical companies for seven years running. However, L'Oréal's commitment to sustainability is not quite as visible to the casual observer as that of The Body Shop. One has to look a bit deeper.

Jean-Paul Agon, L'Oréal's CEO since 2006, noted in 2015's Progress Report on sustainability, "There can no longer be any doubt: companies have to change. They can no longer see their success and long-term outlook in terms of economic performance alone. Sustainability has become the new norm, the new license to do business and even the key to survival. We have continued to dissociate our growth from our environmental impact, proving that economic performance is clearly compatible with a commitment to protecting the climate."

Here's Hope: As the sustainability movement grows and matures, financial performance is aligning with sustainability performance. In 2017, the Ethisphere Foundation compared their top-ranking list of 124 companies across five continents to the S&P 500 over a two-year period. The ethically reported companies showed a 6.4 percent higher return on investment. When ethical behavior and profits align, everyone wins.

Our sixth Sustainability Core Value looks at the idea of leveraging limits as opportunities. Finding new ways to operate within environmental, social and economic limitations tends to push organizations to create better ways to deliver value to employees, shareholders, and customers. Such limitations also create opportunities to innovate. L'Oréal's Agon says, "As we pursue this program, we can clearly see how these social and environmental commitments also provide our laboratories and plants with a source of creativity, innovation and performance. They encourage us to push the boundaries of technology and expertise. They urge us to be inventive."[114]

ECONOMIC SUSTAINABILITY CORE VALUE 3:

CREATIVITY WITHIN LIMITS
Doing more with less

The more you know, the less you need.
— **Australian Aboriginal wisdom**

Overcoming limitations using human ingenuity is a practice as old as civilization itself. Ancient inventions such as the lever and the pulley overcame the limits of man's abilities. Such inventions often take on the challenge of how to do more with less. But while limitless aspiration has delivered many achievements to be admired, our inventions may deliver a dark side of unintended consequences. For example, our appetite for feeding more people with reliably produced, profitable, and perfect-looking crops has resulted in a monster agribusiness industry. This agribusiness is based on unsustainable influxes of fossil-fuel-based fertilizers, GMOs, pesticide-laden foods, and the death of healthy soils and small-hold family farms. Such calamitous side-effects lead us to ask if bigger is always better.

One thread of sustainability's lineage can be traced back to a 1972 report for the Club of Rome. This international consortium of bright minds was founded to "foster understanding of the varied but interdependent components—economic, political, natural, and social—that make up the global system in which we all live."[115] They posed the question "How much is too much?" The four authors delivered the idea of "Limits to Growth," a challenge to a central myth of Western civilization. They asserted that the idea of continual exponential growth, regardless of the cost to the planet, is unsustainable.

The kind of growth they were talking about includes population and industrial output that strains natural planetary systems and resources such as arable land, fresh water, metals, forests and oceans. Limits address the harmful side-effects of associated exponential increases in pollutants, including carbon dioxide. The report suggested that the earth has an upper limit to its growth, also referred to as carrying capacity. Fueling much controversy at the time, their data projections attempted to demonstrate that exponential growth would eventually lead to catastrophic collapse of many of the earth's systems.

Today, many of the report's 50-year-old predictions are coming true. We are experiencing system collapses in areas such as global fisheries and climate. However, there is hope in our ingenious ability to learn from our mistakes and to adapt to Earth's limitations. The concept of Creativity within Limits springs fundamentally from the idea of resource productivity. Understanding resources as finite prompts us to tap into new ways of doing more with less.

In the business world, efficiency shows up as trimming operating costs, or finding the sweet spot that balances cost with benefit. Economic ventures abhor inefficiency, and waste is understood as a "non-value-added" component. The Lean Six Sigma approach systematically eliminates eight categories of waste in order to make business processes more competitive. Some ambitious companies such as Unilever have set an ambitious goal of halving their environmental footprint while doubling revenue.

Creativity within Limits can eliminate the concept of waste altogether, reimagining waste as an untapped resource. Tyson Foods, the world's largest processor of chicken, beef, and pork, created a renewable energy division to turn 2.3 annual billion pounds of chicken fat waste into biofuel, creating a new profit center.[116] A subsequent joint venture produced over 2,500 barrels of fuel per day. Tyson has since sold their share of the joint venture, but still continues to provide fuel feedstock. One of the biggest emerging opportunity areas for such biofuels is sustainable aviation fuel, being tested at the Air Force Research Laboratory.

In order to transition to a true circular economy, everything we use must be completely reusable, recyclable, non-toxic, or compostable.

Ultimately this includes all inputs and outputs, all products and processes, and all supply chains. Ray Anderson, CEO of Interface Carpet, posed the question "How would a forest design a floor covering?" His company's invention of non-directional, random carpet tile patterns eliminated massive amounts of production and installation waste. Such game-changers illustrate the circular economy, or a system that closes the loop of material flows as a way to increase resource productivity.

Another business disruption that creatively overcomes limits is the idea of redefining products as services. Traditionally, manufacturers have focused on one-time product sales. But increasingly, consumers don't need to own a physical thing to obtain the value they desire. For example, leasing commercial modular carpet tile eliminates the need to purchase carpet. Zipcar's pay-per-use model enables us to question the need for everyone to own a car. Sustainability can serve to provide a service versus actual ownership, embracing limitations in order to ultimately provide a better experience for customers. De-materializing the consumer experience is already in effect with music streaming, digital music and books, and cloud-based data storage.

Creative limits can cause us to drastically reinvent what we are doing, getting completely outside the box to transform accepted norms. This can be referred to as boundary disruption. When we respond to limits in new ways, we may be rewarded with innovative and unexpected results. Examples of this abound in the art world.

Igor Stravinsky broke free of traditional patterns of musical meter, contributing to the radical newness of his ballet score for *The Rite of Spring*.[117] More traditional musical compositions by composers such as Mozart or Beethoven generally stuck with one-time signature for each movement. Stravinsky used many unusual time signatures and also switched time signatures repeatedly within a movement, in some places in almost every bar. Stravinsky noted, "My freedom will be so much the greater the more I surround myself with obstacles. The more constraints one imposes, the more one frees oneself of the chains that shackle the spirit."[118]

Visual artist Nina Katchadourian challenged herself to invent artwork during long plane flights using only the materials at hand, with highly entertaining results composed from napkins and food service items. Graphic artist Phil Hansen developed a hand tremor which at first seemed like a tragic occurrence, but it eventually allowed him to entirely re-invent his style, using wiggly lines and improvisation. "Embracing a limitation can actually drive creativity," he said. "We need to first be limited in order to become limitless."[119]

Simply doing things more efficiently will not automatically result in sustainability gains. First, we must ensure we are solving the right problem. Efficiently doing the wrong thing won't lead to sustainability. As William McDonough and Michael Braungart explain in their book *Cradle to Cradle: Remaking the Way We Make Things*, "Our concept of eco-effectiveness means working on the right things—on the right products and services and systems—instead of making the wrong things less bad. Once you are doing the right things, then doing them 'right,' with the help of efficiency among other tools, makes perfect sense."

Sometimes, we have to ask ourselves if the way we have gotten used to doing things merits wholesale reinvention. Given the urgency of climate change, we now know that burning fossil fuels such as coal to generate electricity is not as clever as we once thought. There are cleaner, more renewable, and economic ways to deliver the energy we crave. Throwing off the shackles of tradition can invite new opportunities. Embracing the challenge of Creativity within Limits holds the promise of innovations that can lead to massive long-term benefits.

ENDING NEEDLESS
ANIMAL TESTING TODAY

Our next story explores how The Body Shop championed humane methods for testing cosmetic products, leading to a ban on animal testing in the UK. We will also examine how this regulatory limit later led L'Oréal to invest in innovative laboratory methods that are paving the way toward a worldwide animal testing ban.

The widespread practice of testing cosmetics on defenseless animals was one of Anita Roddick's top activist issues. The world of animal testing is invisible to most consumers who may purchase products, blissfully unaware of the violence they are unwittingly participating in if those products were tested on animals. To raise awareness with their customers, every Body Shop store participated in recurring "Against Animal Testing" campaigns which included public demonstrations led by Anita. She was always accompanied by activists dressed in rabbit costumes. These were not cute bunnies; they were depictions of maimed lab animals with distended 4-foot heads and discolored swollen eyes that stared bleakly into the media's camera lenses.

The following descriptions are not for those with a weak stomach. According to the People for the Ethical Treatment of Animals (PETA), it is estimated that in the US alone, more than 100 million defenseless rabbits, pigs, guinea pigs, rats and mice die in painful laboratory tests each year. They are poisoned, burned, crippled and abused without the use of pain relief. The animals are always killed at the end of each test. One of the most familiar is the eye irritation test, which entails applying a substance directly to the test subject's eye, usually a rabbit, which can cause bleeding, ulcers, or blindness. Another common test repeatedly applies substances to shaved skin for periods of up to 90 days. Oral toxicity tests are conducted by force-feeding substances down the throat using a feeding tube, which may cause convulsions, bleeding from the mouth, paralysis, seizures, or death. The gruesome underbelly of the cosmetics and personal care industry is its lack of transparency. But this is a story that is far from over.

Instead of testing their products on animals, The Body Shop relied on volunteers willing to participate in simple and relatively painless skin patch tests. Shop suppliers also had to declare in writing that they did not conduct animal testing. But this was just the beginning for Anita; she wanted an outright ban on animal testing across the entire industry. By 1998, The Body Shop's campaign petition had collected four million signatures demanding a ban on animal testing.[120] Later that same year, the UK enacted the first national ban in the world, an incredible victory for The Body Shop. By 2003 the EU had enacted an animal testing ban with various provisions to be phased in between 2004 and 2009. (Such judicious phasing gives the market a chance to realistically catch up with alternative options.)

Here's Hope: Further strengthening these moves, the EU Constitution was amended in 2007 through the Lisbon Treaty to recognize animals as sentient beings.[121] Other standards focusing on the compassion for farm animals include veterinary training, animal transport guidelines, and the welfare of sows and laying hens. Thanks in part to Anita's early leadership, alternative testing methods are becoming increasingly available using methods that are more efficient, reliable, and humane. With the EU regulatory changes, finding alternatives to animal testing became an essential competitive business practice in addition to an ethical choice.

Doing the right thing is often about more than just efficiency. Our humanitarian impulse toward empathy tells us that eliminating the pain and suffering of sentient creatures is a prize won by the beating heart of sustainability. Anthropologist Margaret Mead famously told us to "Never doubt that a small group of thoughtful, committed citizens can change the world; indeed, it's the only thing that ever has."

Testing on live animals is commonly referred to as *in vivo*. The alternative is referred to as *in vitro*, laboratory testing relying on tissue samples.

In vitro processes are made possible through something called bio banks. Bio banks collect and store skin tissues for research purposes, in addition to familiar organ donation functions. This allows for the reuse of human bone marrow, heart valves, corneas, blood vessels, and skin. While this practice may sound at first blush like something out of a horror film, the reuse of human tissue serves vital research needs. It also prevents massive amounts of costly waste disposal. Medical waste from US hospitals is estimated to generate 29 pounds of waste per bed each day, resulting in many million tons of medical waste per year.[122] Surgical waste (as much as 30 percent of all medical waste) must be handled with methods that can be ten to fifteen times more expensive than that of other medical waste.[123] The cost of medical waste management is growing, along with population growth and access to healthcare, and will reach a value of $17.89 billion by 2026.[124]

We tend to take our skin for granted, but it has near magical properties. This largest human organ makes up 16 percent of the body by weight and comprises a surface area of between 16 and 25 square feet. Its primary function is to provide a physical barrier to the outer environment, protecting us from toxins, micro-organisms, ultraviolet radiation, and mechanical damage. Human skin has incredible prolific regenerative properties, with the outer epidermal layer entirely renewing itself every two to four weeks. The epidermis is mainly composed of layers of cells called keratinocytes, which synthesize the protein keratin. Cultivated in vitro, a single keratinocyte stem cell from the epidermis can replicate itself 100 billion times over, self-propagating the equivalent of 1,000 adult body equivalents of human skin.

Healthy surgical tissue left over from planned medical procedures can be reframed as a resource that can be recaptured. (Resources are often defined by society as all the materials we need to carry on life as we know it.) With the permission of the donor (or their parents in the case of infants), strips of healthy skin removed during breast surgery, tummy tucks, and circumcisions can be donated for laboratory research. And now the thread of our story picks up again with L'Oréal. Today the company is immersed in innovative practices founded upon the concept of Creativity within Limits. In anticipation of the EU ban, and as an investment in innovation and business development, the company acquired the rights to a biotechnology now known as EpiSkin. L'Oréal continues to invest nearly €1 billion per year in this bio-research business.

The following scenes are drawn from video news stories posted on episkin.com and photo documentation. I've drawn a story with my literary pen here, a fictional account inspired by real events. The names have been changed, but this very real story tells us how corporate investments in R&D can help to advance sustainability in ways we haven't even thought of yet.

It's promising to be a bright, sunny day in Lyon, France, home to L'Oréal's research campus. A thin morning mist surrounding the sun creates the appearance of a lovely golden aureole. This same quality of radiance and light inspired French chemist Eugene Schueller to invent a new hair dye for Parisian hairdressers, which he dubbed "Auréole." Fashionable French women promptly went mad for the stuff, setting the stage for the founding of L'Oréal in 1909, its name derived from that first successful product creation.

On this day, L'Oréal's outreach liaison for research and innovation, Camille Fournier, has arrived precisely on time for work. Her employer's 12,000 square foot gleaming white temple to research backs up to an expansive pleasure garden, flanked by a skateboard park and the Rive Gauche restaurant. Madame is already looking forward to her lunch reservations there later in the day. She is particularly fond of the chef's salmon tartare.

Many of the lushly ornamented green buildings she has passed along her route sport green roofs and living walls, replete with vegetation. In contrast, L'Oréal's building appears to be all business, with little to ornament the exterior of the edifice. The interesting stuff is all inside, as we shall soon see. All of these facilities are headquartered within the Gerland Technopole bioscience park, strategically located near the city of

Lyon's industrial port on the Rhone River. Lyon was first settled by the Romans in 43 BC., serving as an industrial and banking powerhouse for over 500 years now. Here, L'Oréal's bioscience laboratory is engaged in the ongoing work that could end *in vivo* animal testing forever.

Mme. Fournier steps inside to walk along the shining, snowy-colored corridors, a seamless continuation of the building's stark white exterior. A few decorative gestures to potted plants are scattered about the pristine halls. The only other decorative details are large framed scientific illustrations that might appear at home in a university anatomy classroom. Today, Madame is visiting the EpiSkin laboratories to check in on their progress. Much of her job entails responding to media inquiries about the research quietly being conducted here. It seems a publication like *Bloomberg Business Week* or *Wired* contacts her daily. She is famously good at her job, able to manage inquiries with smooth expertise, sharing crisply detailed research facts while creating a glowy, journalistic buzz.

Clicking smartly down the hallway, she clearly knows where she's going. Having arrived in a cavernous space filled with gleaming white lockers, Madame pulls a crisp icy blue lab coat over her dress. Meticulous preparations must be made in order to enter the sterile zone. She exchanges her dainty leather kitten-heel shoes for clunky white slip-ons with thick spongy marshmallow soles. As she smooths back her stylish blonde bob and adjusts a huge pair of clear safety glasses on her nose, she takes a quick glance in the mirror at her flawless complexion, a gift of genetics augmented by a strict skin-care regimen.

Her mind wanders briefly to the lunch that awaits her later today. In conformity to the traditions that are her birthright, her meal will likely include a glass of wine from one of the vintners to the north. Most of them cultivate Gamay grapes used to produce the region's world-renowned Beaujolais Nouveaux. Viticulture is one thing, but could she have ever imagined that her job would involve human skin farmers? These fancy new jobs involve cultivating petri dish skin tissues in space age soil-less laboratories. "C'est merveilleux," she muses.

Madame peers through the sprawling glass wall, past a sign in large official-looking letters. Cell Bank 1 is protected from contamination by a futuristic door lock system that could have come straight out of a James Bond film, protecting Doctor No's underground lair from intruders. Unintimidated by the control panel, she selects a large white button marked "*Overture.*" Immediately, the large green button labeled "*Libre*" lights up, indicating she is "free" to enter. The remaining red button seems to imply that something undesirable might happen if it were to light up. Not a single worker looks up as the newcomer arrives; each is laser-focused on their appointed task.

It is hard to discern any distinguishing personal details since every worker is swathed in lab suits, gloves, and head coverings that leave nothing but the eyes exposed. Mme. Fournier settles herself carefully onto an available stool among the glistening lab tables. Her eyes click around the room, taking everything in. With the exception of a few stainless surfaces, every fixture is spotlessly white. The only sounds are the background hush of the exhaust fans constantly returning air from the outside world to the work stations. (Medical laboratories are notorious energy consumers due to their hunger for fresh air.) Otherwise, the atmosphere is eerily quiet, as though the lab is floating in deep space, alienated from the rest of the universe. The chamber is crammed with crucibles, thermometers, vials, forceps, flasks, graduated cylinders, test tubes, hoses, clamps, and other contraptions that Madame would be hard-pressed to call by name. Microscope sentinels stand crisply at attention at regular intervals along the walls.

The lifeblood of laboratory research is precision, which can only be delivered through absolute control of every possible variable that might create an experiment anomaly. Each technician follows a painstaking series of accurate steps in a complex recipe. Make one mistake, and the skin cells die. Even a minor error could ruin the test trays they are responsible for. A single vessel of reconstructed tissue samples has a cash value equivalent to a month's rent for many of these workers.

Laboratory scientists must have the patience of Sisyphus as well as a fair share of obsessive-compulsive disorder. The exact same procedure must be repeated perfectly hundreds of times, without variation, without annoyance. The more finicky the lab worker, the better. These are a special variety of *homo sapiens*. Their home medicine cabinets are arranged alphabetically in perfect order. They eat the same baguette with butter and jam at the exact same time every single morning, without becoming restless for change.

Mme. Fournier takes a few notes on a tiny silver-cased notepad that she produces from her coat pocket. She watches carefully as each technician soberly manipulates their pipette, applying measured amounts of rosy-colored hair conditioner to trays of skin samples. These trials, which can be completed in short order, are focused on the potential to cause skin irritation. Working with live lab animals is much more time-consuming as well as costly. A similar test carried out on a rabbit's skin or eyes could take two to four weeks to complete. Here, not a furry animal is in sight. The closest thing resembling fur is a pair of bushy eyebrows that peak out stubbornly from beneath one technician's pale blue scrub cap.

Within the labyrinth of L'Oréal's research palace, there are lab rooms conducting "efficacy tests," clinical trials to substantiate product claims. Hair conditioner that will repair split ends! Mascara that will lengthen! Other tests target the effectiveness of an innovative new sunscreen invented here. Aiming to fight back against deadly skin cancer, it contains Mexoryl SX, which screens for UVB rays. L'Oréal invests in R&D to the tune of about 660 million Euros per year. Proceeds from R&D make up 3.5 percent of the company's annual revenues.[125] A significant portion of this comes from the sale of living skin tissue, branded by Loreal as "EpiSkin." Half of the 100,000 units of skin tissue they produce each year will be sold off to other entities, for use in their own cosmetic testing use, or for melanoma or human papillomavirus (HPV) research. Investments in EpiSkin research have created a new profit center for L'Oréal, opening up new markets and disruptive business opportunities for them as pioneers in the field of epidural engineering.

Mme. Fournier snaps her notebook shut with a satisfying click. She checks her watch as she exits Cell Bank 1, to ensure she is precisely on schedule. Her journey down yet another long gleaming hallway takes her toward production rooms where reconstructed skin samples are grown using methods originally developed to help burn victims, using grafts of their own skin to grow more. However, laboratory-grown product cannot exactly replicate how human skin functions as part of a living body, since isolated test samples have no nerves, oil glands, or hair follicles. So just how does the skin farming process creatively overcome this limitation?

Each piece of tissue coming from healthy medical waste is painstakingly stripped apart with forceps, separating the epidermis from the dermis. The remaining tissue samples are the "seeds" which feed the rest of the process. The tissues are placed in a petri dish atop a collagen gel substrate. A mixture of purified water, sugar and amino acids is poured into the dish to nourish the tissue culture and encourage the formation of fibroblasts, the cells that form the structural matrix of tissues, and that play an important role in tissue repair. The cells will eventually grow to form gelatinous, dime-sized discs of living skin somewhat resembling pink Jell-O.

Row upon row of petri dishes placed in minbar-sized incubators are nourished under constant temperature and humidity levels. After three days, the top layer of the growing tissue sample is exposed to air. This replicates real life conditions wherein a rougher outer layer of epidermis forms when exposed to the atmosphere. Air will be wafted across the top of the skin samples, while the bottom layer of skin continues to bathe in a fluid replicating nutrient-rich blood.[126] After ten days, the skin will have grown to a thickness of 12 cells. To replicate the process of sun exposure as it ages human skin, ultraviolet light is then shone onto the tissue.

As Madame's gaze alights on the ultraviolet machine, she can't help but think that it resembles the large restaurant-grade coffee maker at the Rive Gauche restaurant. Satisfied with her morning inspections, she heads away from the hushed glass bubble confines, back to the non-sterile outside world filled with its fascinating mixture of people and places and delicious lunches. Her meal will no doubt feel well-earned by the time she arrives for her assignation.

This tale of *in vitro* lab innovation leverages the idea of Creative Limits by recognizing the limitations represented by unethical animal testing. It demonstrates a willingness to ask difficult questions. How can cosmetics be delivered to the market without causing suffering? How can we use science to overcome limitations presented by outmoded methods? At the same time, these controlled methods deliver a multitude of benefits since they are also more reliably accurate and cost effective than *in vivo* tests. Here, sustainability meets profitability with highly effective methods that are ethical and humane, while delivering business cost savings and new profit centers.[127] It's a win-win-win for sustainability.

MODERN-DAY REVOLUTIONISTS: *IN VITRO* TESTING TODAY

Decades of investment and experimentation at the Gerland Technopole bioscience park are paying off for L'Oréal. After more than twenty years, EpiSkin's *in vitro* testing protocol has been fully validated by the scientific community. If all continues to go well, the unparalleled accuracy and precision of these laboratory methods will allow widespread adoption of the methods across the industry. L'Oreal refers to this as "a great step toward the elimination of animal use."

But there is still much more work to be done. One of the biggest market challenges is China, where animal testing is still mandatory in many cases. L'Oréal's approach is not all or nothing; they have chosen to try to gradually shift China away from animal testing by working with them, as opposed to refusing to sell to them. The company operates a research laboratory in Shanghai similar to the one in Lyon, growing EpiSkin from Chinese medical skin waste. While things are still far from perfect, the company touts its activities in China as "the most active company working alongside the Chinese authorities and scientists for over ten years to have alternative testing methods recognized, and permit the cosmetic regulation to evolve toward a total and definite elimination of animal testing."

Here we can see how the sustainability journey must often occur in an evolutionary fashion. If we expect all or nothing from the outset, we might end up with nothing. Allowing change to happen at a pace that can be accepted and embraced can eventually lead to gains. Trying to change things too fast or too far all at once can feel threatening to the status quo. This can sometimes stymie progress, or reverse progress already made. Proper pacing is critical to the successful revolutionary, able to ride the wave of a series of successive wins to sustainability's shore.

There is still far to go in the widespread banning of animal testing. While the EU has been the global leader, animal testing is still legal in 80 percent of countries.[128] Only a handful of non-EU countries have adopted animal testing bans, such as India in 2014. However, it's hopeful to think that the second-largest country in the world by population has adopted an animal testing ban, and momentum is building.

Here's Hope: While there is currently no animal testing ban in the US, Cruelty Free International polling shows that 79 percent of citizens across all age groups and political views support such action. In addition, some states such as Nevada, Illinois, and California are enacting bills ending the sale of tested cosmetics. The US Humane Cosmetics Act, which would phase out animal testing and prohibit importing animal-tested cosmetics, is gaining support. Corporate endorsers include Paul Mitchell and Coty.

Consumer choice is providing another pathway through "cruelty-free" labels, a common term to indicate freedom from animal testing. Ethical Transparency provides new tools for informed consumer purchasing decisions, including product labeling systems such as *Bunny Free* and *Cruelty Free*. These programs are managed by third party nonprofit organizations People for the Ethical Treatment of Animals (PETA) and the Coalition for Consumer Information on Cosmetics (CCIC). Both of these provide apps with quick-reference information consumers can refer to while shopping. The Environmental Working Group also provides a searchable database called Skin Deep Cosmetics.

Meanwhile, L'Oréal is taking their Creativity within Limits journey into uncharted territory. In 2015 the company announced a new partnership with biotech company Organovo, which uses 3D printing to reproduce living human tissue. Organovo's award-winning bio-printed kidney and liver tissue closely resemble the structure of native tissue found within the living human body, presenting exciting opportunities for more successful organ replacements.

Guive Balooch, Global Vice President of L'Oréal's Technology Incubator, is excited about the possibility of uncovering disruptive innovations across industries that have the potential to transform the beauty business. The partnership will bring about "new advances of *in vitro* methods for evaluating product safety and performance; but the potential for where this new field of technology and research can take us is boundless."[129]

Such new technologies also present their own ethical challenges. Further, some L'Oréal critics claim the company feeds pointless consumerism and therefore should not exist at all. Students at the Ecole Polytechnique, one of the most prestigious scientific universities in France, regularly critique major French companies and urge graduates not to go to work for those who fail to focus on the sustainability transition. The Ecole's student organization published a report which recognized L'Oréal's efforts to reduce their environmental impact, while also questioning the need for such a business. Here we have a group of sustainability revolutionaries, fearlessly asking whether we are spending our energies on answering the right questions.

As with any great adventure tale, the rest of the Creativity within Limits story is yet to be told. Former Assistant Secretary of Energy Christine Ervin observed in a GreenBiz publication, "Just as we've admonished that true energy conservation is not about 'shivering in the dark,' it's time to embrace the abundance that can flow from nature's limits."

The future looks bright for more problem-solving economic ventures that enter the sustainability revolution. As we bring to a close this section of the book focused on the Economic Pillar, we can see the value that a risk-taking entrepreneurial spirit brings to the sustainability journey. When we bring this quality together with key sustainability Core Values, the possibilities are as limitless as our imaginations.

PART THREE

The Social Pillar of Sustainability in Action:

CÉSAR CHÁVEZ AND THE FARMWORKER REVOLUTION

CHAPTER ONE

Who Was César Chávez?

I am convinced that the truest act of courage, the strongest act of manliness, is to sacrifice ourselves for others in a totally nonviolent struggle for justice.

— **César Chávez**

INTRODUCTION TO PART THREE AND THE THREE CORE VALUES OF THE SOCIAL PILLAR

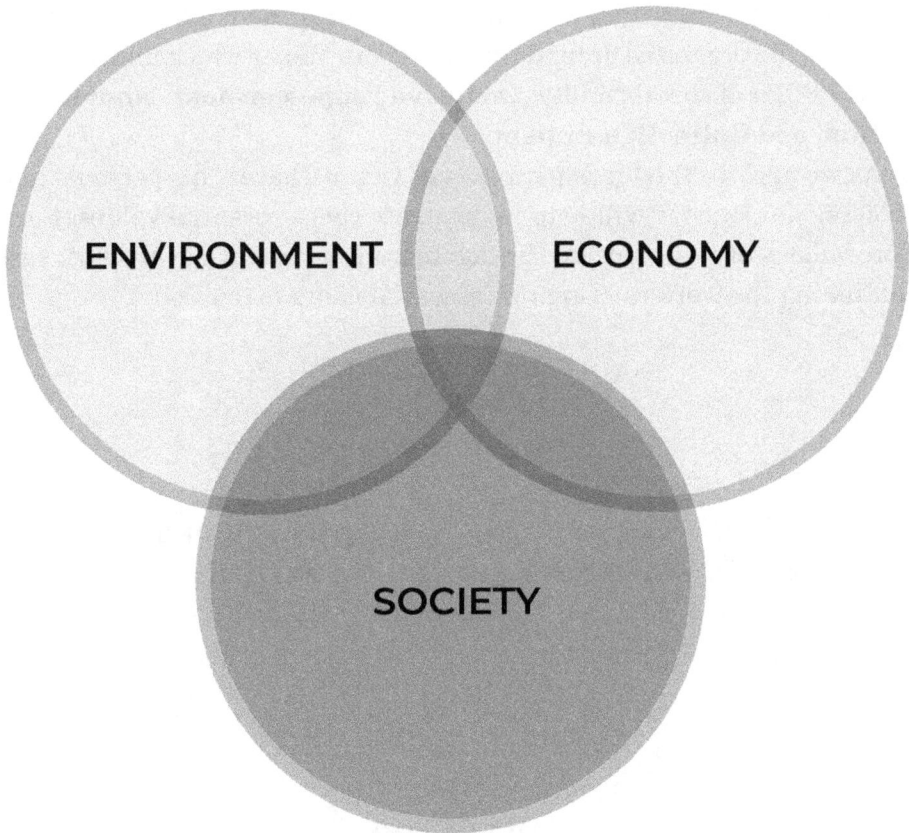

The Three Pillars of Sustainability, Emphasizing the Social Pillar

The **Social** Pillar of Sustainability is the focus of our final section. Social revolutionist César Chávez serves as the primary hero of these next sustainability adventure stories.

THREE SOCIAL SUSTAINABILITY SOCIETY CORE VALUES

The stories in this part's Chapter One provide some background on the Revolutionist known as César Chávez: who he was, and where he came from. Chapters Two, Three, and Four present a series of stories about his life organized around the three Core Values which underpin the Society Pillar of sustainability: **Inclusive Empowerment**, **Nonviolent Action**, and **Collective Impact**.

As we explore the life experiences of César Chávez, his personal and professional journey will help to illustrate these essential values. Each Core Value story will conclude by highlighting a current-day revolutionist continuing the work to bring this essential value to fruition.

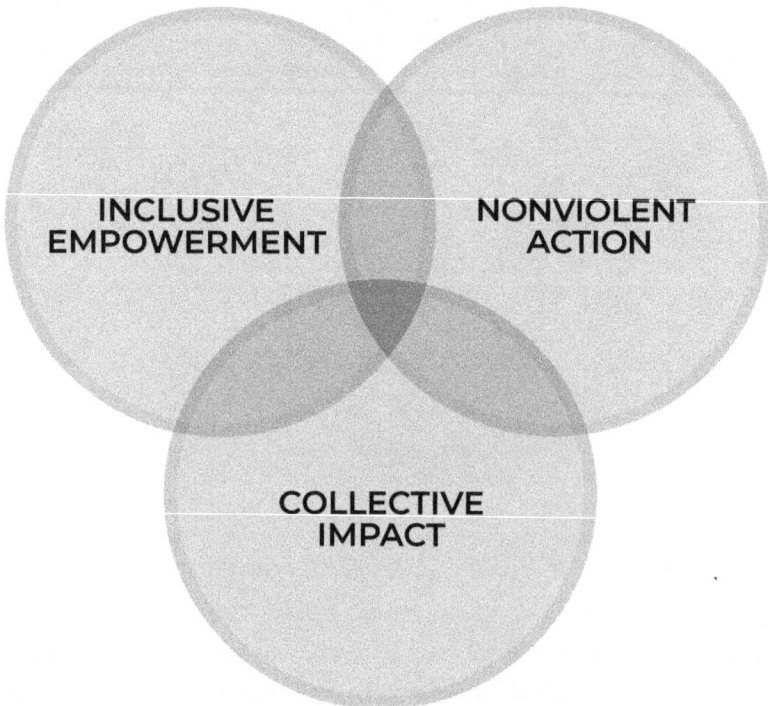

Three Core Values of the Social Pillar

AN INTRODUCTION TO
A SOCIAL REVOLUTIONIST

The hero of our social sustainability story is César Chávez, born in 1927 in Yuma, Arizona. He was a labor organizer, humanitarian, grass roots activist, and nonviolence disciple. A cultural icon, he is one of the most recognized contemporary folk heroes of the Latino community. Chávez rose from the ranks of displaced migrant farmworkers to become a voice for disenfranchised field laborers from many ethnic backgrounds across North America. The causes to which he devoted his life include ending child labor, assuring fair wages, and worker health protections. He staged strikes and boycotts that made themselves known in the shopping carts and kitchens of average Americans, raising their awareness of the plight of the people who grew the food they ate. The grassroots organizing skills that were key to his success led him on a path to challenge powerful labor organizations including the Teamsters Union. The world around him was changed through his nonviolent tactics, as well as through the engagement of his followers to achieve collective impact. His creative organizing tactics forced powerful corporate growers to recognize the union he co-created, representing a new zeitgeist that empowered 50,000 agricultural workers.

Chávez's experiences growing up left an indelible mark on the man who would become the champion of the underdog. A fearless authenticity to his personal beliefs—and his unwavering commitment to spirituality and nonviolence—led him to become a cult-like figure with many followers. Yet many of those followers became disillusioned with him over time. While there is much to admire, Chávez had blind spots. He often failed to understand the organizational development needs of the Union he started, limiting its growth. He could angrily fail to listen to the opinions and advice of others, at times alienating the diverse following he had amassed.

At the same time, many of his successes at union organizing were also due to the contributions of his primary collaborator, Dolores Huerta. But in a male-dominated industry and even to this day, she fails to receive her fair share of the credit or accolades. Nevertheless, the legacy of this great revolutionist continues to reverberate. Across North America, there are roads, parks, buildings, and murals named after him. He was posthumously awarded the Presidential Medal of Freedom by Bill Clinton in 1994. Yet today many young people have little familiarity with his story or understand why his legacy related to the Social Pillar of Sustainability is important.

The legend of César Chávez positions him as a giant of his day, yet his was not a physically commanding presence; he was short and slight of build. His workaholic tendencies were always on behalf of others, never for his own personal or financial gain. He often set an example through his personal sacrifices. He was able to marshal hundreds of followers, yet he was not a powerful public speaker; he was soft-spoken and somewhat shy. What made Chávez great was his skill as a shrewd strategist, his talent for taking calculated risks, and his relatability. He looked and spoke like one of the Hispanic farm laborers he championed. His ability to listen one-on-one to people's problems made him a figure worthy of trust. Chávez was known for building coalitions through "kitchen table" organizing. He empowered humble workers who learned their voices mattered. These followers were able to realize their own agency by organizing and banding together.

In 1962, Chávez formed the National Farm Workers Association with Dolores Huerta, which later merged with another group to become the United Farmworkers Association (UFW). The UFW would become "the first effective national organization to represent agricultural workers and press for political reform."[130] Collectively, they referred to their efforts as *La Causa*. They fought for the right of farm workers to self-organize, receive fair wages, have access to restrooms, regular rest breaks, and protection from unsafe working conditions and dangerous pesticides. Eager to empower farm workers everywhere, César championed social justice causes for decades.

AN ESCAPE FROM COLONIAL RULE

To begin to understand who César Chávez was, one must start with his family history: a story of love, hardship, loss, and the search for human dignity through honest work. Throughout our history, people of color have been robbed of their land, their possessions, their wealth, and their freedom. Today, as we begin to come to terms with our moral debts and the need for reparations, stories of families like this need to be retold yet again. This is part of the journey that sustainability must take us on.

César grappled with the color line throughout his childhood, causing him to eventually become a champion for human and civil rights. He came to stand for worker equality, freedom, and empowerment. His classic family story is one of borders both real and imagined, of multi-generational colonization and abuse, of violent conquest and expropriation of indigenous lands. The genealogy of the *familia* César Chávez followed the pathways of hope for the future, the search for fertile fields for growing food, and the courses of rivers bringing life-giving farm irrigation. Today when we fly over such landscapes, the rivers and the fields they irrigate paint the landscape with squares and circles in varying shades of green, a mosaic laid out in careful patterns along the boundaries of fields that feed millions of people. We have come to take for granted the contributions of those who allow us to be fed. It is time to remember, to honor, and to value these essential workers who are most often people of color.

César Chávez is the namesake of a man he never knew, his grandfather Césario Chávez, who came from a small village in the Mexican state of Chihuahua. Born into Mexico's feudal hacienda system, he was an indentured servant, laboring from a very early age on a *hacendado* ranch. A *hacendado*, similar to a plantation owner, heads a large land-holding called a *hacienda*. The name derives from the Spanish word *hacer* meaning *to make*. Money-making activities included ranching, farming, and mining. This feudalistic system began with "land grants" based on the theft of indigenous lands, awarded to the conquistadors by the imperialistic

Spanish crown. The crown overthrew the Aztec capital of Tenochtitlan in 1521, and the earliest Mexican land grant occurred in 1529.

Fast-forward through hundreds of years of servitude to 1898, where we find César's grandfather, Papa Chayo, seeking freedom from the harsh hacienda system of indentured service. He fled through El Paso[131] to the United States in that year with his wife, Dorotea, and eight small children in tow, at a time when the border "was more of an idea than an actual border. There was no barbed wire and no immigration department. The [family] settled near this valley because the land was very rich."

After entering into the US, the Chávez family would eventually settle in the far southwest corner of Arizona near Yuma, an area that was once part of the vast Aztec empire. This corner of the state sticks out from the border like a puzzle piece, surrounded by California a few miles to the north, and Mexico to the west and south. Rooted in his life experiences working the lands of the hacienda, Papa Chayo had a deep instinct for the kind of place that would make a good farm. Here, sediments deposited by the Colorado River and its tributaries provide fertile agricultural soils. In today's winter growing season, 90 percent of all the leafy vegetables eaten in the US come from the Yuma area, often referred to as the winter vegetable capital of the world. This is partly due to 350 days of sunshine per year, which the town calls "the longest growing season in the country."

While this area of the Sonora desert has an annual rainfall of only three inches, it is blessed with access to precious irrigation water from the Gila River, a tributary of the Colorado. In the days of César's boyhood, simple irrigation ditches supported the fields. Today 230,000 acres of fields are irrigated with a sophisticated system governed by seven different irrigation districts, all fed from the Colorado River.

Each field is leveled and graded using laser and GPS technology to increase efficiency. This might seem impressive, unless you understand that communities in this general area were practicing agriculture as early as 2100 BCE, with evidence of irrigation canals dating as early as 1250 BCE. In fact, the Aztec empire gained its economic power base from growing hydraulically irrigated crops such as corn, beans, pumpkins, tomatoes, cocoa, tobacco, and cotton. To the north, in the years pre-dating the arrival of Spaniards, the Hohokam peoples had built a canal system with more than eight hundred miles of trunk lines, many lined in leak-proof clay, with a single canal estimated to feed ten thousand acres of irrigated fields.[132]

Agriculture was not "introduced" to lazy and unsophisticated indigenous tribes by Spanish colonists and missionaries, as revisionist history tries to claim. History is often rewritten to support the stories and the wealth of the powerful, while removing legitimacy and empowerment for traditional cultures, indigenous peoples, or non-whites. In today's revolution toward social sustainability, peoples across the globe are seeking to reclaim indigenous agency. They strive to recalibrate centuries of injustice. The Chávez family journey is a part of that ongoing story. In the next chapter, we'll see how the family temporarily finds freedom from centuries of colonial subjugation—only to succumb eventually to power structures beyond their ability to battle.

CHAPTER TWO

Inclusive Empowerment

Once I had asked God for one or two extra inches in height,
but instead he made me as tall as the sky, so high that
I could not measure myself.

— **Malala Yousafzai**, Pakistani activist, Nobel Prize Laureate

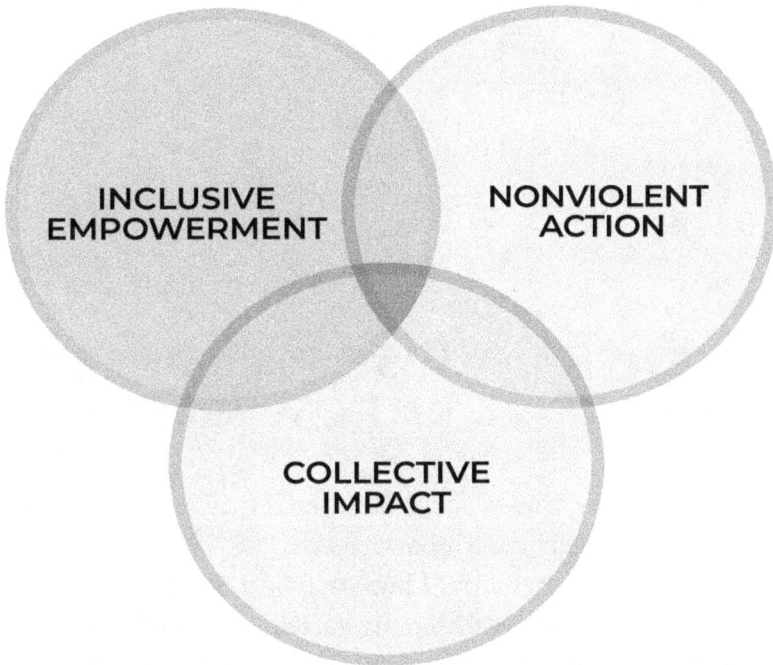

Three Core Values of the Social Pillar,
with an Emphasis on Inclusive Empowerment

SEVENTH COURSE: A COURSE IN INCLUSIVE EMPOWERMENT

Back at my imaginary dinner party, it's time for the seventh course to be served: a course in Inclusive Empowerment.

I have whipped together what I hope will be a delicious potato galette, prepared with shallots, chives from my garden, and cream from the local dairy. I had slipped into the kitchen earlier in the evening to pop it into the oven, so it would be ready at the appropriate time. The delectable scent had been tantalizing us for some time, and now the moment has come to break through the beautiful golden crust on top to sample the velvety hidden layers beneath.

As my guests are digging in, we are accompanied by a playlist of my operatic favorites. One of Puccini's most famous arias begins to play: "*Quando M'en Vo*" (When I Go Along).

Cousteau leans back in his chair, breathing in the delicate soprano voice. "La Boheme! Such a lovely opera. Such a tragic ending."

"I'm glad you know it. The libretto tells the tale of four struggling bohemians—a painter, a poet, a musician and a philosopher. Their story is set in Paris, on a freezing Christmas eve that will change their lives forever. They are so poor they can't afford rent or fuel to keep them warm in the middle of winter. As I recall, at one point the writer burns part of the play he is writing in an attempt to stay warm."

Cousteau is nodding. "I believe they are also drinking Bordeaux, just as we are this evening. Just as we are four souls gathering together on a magical night that may well go down in history. My favorite line, by the poet character Rodolfo, translates as 'I'm a millionaire in spirit.'"

"That's a beautiful thought," says Anita. "I feel rich tonight with the possibilities of this conversation. And it's lovely to think about music as a universal language. It can speak to anyone, even if they can't understand the words. I typically don't understand the language, but opera always makes me cry."

César finds it easy to plug in to this conversation. "Music has always been one of my community organizing tools. It speaks to our heart. A good song can lift the spirits of even the weariest traveler, no matter where they come from or what language they speak. It is the language of the spirit."

I'm excited at how these musical notes have sparked conversation. "I've always enjoyed hearing music from other places and cultures. It's like being able to travel without actually getting out of your chair. And travel is so eye-opening. I think it was Mark Twain who said in *Idiots Abroad* that more people need to travel in order to benefit from the way it proves fatal to prejudice and narrow-mindedness."

Cousteau finds it easy to pick up this thread. "To be able to travel for pleasure is a gift, and I have been lucky enough to travel more than most. In return for the privilege, I felt it was my responsibility to share it with others. Television enabled me to empower everyday people with new information, and to delight them with wonder. Without the need for them to leave their home, everyone could become travelers on the same voyage."

A GRAPES OF WRATH FAMILY STORY

At the time the Chávez family arrived in the US, Arizona was seven years away from having its territorial status converted to statehood. Much of the state's land had been acquired from Mexico by the US in 1854 as part of the Gadsden Purchase. At the time, land policies were being driven by the political views of Northerners, part of an ongoing conversation about what equality and freedom from oppression should look like. These views opposed slave ownership and large plantations, which Northerners saw as a way to shut out small-hold farmers. This was an ideological holdover from the ideals of Jeffersonian democracy. The Jeffersonians valued the "yeoman farmer" and "plain folk" over the interests of an artificial aristocratic elite class, people thought to be subject to corruption and an unfair concentration of power. Shared power is a fundamental tenet of sustainability. When power is shared, many voices are elevated into inclusive forms of dialogue, such that no voice is left out.

The concept of homesteading was conceived as a public policy based on sustainability inclusiveness, theoretically giving everyone a chance to be a landowner. A series of variations on the original Homestead Act of 1862 was enacted through the 1930s, creating the Federal Homestead Program. In order to be a homesteader, an individual had to be the head of the household, at least 21, live on the designated land, build a home, make improvements to and farm the land for at least five years, and pay a fee of $18. Immigrants who had filed for citizenship, single women, and former slaves were all eligible, a powerful public statement about equality.

These homestead dreamers, who dreamt of a better life, share much in common with the social sustainability dreamers of today. They strive for quality of life for everyone, regardless of their background, the color of their skin, or their income. They dream of dignity and equity as the backbone of finding more sustainable ways of inhabiting our planet. Indigenous land acknowledgements, land reparations to redress theft, and the idea of wealth redistribution to address decades of inequity are beginning to take hold in public discourse and practice. Even though we are far from resolving those issues, we are beginning to make progress. As prominent democratic intellectual Cornell West puts it, "Justice is what love looks like in public."

Just as 1905 was coming to a close, Papa Chayo filed a homestead claim for a 120-acre plot in the North Gila River Valley. His choice of the location was well-informed by the fact that the property was intersected by the main North Gila irrigation canal, a 6-foot-wide ditch that delivered precious water to the property. He quickly got to work building a home and a life of freedom for his family. He chose to set their house on a small hill, facing west, with a wide breezeway to capture cool winds. He made the earthen adobe walls extra thick to withstand the scorching summers. The irrigation ditch delivered water to the fields with gravity controlled by opening small wooden gates, allowing the family to cultivate 80 acres in cotton, alfalfa, and watermelon. The plough horses were penned in a wooden corral. An outhouse, a small family vegetable and herb garden, and eventually a milk cow and some chickens completed the basic needs of the family.[133] Such self-sufficiency, and the ability to live within the means of available local resources, are important tenets of sustainability.

Over the next three decades, Papa Chayo and Dorotea's eight children grew up. Some acquired land of their own nearby. Some moved away. Eventually, Dorotea, or Mama Tella as she was called, inherited the farm after the death of Papa Chayo. She lived in the main farmhouse with her last unmarried daughter to care for her. Her son Librado also stayed behind to help manage the homestead. Librado was still unmarried at 37 when he asked Juana Estrada, a petite raven-haired woman and a family friend, to join the rest of her life with his. A bride at 32 years old, very late in life for the time, she was to become a powerful matriarch in the family following the tradition of Mama Tella.[134] César was the second of their five children, born into the safety of a large extended family including aunts, uncles, and cousins. The adults had all been born in Mexico; the children had all been born on US soil.

The men formed the patriarchal structure of familia, but the women were the spiritual and cultural guideposts. While Papa Chayo was illiterate, Mama Tella had learned to write in both Spanish and Latin while she was living in a Mexican convent as an orphan. As the family elder, she demanded obedience and schooled her many grandchildren from her bed until well into her nineties with stories of the saints, preparing them for confirmation in the Catholic church. The rituals, traditions, and obligations of the church were paramount.

Juana, the children's mother, was considered by some to be a curandera, or traditional healer, known within the local community for her knowledge of using medicinal herbs.[135] The herb garden she kept included many plant remedies for everything from toothaches and dandruff to kidney stones and snake bites. Her knowledge of plant use followed a rich tradition passed down from generation to generation since the days of the Aztecs, who had recorded their knowledge of herbal medicine in codices. Most of these were considered heretical and were burned by the Spanish missionaries. One of the few remaining, the *De La Cruz-Badiano Codex,* was written in both Latin and Náhuatl (Aztec language).[136]

Juana was a strict disciplinarian. She forbade any form of physical violence and instructed her children not to fight back against schoolyard bullies, despite the predominant culture of machismo. She would tell her children, "God gave you senses, like your eyes and mind and tongue, so that you can get out of anything."[137] In addition to her belief in nonviolence, Juana also believed in helping those in need. She regularly required her children to go out in search of the hungry to bring them home for a meal. At the time homeless people were often white and referred to as hobos or *trampitas*.

Even though they had no electricity or running water and wouldn't have been considered well off, their family life was relatively secure, comfortable, and independent. The Chávez family was able to feed themselves from their subsistence farm, even as the Great Depression was taking hold. There were always ample beans, rice, and homemade tortillas. Their diet was supplemented with fresh vegetables, eggs, milk, and occasionally chicken meat. César attended mass and school with his siblings and cousins, and tended to farm chores caring for the chickens or horses, and picking watermelons.

There was also time for play, riding through the fields, swimming in the irrigation ditches, and enjoying celebrations and feast days such as Todos los Santos, Noche Buena, and the feast of Nuestra Senõra de Guadalupe. One of César's favorite activities was roasting fresh ears of corn around a bonfire while listening to stories of Mexican heritage. "We heard tales of the Mexican revolution, the battles fought by farmworkers," he said, "how they won and lost. We learned that when you felt something was wrong, you stood up to it."[138]

Dispossession and Disempowerment

Unfortunately, the idyllic days of César's childhood were not to last. His family would suffer the same injustices that sustainability battles today when it fights inequitable divisions of resources, as well as an ongoing burden that the disempowered must bear, all to shore up the wealth of the few. Dreaming of a better life for his children, Papa Chayo and his father tried to start up several businesses, taking out mortgages to invest in nearby properties including a gas station and general store with post office. These ventures ultimately failed, perhaps due to the family's generosity. During the Depression, they loaned money to friends and relatives who were unable to repay the debts. Eventually, the family owed seven years of unpaid back taxes on the farm, and time was running out.

Neighboring property owner Archibald D. Griffin was a bank president and a powerful local grower. He wanted the Chávez property for himself. In 1939, the land was sold to Griffin as the highest bidder for $1,750. The Chávez clan simply couldn't scrape up enough cash to outbid him.

As events similar to these repeat themselves today, families and businesses subject to hardships might find some forms of institutional relief from the pandemic, economic downturns, gentrification, and predatory lending practices. Social sustainability values grounded in equity and fairness have driven the creation of a myriad of social programs with varying levels of success, at both the federal and local level. These include debt relief programs, small business grants, nutrition support, free healthcare, and affordable housing. All are designed to help address wealth and other gaps that have been cemented into place through centuries of discriminatory practices.

César was twelve when his family lost the farm, and things would never be the same for him or his relations. Let's imagine the family's forced departure from their land and the events that set César on his path to become a champion of social sustainability, based on César's own accounts of what happened. Some of the details are augmented through literary imagination.

The crunch of metal against the wood rails of the corral was the most horrible sound that young César had ever heard, worse even than the noises of a chicken being slaughtered for Sunday dinner. The big shiny red tractor was mercilessly tearing down everything they had worked so hard for. When Mama came out of the house, her broad face, usually alight with some piece of wisdom or a remedy to share, was awash with tears. César had never seen her look so heartbroken, except perhaps the day his abuela had died. The beautiful, cloudless afternoon didn't seem to match the horror of the scene. Water flowed by in the irrigation ditch peacefully, just as always. His favorite climbing tree stood as tall as ever. How could these sentinels of his childhood appear so unmoved?

He had begged his grandfather to let him help build the fine corral out of the timbers they had hewn by hand. Papa Chayo had been patient, showing him how to swing the ax just so, to chop away sections of the tree trunks until a plank emerged. His shoulders had ached, but he had been proud to be allowed to help build an enclosure for the horses he treasured. The sweet red mare Rosado was his favorite. His father preferred the muscular stallion, the horse that he allowed César to name Canción. Galloping bareback with his sister Rita, they would ride the two horses out to discover new spots to build secret forts. Hand-feeding the majestic animals carrots from their garden always brought joy to his heart. But the horses had already been auctioned off along with their farm tools and plow. The $40 this sale yielded was all the money they had now.

César was trembling with fear. What would happen to them now? This family piece of land was the only home he had ever known. Far off in the distance, the rounded peaks of the Fortuna Foothills gave no sign of what the future might hold. The Anglo sheriff had visited several times over the past few days, his tone growing increasingly harsh. But César had seen this before, and he had been sure that his Papa would fend off the threats just as he always did.

His mother had always told him, "Con virtud y bondad se adquiere autoridad." (With virtue and goodness, authority is acquired.) It was hard to see how this could be true now. His family were good Catholics, always ready to help others in need. But now they were being punished for no good reason César could surmise. He held his sister Rita's hand tightly, not wanting to lose his grip on the family he would never allow anyone to force him to give up.

The house was spared from the demolition for now, but over the years its adobe walls would disintegrate into the earth from which they had come. Eventually there would be no sign that the Chávez family had married their lives to this place and loved it as one of their own.

The bulldozing of the family farm would be seared into César's memory for the rest of his life. "Just a monstrous thing, knocking down trees. We left everything behind. Things belonging to my father's family and my mother's as well. Everything." In future years, he would say, "Maybe that is when the rebellion started."[139]

His family packed up all the belongings they could fit into their massive 1930 Studebaker President sedan, which his father bought second-hand a few years earlier. They were only allowed to bring a few clothes and bedding. Mama had secured two mattresses to the roof and strapped on a few big washtubs and cooking pots. Papa brought along his smaller tools and some mysterious valuables wrapped in rags, items that rode in the big metal box over the back bumper, fat leather straps holding it in place. The children were not allowed to touch anything in there. Papa had declared they would go to California to find work. For years, he talked about buying back the land. As an adult, César would talk about it too, but this would never come to pass.

There could not have been a worse time for the Chávez family to join the stream of people desperately looking for work in California as part of the great Dust Bowl exodus. Between 1934-1940, the Great Depression's farm foreclosures combined with the worst sustained man-made environmental disaster in US history. A failure to pay attention to drought conditions and poor agricultural practices stirred the Dust Bowl. The mistakes caused mass migration of tens of thousands of desperate farmers in Oklahoma, Texas, Northeastern New Mexico, Colorado and Kansas. The Dust Bowl was littered with inky black maelstroms of dirt a mile high and 2 miles wide, creating blackouts, killing livestock, and choking the air.[140]

In the ten years following the Chávez's family's dispossession, their family history would trace a course to the Salinas Valley of California, following farm work and the life-giving irrigation waters of rivers and their fertile deposits of soil for growing food. Over the years, César would learn there were a lot of people that couldn't be trusted and who might try to cheat you or steal from you. He would realize that he had taken home for granted, and that sometimes the only shelter available was a soggy tent in Oxnard, a barn in Beaumont, or an abandoned dirty tarpaper cabin in the San Joaquin valley. He would learn that the color of his family's skin was reason enough for them to be pulled over by police officers and harassed for hours.[141] He would see their skin color would also preclude his family's access to wealth, power, privilege, and sense of agency.

From this point on, the Chávez family, including the older children, worked as migrant farm laborers. They often toiled for corrupt employers, earning meager wages that didn't provide enough for the family's basic needs. They drifted from farm to farm, between various labor camps,

always following the crops. Sometimes it was cotton, sometimes tomatoes, grapes, plums, lima beans, chiles, melons, or cherries. The work
was merciless and, in the ultimate irony for people who toiled producing
edible crops, the family was often hungry. In a truly sustainable world,
this would never happen.

MISERY IN THE FIELDS

L et's imagine what might have been a typical day in the fields for the Chávez family, using details from historical sources about immigrant working conditions in those fields.

The rich valley farmlands of the Salinas River create a mosaic of wealth, patches of green stretching away into the disappearing point of countless artists who have attempted to recreate its beauty on canvas. Spring is cantaloupe planting season in the valley. Bruce Church and the D'Arrigo Brothers were some of the biggest growers. Their growing and packing operations were flung across Southern California and Arizona, but the main offices were in Salinas.

On a typical day in April of 1942, the Chávez family had arrived before dawn to get in line to join the field crews. They had learned the hard way that if you arrived too late, the work was all already assigned out. They had been awake since 3 a.m. Work was paid at a piece rate per box or basket harvest. If you complained about what they were paying, there was always someone hungrier or more desperate standing behind you in line who would take it. The field bosses were middlemen, working for absentee corporate overseers. They often skimmed off the top or cheated the workers, and the wages they offered varied from day to day depending on what they thought they could get away with. On this day the work was thinning cantaloupe seedlings, paid by the hour, for as many daylight hours as the workers could withstand.

It was finally light enough to see the soft lusciousness of the hills beyond the field. Everything appeared covered in the green fuzz of spring, the air thick with moisture and the season's distinctive perfume. The Chávez family was bending low, thinning crop rows that seemed to go on for miles. Their crew consisted of both parents; Rita, 17; Cesar, 15; and Richard, 14. The youngest members of the family, aged 6 and 8, had to wait in the car all day.[142]

Each worker was forced to use a thinning tool which became infamous for the abuse it leveled. The short-handled hoe was called *el cortito* or "the short one." At twenty-four inches long, it forced workers to stoop low, doubled over, hour after hour. Growers preferred it because they could easily spot the workers who stood up to take a break, making it easy to reprimand them. After successive hours and days of using the short-handled hoe, a worker's ability to stand upright could be permanently marred, and they might end up with a permanent limp. For the rest of his life, César would struggle with debilitating back pain that doctors would blame on his use of *el cortito*. The tool, also referred to as *el brazo del diablo* (the devil's arm), became a symbol of farmworker oppression and abuse. César would later say, "It's just like being nailed to a cross. You have to walk twisted, perpendicular to the ground."[143]

Each day seemed no different from the next. After a typical toilsome ten hours, they would count up their earnings. The hourly wage for children was 8 cents, 12 cents for the adults,[144] the equivalent of about $1.30 and $1.95 per hour today. (For comparison, the average hourly wage for a manufacturing worker at the time was 85 cents, or about $13.80 per hour in today's dollars.[145]) Between the five of them, they had earned $4.32 on that April day. But almost half of their day's earnings would be deducted for what they owed the company store in groceries, and for rent at the labor camp. Bone-weary, the family piled into their car where the little ones had long since cried themselves to sleep.

Half an hour later, they arrived back at the migrant camp to regroup. Their shelter was a grubby 10-by-12 windowless tarpaper cabin that leaked when it rained. Juana had always kept a spotless home, but here there wasn't a remote possibility that this place could ever feel clean, no matter how much she scrubbed. The only furnishing other than the two mattresses they carried with them was a little wood stove in the corner that could be used for cooking. When in use, the air inside the cabin would make your eyes burn and your lungs ache. The two youngest children were sent to refill their drinking water jugs, a couple of old vinegar bottles wrapped in burlap as insulation.[146] There was one water spigot on the far side of the camp that had to serve everyone's needs for drinking, cooking, and washing. A separate area behind some flapping pieces of dirty canvas had a spigot for cold showers.

The life of anonymity in a crowd of thousands of migrant workers was unfamiliar to young César. Watching his parents struggle in these harsh conditions would influence him for the rest of his life. His early childhood days growing food to feed their family, on their own land, had been hard work, but it was an honorable life. He missed the ranch bitterly. "Some had been born into the migrant stream. But we had been on the land, and I knew a different way of life. We were poor, but we had liberty. The migrant is poor, and has no freedom."[147]

On the days they were able to get away from the fields, César and his siblings would attend school. Constantly on the move, they were never able to stick with one school for very long. As soon as the crops were harvested, the migrants' presence immediately became unwelcome. One young migrant boy said, "When they need us, they call us migrants, and when we've picked their crop, we're bums, and we got to get out."[148]

Eventually, César would attend thirty-six different schools across California. He spoke Spanish with his family, but English was the only language that was allowed in school. Both girls and boys were paddled with a piece of wooden two-by-four for speaking Spanish, sometimes referred to as "dog language." Once a teacher hung a sign around César's neck that said "I am a clown. I speak Spanish." The pain and humiliation stayed with César. "Words can be painful as a switch, and many times those who say them are unaware of how painful their words can be."[149]

César and Rita would never graduate high school. After their father was injured in a serious car accident, César dropped out right after eighth grade so he could take on more work to help support the family. Ashamed that she had to attend school without shoes, his sister Rita refused to return to the classroom. Over the years, the Chávez family experienced many forms of discrimination and loss of dignity, including being refused service in diners where they were belittled by waitresses for being "dumb Mexicans."

The Chávez family lacked basic civil rights protections which might have shielded them from repeated discrimination based upon their racial, cultural, or socio-economic status. In addition, they were deprived the dignity of basic human rights including access to adequate food, clothing, housing, wages, and medical care.

Eventually, César Chávez would come to tell the story of how he defiantly sat in the Whites Only section of a movie theater, for which he was arrested. For years to come, confrontations with the police would become familiar territory for him. César would be arrested repeatedly on charges of strike-breaking and disturbing the peace. Through these many experiences, his sense of dignity and defiance would take him on an increasingly public and unapologetic crusade.

SOCIAL SUSTAINABILITY CORE VALUE 1:

INCLUSIVE EMPOWERMENT
Dignity and self-determination for all

If they don't give you a seat at the table, bring a folding chair
— **Shirley Chisholm**, First African American
woman to serve in the US Congress

Sustainability calls us to identify and repair systems based on prejudice. We are finally taking steps as a society to acknowledge centuries of abuse and exclusion of people of color, paired with centuries of privilege and entitlement for whites. For white people such as myself, at times the journey can feel fraught, requiring us to strap on our courage. Looking backwards through history, we can see that the freeing of slaves, followed by the Civil Rights movement, were pivotal moments in our journey toward racial equality. Yet we find ourselves in a current era that points out how far we have yet to go in order to fully realize social justice. In the dynamic human metamorphosis toward inclusive empowerment, we are learning as we go. This first Core Value of Social Sustainability brings together two powerful ideas: inclusion combined with empowerment. Let's examine the concept of inclusion first.

Inclusion

The practice of inclusiveness is firmly grounded in the rainbow of social diversity. The unique differences among individuals comprise a wide array of elements including ethnicity, race, religion, age, gender and gender identity, socio-economic status, immigrant status, physical or mental characteristics and abilities. Our impulse to put differences into such categories is a normal human tendency. But taken too far, the need to categorize can provide grounds for discrimination and exclusion.

Inclusion requires us to include or accommodate those who have historically been left out and left behind. So why is increasing diversity and eliminating bias such a powerful set of sustainability practices? First and foremost, eliminating racial prejudice and discrimination must occur to achieve justice. Hundreds of years of history spent marginalizing and exploiting people of color requires us to undo these wrongs. It is simply the right thing to do. In addition to achieving racial and social justice, embracing diversity also brings with it a multitude of benefits—not unlike the way ecological diversity increases the resilience and stability of ecosystems. Embracing diversity tends to make us more open-minded, less rigid, and more elastic to change.

Diversity can bring many challenges, particularly if the differences are only among a limited number of groups. Negative bias among groups, which can occur either consciously or unconsciously, tends to pit people against one another. This can create relatively small, exclusive camps. A narrow view of inclusion can also breed tokenism. It requires far more than checking a diversity box represented by simple numerical tallies.

The term super-diversity was coined by social anthropologist Steven Vertovec in 2007, based on research in an area of Britain where high diversity levels were present. The super-diverse area began to accrue many benefits. As immigration shifted the overall British population, super-diversity increased socializing, communication, and collaboration "beyond and across ethnic and cultural barriers."[150] This was the exact opposite of typical patterns where only one or two ethnic or national identities predominated.

Diversity has increased well-being and expanded influence at the Danish super-diverse facility services company ISS. Workplace research from Science Nordic showed that a high density of differences in ISS workplace teams nurtured high levels of social cohesion. Cohesion improved levels of workplace well-being. In many cases, the presence of super-diversity allowed more group members to influence team dynamics and group behavior.[151] Super-diversity can contribute to lower staff turnover, higher employee morale, increased creativity and innovation, and better organizational flexibility.[152] Where inclusion thrives, sustainability blossoms.

The differences between diversity and inclusion need to be articulated. In simple terms, diversity means being allowed to attend a dance. But just being present doesn't automatically mean an individual won't be excluded, or that they will be treated the same as everyone else. Inclusion means also being asked to dance.

One of the most familiar examples of removing inequality is the Americans with Disabilities Act, which requires wheelchair accessible ramps to public buildings and parks. Advocates for the rights of the differently-abled pushed for national legislation to protect the rights of those with physical, mental, cognitive, and developmental abilities. However, the legislation's success is limited. It addresses diversity, but not full inclusion. This is because the resulting wheelchair-accessible ramps are often separated from mainstream routes of access. A person in a wheelchair receives equal but separate treatment, falling short of full inclusion.

If we look at efforts to achieve diversity within a corporate workforce, simply hiring to meet racial or other quotas, this alone won't achieve inclusion. If people are hired into a company with a toxic culture related to race and social justice, nothing will change. Change must go deeper in order to achieve transformation and healing.

Embedded, institutional practices can serve to exclude people, often without our being fully aware that this is happening. Achieving equity entails addressing and dismantling institutional practices that reinforce racism and inequity. The national research and action nonprofit PolicyLink defines equity as "just and fair inclusion into a society in which all can participate, prosper, and reach their full potential. Unlocking the promise of the nation by unleashing the promise of us all."[153] The achievement of true equity leads to empowerment, our next topic.

Empowerment

Empowerment is a basic tenet of human dignity defined in Duhaime's Law Dictionary as "an individual or group's sense of self-respect and self-worth, physical and psychological integrity and empowerment." Inequality often appears in our society as differing levels of access to resources. Individuals without access to resources such as social services, housing, adequate food, medical care, and different forms of capital including economic, social, and human capital, are unable to participate as full members of society.

Fair treatment and access to resources are defined by the United Nations as fundamental human rights. They define human rights as "inherent to all human beings, regardless of race, sex, nationality, ethnicity, language, religion, or any other status." Human rights—many of which continue to be violated around the world—include freedom from slavery, torture, and exile; the right to equal protection under the law; the right to equal pay and reasonable working and living conditions; and the right to education and an adequate standard of living.

In Germany, inclusive soccer programs are targeted at welcoming the vast inflow of migrants into the country. Soccer aided the 2017 social integration of the 890,000 new arrivals expecting to become permanent residents. The Heimstärke (Home Power) program in the Rhine-Neckar region supports young male refugees. These men are trained to play in mixed soccer clubs; the inclusion aims to increase contact with local residents, improve participants' health, and increase German language skills.

In one snapshot, one-third of the participants were born in Afghanistan, with the rest coming from Gambia, Syria, and Iran. "The aim is to provide young people with a social skill set," said an article in the *Journal for Labour Market Research*, "by addressing social topics such as fairness and mutual respect, health and peacebuilding, communication and leadership as well as gender equality and teamwork."[154] The program seeks to improve chances for participants' success in the local labor market, thus empowering them economically. Positive preliminary results are positive, pointing toward sustainability's promise of successful, well-adjusted communities adapting to change.

The Home Power program's economic success is an example of how inclusion can lead to empowerment. A truly inclusive society brings with it a sense of empowerment to all its diverse members. Empowerment can be thought of as the power, right, or authority to do something. It implies a sense of liberty or freedom to act. Empowered individuals and communities have control over their own destinies as well as the license to do something about it. Empowered people don't have to wait for someone else to take action on issues they define as important. Such issues run the gamut of the human experience, from where to live, what school to attend, how to vote, who to work for or marry, whether to have children, and what church to attend.

Empowerment is fundamentally a social process because it occurs in relationship to others; it cannot exist in isolation. Power is defined by relationships, influence, and control. In hierarchical dominant power structures, power is about the ability to force others to do what we want, whether they wish to or not.[155] Dictatorship and white supremacy are extreme examples. Toxic power structures tend to produce intergenerational legacies which we have only just begun to dismantle.

Ensuring the empowerment of the LGBQTI community is a journey still underway. Damian Barr, the out Scottish author and journalist, once noted, "We are not all in the same boat. We are all in the same storm. Some are on super-yachts. Some have just the one oar."

No city is better known than San Francisco for its journey to create a level playing field on behalf of the gay community. Harvey Milk was a gay American revolutionist who worked to make local government more responsive to the rights of individuals, and to empower people of diverse sexual orientation and gender identify. The brash, outspoken Milk was elected city supervisor, determined to tackle lack of legal protections for those experiencing homophobic discrimination. Gay San Francisco residents were regularly being denied access to fair housing. During a brief eleven months in office, he sponsored and successfully passed a bill banning public employment and housing discrimination based on sexual orientation.

Sadly, Milk was assassinated soon thereafter. However, his legacy continues and his vision lives on. His power as an orator telegraphed his vision of a righteous world. He called it "hope for a better world, hope for a better tomorrow, hope that all will be all right—because if a gay person makes it, the doors are open to everyone." These doors can continue to open only if the privileged few are brave enough to remove their blinders of entitlement and power. Only then can we begin to realize the promise of inclusive empowerment.

We're making progress toward elevating those who have been historically excluded. At the same time, we realize that even a well-intentioned inclusive act assumes that someone has the authority or right to invite others in. But who gave them the power or authority?[156]

Toxic norms help to maintain the status quo power structure in many organizations, systems, and cultures. The training collaborative known as Dismantling Racism Works provides an excellent primer for undoing institutional racism in their publication "White Supremacy Culture in Organizations." The authors note white supremacy culture as "the idea that white people and the ideas, thoughts, beliefs, and actions of white people are superior to People of Colour and their ideas, thoughts beliefs and actions."[157] Some of the white cultural norms they address include power hoarding, a cult of perfectionism, worship of the written word, and paternalism.

Once we realize that power over others is not inherent within any individual or group, we also realize that power and power relationships can be changed. New models of shared power go beyond a win/lose, zero sum gain state. Relationships based on respect, collaboration, mutuality, and sharing are taking hold across and among many groups. Such transformational acts, tempered by love and compassion, begin to realize the full potential of our human race.

MODERN-DAY REVOLUTIONISTS: EMPOWERING THE NEEDY

The next section takes up the story of an immigrant who has become a powerful leader in his own right. In work that also focuses on food systems, Chef José Andrés' life work revolves around empowering those in crisis situations. He is one of today's heroes working toward supporting basic human dignity, by addressing hunger in communities grappling with climate-related disasters.

Chef Andrés is a passionate man. He is passionate about food, passionate about people, passionate about giving back, and passionate about what it means to be an immigrant. Andrés exudes an earthy warmth and humility, even though he'd be well within his rights to put on airs. He is a celebrity in the food world, an award-winning culinary genius with dozens of restaurants, some Michelin-starred. Born in Spain, he came to the United States at the age of 21 and still speaks with a delightful thick accent. Chef made waves when he decided to pull his restaurant out of the Trump International Hotel in Washington DC after the US President by the same name made disparaging comments about immigrants. The dispute was later settled after a lawsuit was filed. Never hesitant to let his views be known, Chef also set up a kitchen in DC to give free meals to federal workers during the 2019 government shutdown and worker furlough. Chef Andrés gesticulates forcefully when he speaks to emphasize his points.

"I am a proud immigrant. I do believe we are all immigrants, and we are all from somewhere else. Anytime you move away from your comfort zone, you become an immigrant.[158]

Chef Andrés can often be seen wearing a t-shirt that says "We are all Dreamers." He was nominated for a Nobel prize for humanitarian aid through his nonprofit World Central Kitchen. He founded the organization after the 2010 earthquake in Haiti, "with the belief that food can be an agent of change."[159] And change is the lifeblood of sustainability as we have realized the way we inhabit the planet today is inherently unsustainable. As we have seen in story after story, sustainability is fundamentally a revolutionary change movement.

Chefs such as Andrés have a unique skill set far beyond creating delicious food. According to London's Chef Academy, they are masters at organization, leadership, stamina, flexibility, multi-tasking, frugality, and finding creative ways to use what they have. These skills are all transferable to responding to disasters. Since Haiti, World Central Kitchen has performed massive food relief efforts in Afghanistan, Brazil, Cambodia, Cuba, Dominican Republic, Haiti, Mozambique, Nicaragua, Zambia, and the United States. The success of their efforts stems from their ability to mobilize a massive chef network, supporting the ability to empower local people to be part of the solution. The organization's focus is expansive and has evolved far beyond providing feeding hungry people as an isolated solution. Their programs include health, education, jobs, and social enterprise, all tied back to using "the power of food to empower communities and strengthen economies."[160]

Natural disasters and extreme weather events disproportionately impact low-income communities and other vulnerable groups who don't have the resources to bounce back. Low-income communities are more exposed to environmental hazards such as extreme heat and flooding, and already have higher rates of poor health conditions. According to the Fourth National Climate Assessment, climate-related disruptions will be most extreme for people with economic inequality living in areas with aging or deteriorating infrastructure. Climate change will exacerbate these existing inequalities. Such conditions have led to a massive focus on shoring up the resilience of communities, or their ability to bounce back better and stronger after experiencing shocks or disruptions such as natural disasters. Resilience to disruption has become a recurring theme in sustainability change management efforts.

On a lush island in the Caribbean where coffee and bananas usually grow with abandon, climate change has barreled down to decimate a way of life. In September 2017, a Category 5 Hurricane hit with such power that virtually every tree across an entire 3,400-square-mile island was toppled or denuded. Hurricane Irma battered this island in the Caribbean that many people still don't realize is part of the United States: Puerto Rico. The tornado force winds, followed by a second deadly hurricane named Maria, wiped out bridges and homes, flooded neighborhoods, and devastated the island's entire power grid. Darkness fell on over three million Americans. The eventual death toll reached almost 3,000 people whose lives were lost either as the direct result of the hurricane, or from the indirect results in the aftermath.

The following vignette is based on Andrés' 2018 book *We Fed an Island: The True Story of Rebuilding Puerto Rico, One Meal at a Time,* as well as various photographs, and written records. Some of the details are imagined to help the story come alive.

José Andrés sprang into action within days after the first disaster hit, hopping a flight to arrive at the near-deserted San Juan airport. He headed immediately to the Homeland Security makeshift headquarters at the Convention Center. After sitting in on a few FEMA meetings, he quickly realizes that the government officials are hobbled by a well-meaning but entirely ineffective bureaucracy. Five days into the disaster, they seem more focused on contractual procedures and next week's scheduling challenges, rather than on immediate aid for people going hungry and thirsty today.

Andrés is not a patient man when it comes to reaching those in need. He wants action versus action plans. Like-minded local chef José Enriques is the perfect co-collaborator for revolutionizing the hurricane relief approach. Long after the nighttime curfew had ended, the two Josés plotted by candlelight. Within hours of the next day's dawn, they started cooking up massive pots of food in the kitchen of Enriques' namesake restaurant, located in San Juan's Santurce neighborhood. The volunteers in the dining room quickly became a sandwich-making army. And thus,

Chefs for Puerto Rico was born, serving 500 sandwiches and 2,000 hot meals to hungry Puerto Ricans on its first day of operation.

Let's imagine the first day of the chef's relief efforts.

The hot pink façade of restaurant Enrique positively glows in the afternoon light. The masonry walls wrap around the building's front patio like a warm abuela's embrace. Standing at attention within, the two perspiring chefs stand grinning over gigantic stock pots full of *sancocho*, a fragrantly rich beef stew that is the national dish of Puerto Rico. Chef Andrés is wearing a t-shirt and the khaki multi-pocketed fly-fishing vest that has become his signature look. His apparent joy as he ladles out dishes of stew masks his exhaustion from having been up most of the night.

The Santurce neighborhood, sometimes referred to as the Brooklyn of San Juan, had been uncharacteristically quiet in the days since the two recent hurricanes, the streets deserted and eerily quiet. Normally, this lively community is awash with activity in the mercado by day, or at the hard-partying bars at night. The sound of salsa music is always drifting through the air. Merengue or bomba dancing often erupts spontaneously in the streets. The narrow thoroughfares are a favorite spot for tourist selfies, providing a colorful photo backdrop: robin's egg-blue shutters, canary yellow facades, and fuchsia-painted brick street pavers.

Since the storms knocked out electricity, at night the streets are black. The curfew contributes to the feeling of a city that is dying. Chef still has a charge on his cell phone. He tweets out *#SanJuan community in need come to Jose Enrique restaurant 4 pm for sancocho! Spread the word! #ChefsforPuertoRico*. Word spread quickly. Enriques' restaurant is so popular that he normally doesn't advertise or even post a sign announcing his restaurant. But today, he has taped up a handwritten sign announcing *Hay Sancocho*. Locals gather together like clusters of flotsam in a flood. They huddle around the stew pots, eager for bowls of the spicy comforting concoction. As they eat, they share stories of unexpected tragedies, miraculous rescues, relentless nightmares, and their effervescent prayers for the future.

In a disaster, people revert to their most primal and basic needs as they struggle to survive. Chef Andres believes that in addition to the basic needs of shelter and water, food that is cooked by the community helps bring scattered people back together. In the aftermath of Hurricane Maria, FEMA's immediate food strategy was to supply military MREs (Meal Ready-to-Eat), which are calorie packets designed to sustain soldiers on the battlefield. MREs contain enough preservatives for them to last three years without refrigeration and to survive parachute drops.

While they are effective at staving off starvation, they are far from a satisfying experience. Chef Andres does not see them as any kind of solution. "An MRE is a matter of survival. A freshly cooked plate of local food is a meal you're sharing with your family and community. A hot meal is more than just food; it's a plate of hope. When you serve a plate of food, you gather intelligence about who needs feeding. When you dump a pile of MREs, you learn nothing about the true nature of the crisis."

Andrés hopes to bring the island "slowly back to life, one ladle at a time" with familiar foods that provide nutrition and comfort. Recipes for traditional *sancocho* can be found in the cuisines of Honduras, Ecuador, Colombia, Cuba, Panama, the Dominican Republic, and Venezuela.[161] The one-pot meal shows its indigenous roots with ingredients such as yucca (cassava) or calabaza (squash), favored by the original native Taíno inhabitants or African slaves imported by the Spanish colonists. (The Taino language gave us the word "hurricane.") European invaders, by way of the Canary Islands, introduced the idea of stews prepared in large clay cooking pots. Chef José Enrique wears his deep feelings on his sleeve about the dish. "When you eat sancocho, you think of your grandmother, and it puts a smile on your face." Sustainability can feed our physical as well as our spiritual needs.

Chefs for Puerto Rico assembled a team of local chefs, able to gather intelligence on-the-ground, determining where the most need existed. This empowers local people to solve their own needs, grounded in the skills of local chefs and the cuisine of the local culture. It is an antidote to the white savior mentality that often takes hold in crisis situations. This approach may leverage outside help such as that provided by Chef

Andrés, but it also requires teaming with locals and relying on their own expertise and knowledge of the situation on-the-ground.

A diverse team approach is often needed to tackle sustainability challenges. Complex, enormous problems will require us to enroll many others to roll up our sleeves together. Based on real-time information, this team sent meals to people waiting in line for ten hours at gas stations. They divvied up assignments to secure food supplies, delivery vehicles, fuel, and more volunteers. They expanded their operations, initially enlisting food trucks to deliver meals to hospital workers and the elderly. They worked with food suppliers such as Goya, founded by Spanish immigrants in Puerto Rico, to provide large quantities of rice and yucca as meal ingredients, spreading their operations out across the entire island. In time, 20 volunteers became 20,000; one tiny kitchen grew into 25, and 2,000 meals a day grew to serve 170,000 in a single day. In an interesting turn of events, they became the meal suppliers for the Salvation Army.[162]

Puerto Rico was subjected to the longest blackout in US history. In the end, Chefs for Puerto Rico served more than 3.5 million meals to Puerto Ricans who were not only hungry, but also suffering from the lonely feeling that they had been forgotten by their own countrymen.

But even as the lights were beginning to come back on and Puerto Ricans were starting to bounce back, many suffered from feelings of helplessness compounded by Post Traumatic Stress Disorder. In the months following the disaster, psychologist and Associate Professor Domingo Marqués of the Albizu University of San Juan estimated that 30 to 50 percent of the population was experiencing PTSD, depression, or anxiety. "The storm takes away the foundations of society. Everything you thought gave you certainty is gone. We saw a lot of resiliency. We're not going anywhere. We're rebuilding. We'll be okay. But we shouldn't try to get back to normal, because things will never be normal again."[163]

World Central Kitchen continues its work in Puerto Rico today, but it looks different. Once the initial aftermath of the disaster was handled, they pivoted to support designed to help get communities back on their feet over the long haul. Such nimbleness is often needed to address sustainability challenges. We may try out one solution only to find out fairly quickly it doesn't work. We must learn to quickly pivot toward different approaches until we find the one that works. Mistakes are a part of the journey. According to their website, today World Central Kitchen invests in social enterprise food ventures designed to *"strengthen economies and transform communities."* In multiple countries where they have performed initial relief work, they provide financial support for fishermen, beekeepers, coffee growers, cooks, and farmers, particularly those who use sustainable eco-agricultural practices, and share their equipment and knowledge with their neighbors. Their culinary schools help people learn job skills. Initial relief as well as long-term recovery efforts are all part of the work toward community resilience.

The Chef Network continues to expand as it "engages socially conscious chefs skilled in a wide range of culinary arts and matches them with communities in need around the world." World Central Kitchen uses food—growing it, cooking it, sharing it—to empower people in the communities where they work. In the end, everyone involved is transformed. As Chef Andrés says, "Charity should not be about the redemption of the giver but about the liberation of the receiver."[164]

Voices of Empowerment

Sustainability's empowerment Core Value must include the ability to speak up. The right to vote, expressing individual views through the power of democracy, is a critical form of empowerment. Even though they are US citizens, Puerto Ricans are unable to vote in presidential elections, justified by those who assert that they are residents of an unincorporated territory. They have only one non-voting congressman in the US House of Representatives. They have little to no voice in Washington on important policies that directly impact them. The island's massive debt and fiscal woes are compounded by high unemployment (only 40 percent of the labor force are employed, which puts them in the bottom 3 percent globally.[165])

Arcane importation laws and prohibitions on bankruptcy declaration continue to hobble the island's economic recovery and send clear signals that they are looked on as second-class citizens without the same rights and privileges as other Americans. Some Puerto Ricans want to secede from the US, while others desire statehood. Some believe the most likely path to join in the rights that states share is to be annexed by Florida.

Chef Andrés feels strongly about exercising the right to vote. Through a nonprofit called When We All Vote, started by Michelle Obama, Andrés entreats immigrants to exercise their voting rights. He talks about how being a naturalized American citizen makes him part of something larger than himself, with the ability to make a difference. "As a chef, when I see a dish that can be improved, I take the time to improve it. It's the same with our country. When we all vote, we decide our future."[166]

CHAPTER THREE

Nonviolent Action

Civilization and violence are antithetical concepts.
—The Reverend Martin Luther King Jr.,
Civil rights leader, Baptist minister

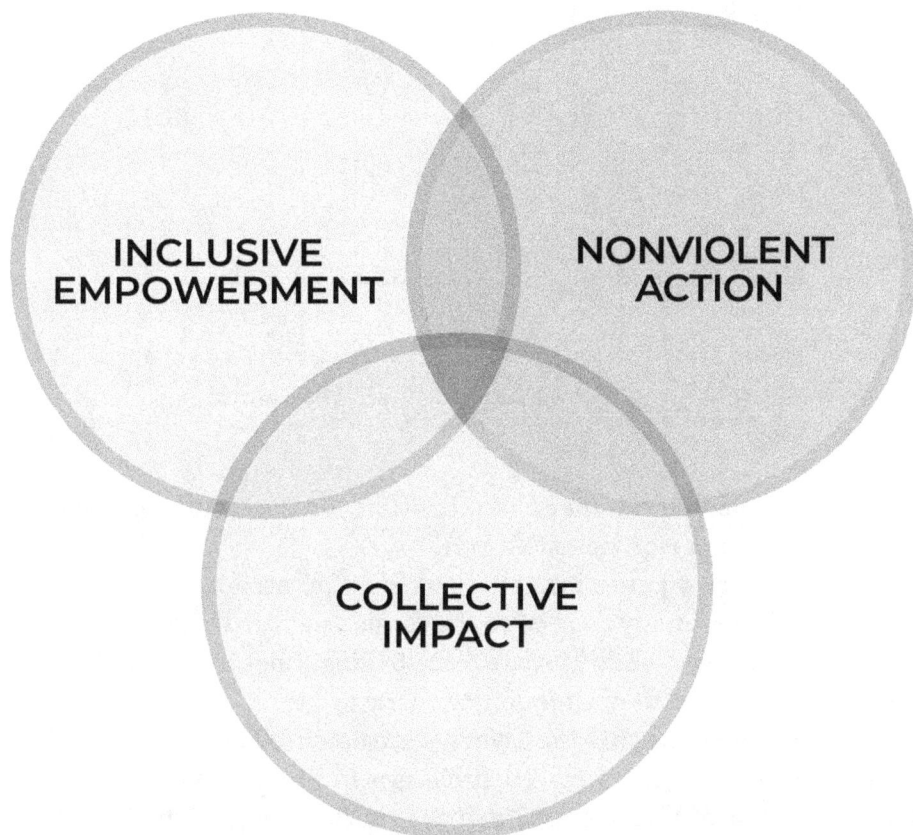

Social Sustainability Core Value Two: Nonviolent Action

EIGHTH COURSE: A COURSE IN NONVIOLENT ACTION

Back at my imaginary dinner party, it's time for the eighth course to be served: a course in Nonviolent Action.

My guests are digging into slices of the almond apricot tart I have prepared. With so many courses to the meal, a light fruit dessert seemed the only choice. And while I love to cook, baking is not my forte. Over the years, I've managed to master simple rustic tarts.

My guests are savoring the layers of caramelized sugar and luscious fruit. As the evening has worn on, it has grown warm in the dining room. The luscious roses I have placed in a vase in the center of the table have grown increasingly fragrant, their heady odor hanging heavy in the air. Between his bites, I see Anita lean forward in her chair, inhaling deeply, her eyes momentarily closed.

"Are you enjoying my roses? It's quite a labor of love to grow them. I only plant the sweetest-smelling types. This variety is called Peace Rose."

César's gaze lands on the blooms, the petals a delicate cream color, flushed at the edges with crimson-pink. "Beautiful, Lucia. Roses are very special to me, as a symbol of Our Lady of Guadalupe, the patron saint of Mexico. Her appearance is associated with the Miracle of the Roses."

I knew the legend, but I wanted to hear it told in the oral tradition which helped make it famous. "That sounds like a fascinating story." César needed little encouragement.

"It happened ten years after Cortes conquered and enslaved the Aztec empire. The imperialists stole their land and committed genocide against the indigenous peoples. The story takes place in wintertime. Diego was a young Aztec Christian convert. He is visited by a magical apparition of Our Lady. She was mestiza, a dark-skinned, half-blooded woman. She asked him to take her shawl to the local bishop and share the news of her appearance."

I imagined generations of families retelling this story around a fire.

"When Diego presented Our Lady's shawl to the Bishop, roses that could not have been growing in the middle of winter came spilling out. That is the Miracle of the Roses."

I wanted to make sure the group understood the importance of this event within the context of the subjugation of the Aztec by the Spanish invaders. Her story was seen as legitimizing the indigenous people crushed under Spanish colonization.

"The Lady of Guadalupe being of mixed race was a sort of symbolic rebuke to the violence of the times, right?" I watched his face for a cue to continue. "The mestiza offspring of indigenous women raped by Spaniards were often left to starve. It must have felt to the Aztecs like their dignity was finally being acknowledged."

"Exactly. Our Lady of Guadalupe is the patroness of the ostracized and rejected.[167] Today, she represents empathy for the poor and suffering, acceptance, and unity. She is our symbol of love and nonviolence. For some who may not relate to her Catholic origins, she has become more a symbol of Mexican nationalism than a religious figure per se."

ROOTS OF NONVIOLENCE

The nonviolent battles our social revolutionist Chávez waged most often relied upon a grassroots army, tilting at the windmills of organized labor and modern agribusiness. Chávez was a formidable adversary with the perseverance of a marathon runner. His patience often delivered victory in many seemingly unwinnable battles. While the campaigns he led could at times appear to be a matter of life and death, he never resorted to violent tactics, even when violence was used against him and his followers.

Chávez never allowed anyone accompanying him to be armed. When federal agents notified him that a hitman had been hired to assassinate him—one of many death threats he would receive over the years—he responded by adopting a rule of never sleeping in the same place twice.[168] He eventually conceded to the idea of bodyguards in the form of two German Shepherds, which he named Boycott and Huelga (Strike).

Over the years, UFW strikers were attacked with chains, bulldozers, cars, ice picks, tire irons, rocks, tear gas, and bullets. There were many physical assaults. Chávez was sometimes burned in effigy. 1973 was one of the deadliest years for the union, with the death of two supporters. Nagi Daifullah, a 24-year-old Arab picket captain, was clubbed with a flashlight by police and dragged, head bouncing, across pavement. Sixty-year-old Juan de la Cruz was shot on the picket line by someone firing from a speeding truck. In the year of these losses, 3,500 farmworkers and their supporters were apprehended. The arrests were often conducted using a good measure of police brutality, with strikers thrown to the ground, maced in the face, or struck with billy clubs before being handcuffed and hauled away.[169]

In stark contrast to these horrific proceedings, Chávez was a devout student of nonviolence and Christian mysticism. He revered the teachings of Gandhi and St. Francis of Assisi. The religious teachings of these two men helped form his value system, based on love and compassion. The spiritual teachings of St. Francis must have felt comfortably familiar to

Chávez, whose upbringing was rooted in the Catholic traditions of his familial matriarchs.

In one often-retold legend, St. Francis explained that "Brother Wolf" was attacking the villagers and their livestock only because it was hungry. The wolf was tamed once Francis blessed it and the villagers agreed to feed it regularly. The wolf could represent the hungry farmworkers in César's story, who only wanted enough to eat and to be treated with respect. Erasing hunger is one of the many problems that sustainability strives to resolve.

César's study of Gandhi, a religious Hindu, was something he referred to often. Gandhi's philosophy of non-violence in action provided an important underpinning for César's union tactics. Hindu belief in nonviolence extends to the slaughter of animals. Even though he wasn't Hindu, Chávez was also a vegetarian.

Although they never met, Dr. Martin Luther King Jr. once said of Chávez, "You stand today as a living example of the Gandhian tradition with its great force for social progress and its healing spiritual power."[170] He also wrote to him, "As brothers in the fight for equality, I extend the hand of fellowship and good will and wish continuing success to you and your members . . . You and your valiant fellow workers have demonstrated your commitment to righting grievous wrongs forced upon exploited people. We are together with you in spirit and in determination that our dreams for a better tomorrow will be realized." Both Chávez and King were deeply spiritual men, although César may have sometimes wished that he shared the Reverend's gift for oratory.

Portraits of Gandhi and Martin Luther King Jr. were among the posters adorning the shabby UFW office.[171] A large image of the Virgin of Guadalupe also graced the walls. Crammed with papers and beat-up second-hand furniture, this tiny space was where the union masterminded many of its chess moves. A treasured telegram from King was also on display. "We are together with you in spirit and in determination that our dreams for a better tomorrow will be realized."[172]

In practical terms, Chávez learned many of his tactical political action skills from the godfather of modern community organizing, Saul Alinsky. In his early days of community organizing, Chávez worked under the tutelage of a disciple of Alinsky to register Latinos in California to vote. Alinsky's most famous publication was *Rules for Radicals*. The author explained the purpose of his book by saying, *"The Prince* was written by Machiavelli for the Haves on how to hold power. *Rules for Radicals* was written for the Have-Nots on how to take it away."[173] Alinsky's Industrial Areas Foundation continues its work today, embracing sustainability through training community organizers to understand power and develop leadership skills.

Alinksy's 1971 *Rulebook* as well as Gene Sharp's 1973 passive resistance follow-on, *The Politics of Nonviolent Action*, provided a wealth of nonviolent tools to spread messages and garner support for causes. Chávez drew on the book's catalogue of action: consumer boycotts, picket lines, marches, demonstrations, banners, symbols, display of portraits, pilgrimages, religious processions, underground newspapers, spiritual fasts, music, guerilla theater, and labor strikes.[174]

The most overarching reformation sought by Chávez and Dolores Huerta was for farmworkers to be included in labor union organizing. This would afford them the same access to voting rights in union elections and the associated labor rights and protections awarded to union members. Chávez and Huerta knew this was the best way to ultimately improve working conditions in the fields, earn better wages, and receive rest breaks, access to toilets, housing, and medical care.

Three years after the formation of the UFW, actions by the Filipino American Farm Workers working in California would change the course of union history. Huerta was no stranger to Filipino workers. She grew up in Stockton, where her mother offered affordable rooms in the seventy-room hotel she owned to a diverse array of Mexican, Filipino, African-American, Japanese, and Chinese working-class families.[175]

In 1965, in pursuit of better pay, the Filipino union was preparing to stage a grape worker labor strike in Delano, California. A patchwork of grape-growing farms populated the area, including the 4,400-acre DiGiorgio Sierra Vista Ranch.[176] Many of these growing operations included worker camps with army-style mess halls and dormitory housing where men slept four to a room. Thirsty workers might be charged twenty-five cents for a drink of water in the field, served in a shared rusty cup or old beer can.

The Filipino union wanted the UFW to join their strike. If not, when the UFW members crossed the picket lines, they would become strikebreakers. Chávez and Huerta couldn't stomach this idea, so they decided the UFW would join in a walkout. While perhaps not the most logical decision, this move changed the course of history. What would become the five-year Delano Grape Strike had begun.

The sustainability revolution can rely on logic, but it can also rely on intuition. To use a card game analogy, sometimes, we have to know when to hold 'em, and when to fold 'em. There are times when no rulebook is available other than our own instincts.

THE DELANO GRAPE STRIKE

Grapes are the perfect crop for an agricultural labor strike. Unlike seasonal crops such as lettuce that rely on short-season laborers, grapes need care and cultivation ten months of the year. This requires near-continuous skilled attention to spraying, trimming, and a process called girdling to prompt grape production. Picking is also highly skilled, with the need to determine when grapes are ready and careful handling to prevent damage to grapes headed to the table. The grape crop relies on a relatively stable workforce, less subject to monthly migrant farm workers looking for a new crop to harvest.

During the Delano grape strike, Chávez would walk the picket lines, yelling encouragement from a bull horn. Growers and their bosses bullied the strikers, spraying them with pesticides and fertilizers. They created physical barriers so strikebreakers couldn't see picketers. They played loud car radios at top volume to drown out the strikers' shouts of "Huelga!"[177] Sometimes, children were exploited as strikebreakers.

Chávez and Huerta were beginning to frame the strike as a civil rights struggle. Chávez proclaimed, "We need to be recognized; not just in the union sense, but as human beings with human rights."[178] Just six months into the strike, the political ground was starting to shift. An impossible-to-ignore dialogue was growing about the dignity and human rights of farmworkers, and their need for better living and working conditions. Such public discourse is critical to the sustainability revolution. A Congressional Subcommittee on migrant labor was formed. In March 1966, a series of California-based hearings began. At this time, local police were pre-emptively conducting arrests based only on the suspicion that strikers were poised to break the law.

Sen. Robert F. Kennedy attended the final Congressional hearing. The day before, Chávez had accompanied him on a visit to a labor camp, followed by a large gathering in a farmworker union hall. Kennedy questioned Kern County Sheriff Roy Galyen about the arrests that were occurring without cause.

> **Kennedy:** *This is a most interesting concept . . . that you suddenly hear talk that somebody's going to get out of order, perhaps violate the law, and you go in and arrest them, and they haven't done anything wrong. How can you go and arrest somebody if they haven't violated the law?*

> **Galyen:** *They are ready to violate the law, in other words.*

> **Kennedy:** *Could I suggest that the Sheriff and the District Attorney read the Constitution of the United States?* [179] [180]

At this point, the room erupted into thunderous cheers. The moment was to prove pivotal for the UFW, buoyed by Kennedy's support.

According to Miriam Pawel, the authoritative Chávez biographer, as fellow Catholics "Mexicans felt a strong affinity for the Kennedy family" as a part of groups who "worked hard for the election of the first Catholic president in 1960."[181] The UFW was adept at using images and words that appealed to those with a shared Hispanic culture. Their events were often accompanied by an iconic banner of Our Lady of Guadalupe, the national folk saint of Mexico.

Soon after the hearings concluded, Chávez launched a processional three-hundred-mile pilgrimage from Delano to Sacramento, the California state capital. With Lent approaching, Chávez saw the march as a spiritual pilgrimage, one designed to raise awareness of the strike far beyond California. The focus of the march was the grape strike, and the focus of the strike was a fifteen-cent increase in hourly wages as well as more pay for each box of grapes picked.

Sustainability must be a journey of the head as well as the heart. Chávez's spiritual journey provides inspiration for the non-corporeal aspects of the sustainability revolution.

THE PILGRIM'S ROAD
TO SACRAMENTO

L et's imagine the march to Sacramento, based on recorded facts. Some events in this creative nonfiction account are blended from other related union organizing activities.

The road ahead was long. It would be many hours before sleep, if it came at all. Fifty followers trudged along, carrying sleeping bags and paper bags of spare clothing. Chávez had hurriedly planned the event, which he referred to as *"Perigrinacion, Penitencia, Revolucion."* (Pilgrimage, Penance, Revolution.) He wished to instill hope in the farmworkers, but more importantly to plead for God's mercy and to offer atonement. On his mind was "public penance for the sins of the strikers, their own personal sins as well as their yielding perhaps to feelings of hatred and revenge in the strike itself."[182] Chávez insisted that those who joined in the strike take a vow of nonviolence.

He hoped that the march would help his pilgrims find peace with the Lord, and for their cause to be purified. After all, it was the Lenten season of reflection on the sacrifices of Jesus, and he was hoping to reach Sacramento by Easter. In addition, there was comfort in following a centuries-old tradition born of Spanish culture, "springing from the spontaneity of the poor, the downtrodden, the rejected, the discriminated-against baring visibly their need and demand for equality and freedom."[183]

César could feel the blisters on his feet bursting as new ones formed on top of them. He always refused bandages or a change of shoes. More comfortable sneakers, which were offered to him repeatedly, were out of the question. Experiencing pain was part of the penitent's process. Reverend Jim Drake, an early ally of Chávez, noted "Mexico is a poor land with a great deal of suffering . . . Mexicans believe that from suffering you get strength . . . We've always suffered. Now we can suffer for a purpose."[184] While his followers generally didn't complain, Chávez could overhear a few distant grumbles from among the crowd. "Tengo hambre?" and "Quánto más lejos hoy?" or Spanish for "I'm hungry. How much farther today?" But César's attention barely registered on these. Instead, his focus was on the glorious banner above his head.

Our Lady of Guadalupe, hands folded in prayer, her image resplendent in shades of green and rose, was framed within a golden mandorla adorned by images of voluptuous rose blossoms. César never conducted an important event without Our Lady of Guadalupe's banner nearby. The dusty reality surrounding him drifted away as he fell into a reverie surrounding her lessons of compassion.

Our Lady of Guadalupe no doubt looked down on César's suffering and longings with tenderness. The premier symbol of Mexican national identity, she is often referred to as *"La Morenita"* or *"The Dark Woman,"* a reference to her mixed blood. Given the potency of her symbolism, the carrying of her banner on the march to Sacramento was *"the first hint . . . that the pilgrimage implied social revolution."*[185]

The Dark Virgin's message of love and compassion was a natural fit for César's cause, grounded in his fervent belief in nonviolence. During one of their many farm strikes, his followers fashioned a makeshift wooden altar to Our Lady of Guadalupe on the back of Chávez's old Mercury station wagon.[186] The women who hatched the idea had suggested the idea of praying instead of picketing. Migrant farmworkers visited the roadside altar nightly, enchanted by its flowers, flickering candles, and images of La Morenita. Local Spanish language radio stations helped to swell attendance by promoting the prayer vigil on the airwaves.[187] All were welcomed and embraced, regardless of whether they had crossed the picket lines.

Back along the pilgrim's way, César stumbled on a loose stone, catching himself from falling with the help of his cane. After so many years of stooped-over field labor, the work had ruined his back such that he often relied on the cane to help him walk. Drawn out of his reverie, he began to think of how far they needed to walk before dusk would seal the miles covered today. He drew forth a mental image of the huge crudely drawn map hanging on the wall of his headquarters, plotting their route. Covering about eight to ten miles per day, the pilgrims' path had been planned to pass through many of the small towns that might bolster the numbers of their supporters. His penitents had already traversed Farmersville, Fresno, Madera, and Chowchilla. He hoped to lead them into Modesto before sundown.

If all had gone well today with his supporters in their advance work, there would be a bed and some hot food to greet their arrival. If not, he was content to sleep in a car. Thus far, each town's priests had opened their doors to them, offering mass and blessings. Would the Modesto priests prove as open-hearted? But there was no point in thinking about that now, he told himself. La Morenita would provide, if she was able.

César began to hum a tune, recalling music as one of the inspirational tools in his nonviolent playbook. Familiar religious or folk melodies never failed to take a pilgrim's mind off their aches and hungers. Maybe it was time for a round of the ever-popular Mexican folk song De Colores (All the Colors), to help keep the faithful motivated. The song was quickly becoming the Union anthem.[188] Each penitent had been given song sheets, although he doubted anyone but the Filipinos would need them. Everyone he grew up with had learned this song when they could barely walk.

> De colores, de colores es el arco iris que vemos lucir
>
> (All the colors, all the colors in rainbows we see shining bright in the sky)
>
> Y por eso los grandes amores de muchos colores me gustan a mí
>
> (And that's why a great love of all colors makes me feel like singing so joyfully . . .)

The melody always brought a smile to his face, first with memories of his childhood, and then with thoughts of how all of his allies in this fight, whether Hispanic, Black, Filipino, or Anglo, whatever their color, were all unified in a worthy cause. The spirit of the song fit César's mood perfectly.

He hoped that the pilgrimage experience would prepare the farmworkers for "the long, long struggle ahead. We wanted to be fit not only physically, but also spiritually, and we wanted to stress nonviolence even more, build confidence, and have more visible nonviolent tactics."[189]

An hour later, dusk was falling and along with it the pilgrims' spirits. Just when hope's glimmer was fading, the Modesto city lights came miraculously into view. A cheer materialized from the limping crowd, which included those who had started out with him from the very beginning, referred to as the *originales*. Many others had joined along the way, walking for a few hours or for the duration.

The city limits gradually fell behind as their way became lined with a welcoming crowd of supporters, holding alight flickering candles to light their path. They trudged along, gratefully allowing themselves to be led to the local town hall where a hot meal awaited them. The food was simple: tortillas, arroz, and frijoles, but nothing had ever tasted better to César. Even if they had been serving meat, he wouldn't have eaten it. He was a vegetarian, and this peasant fare fit his idea of sacrifice and penance. In future times, César would go on many spiritual fasts, following again the example of Gandhi, to reinforce his commitment to nonviolence. During one of these fasts, he would not eat for 25 days and lose 35 pounds.

Once the penitents' prayers of thanks had been offered and the pilgrims' bellies were full, it was time for some entertainment. Offsetting hard work with relaxation is essential to a balanced life, and to the long sustainability journey. We must take the time to pause, to rest, to celebrate each victory along the way. Entertainment is one of the ways we can recharge our batteries and lighten our load. The passionate Luis Valdez, who had become his dear friend, was preparing to lead what had become a nightly guerrilla theater performance dubbed Teatro Campesino, the Farmworker's Theater. The Teatro Campesino performance plots came from Luis's own experiences. One emerged while working the Delano grape strike, when he had been ordered at gunpoint by an enraged non-striking farmworker to stand down.[190]

Guerilla theater-of-the-people can be a tool of nonviolence. In each Valdez play, a short improvisational skit used satire and humor to teach, using story. These simple parable-like performances were meant to inspire and uplift the marchers by helping them to find humor in their circumstances, and solidarity in their cause. The Teatro Campesino players were not trained actors. Luis recruited company members by telling them, "If you can sing, dance, walk, march, hold a picket sign, play a guitar or harmonica or any other instrument, you can participate: no acting experience required."[191]

On this night, it felt like a luxury to be staging the play indoors. Since the march had begun, they had performed most nights on the back of a flatbed truck. The gathered crowd became hushed as they sensed the play was about to begin. The only stage decoration was a huge United Farmworkers flag, painted on an old sheet, the union logo blazing in vivid splashes of color. The symbol that César and his cousin had selected for the Union was a bold red and black Aztec-style eagle, designed simply using squares, with the idea that it could easily be reproduced by anyone. The eagle was a familiar symbol that also appeared on the Mexican flag. To any free-associating mind, the blocky shape of the eagle's body also looked like an inverted Aztec pyramid. Red symbolized the farmworkers' sacrifice, black their struggle, and white their hope. The eagle design had been unveiled at the first mass meeting of the UFW. It had now become a highly recognizable symbol of their struggle.[192]

In every Teatro play, the identify of each actor was announced with simple hand-drawn signs, painted on cardboard and hung with twine around the necks of the players. They would be labeled variously as "Patroncito" (Boss), "Huelguista" (Striker), "Rotten Grape" and "Esquirol" (Scab). The well-fed Boss wearing sunglasses holds a toy wooden gun to the head of the skinny Huelguista, hurling insults and demanding he stop striking. The Huelguista hurls his own insults, accompanied by cheers from the crowd. Hoes, shovels, and picket signs are used as simple props. Laughter is a must, such as when the Boss threatens that he will take away the

Huelguista's worker seniority. The wide-eyed worker responds densely. "Mi senora (wife)? No, you're not going to take away mi senora."[193]

Tonight's play is called *Las Dos Cara del Patroncito* (The Two Faces of the Little Boss). The Boss arrives on stage wearing a paper maché pig mask in order to confront the striker, Pedro. The Boss argues that his life of housing and feeding farmworkers and providing for a spendthrift wife is much harder than the plight of the toiling farmworker. Hoping to teach Pedro a lesson, the Boss demands he don the Pig mask. Once the role reversal is complete, Pedro becomes a domineering, abusive boss, and thus both characters learn that they share the same humanity. As the play comes to a close and the players take their bows, the exhausted crowd appears to revive. Shouts of "Viva la causa!" and "Viva la huelga!" ("Long live the farmworker's cause," and "Long live the strike") erupt as a few marchers spring to their feet, waving their arms in spite of the weariness in their bones.[194]

With dreams of the Teatro dancing in his head, César falls into an exhausted slumber at the home of a local family who have offered him shelter. Almost two hundred miles of dusty road have passed beneath his feet. He has trudged past fields of lettuce, asparagus, artichokes and grapes. He will never give up. Little did he know that on the following day, the first grower subject to the boycott would fold, signing a deal to recognize the rights of the farmworkers to participate in contract negotiations. The Delano empire was starting to topple, just as Sacramento was drawing near. La Morenita must be smiling on them.

According to plan, they arrive in Sacramento on Easter Sunday. Leaning on the shoulder of a fellow marcher, Chávez limps across the Tower Bridge, high above the Sacramento River. It would take over an hour for everyone behind him to make it across. The dozens of red and black United Farmworkers flags snake from the rear of the march and out of sight. A huge *BIENVENIDOS* banner on the bridge announces a welcome to the crowd. Cars are still being allowed cross the bridge in the lane alongside the marchers, allowing a VW Beetle's white driver to honk his support as he passes the throng.

As a man of few words, now César's mind turns to what he will say to the crowd once they finally reach the capitol steps. There are only nine more blocks to go, little time for him to choose his words. It was raining, sure to ruin many a planned Easter picnic. Would the rain dampen the spirits of his followers? As they arrived, he could see that the green lawn surrounding the white-domed capitol could easily hold the decent-sized crowd. But this was not exactly how he'd planned it. He had wanted to arrive to a meeting with Governor Pat Brown so they could roll up their sleeves for a discussion of unionization and worker's dignity. But the Governor had turned him down in favor of spending the holy day with Frank Sinatra in Palm Springs, at his swanky 4,500-square-foot modernist home, featuring seven bathrooms and a piano-shaped swimming pool.[195] Such a home sends clear signals of privilege and power that excludes everyone but the glitterati.

Now that they had finally reached the Sacramento capitol steps, the penitent pilgrim mood shifts toward exuberance. One thing Chávez was not disappointed with was the turnout: eight thousand cheering supporters, of all colors and all walks of life. The fifty-odd *originales* had been provided a place of honor on the platform.[196] A few mariachis sporting huge black sombreros ride in on horseback, ceremoniously waving flags. The exhausted César can find only a few words to say. "It is well to remember in defeat that there must be courage, but also that in victory, there must be humility."[197]

As sustainability revolutionists, we must believe devoutly in our cause, and be brave enough to shout it from the rooftops. Coming to the table with an attitude of grace and humility can win over opponents and bring them to your side. As the saying goes, you can catch more flies with honey than vinegar.

An undaunted Huerta takes the mic next. She wears a rakish cowboy hat, her face flushed with excitement. "On behalf of all the farmworkers of this state, we unconditionally demand a collective bargaining law for the state of California. You cannot pretend that we do not exist. You cannot plead ignorance to our problems, because we are here and we embody our needs for you. And we are not alone."[198]

The galvanizing events of the March to Sacramento would bolster the farmworkers' morale for many months to come. They would need every ounce of the strength of their commitment to nonviolence for the work ahead. Following in Gandhi's footsteps, Chávez would undertake a spiritual fast to reinforce that violence was not the answer. The union would continue its work, eventually discovering how to enroll more supporters in their nonviolent efforts by conducting peaceful consumer boycotts.

"Once social change begins, it cannot be reversed," Chávez said in a famous speech. "You cannot un-educate the person who has learned to read. You cannot humiliate the person who feels pride. You cannot oppress the people who are not afraid anymore."[199]

The big tent of sustainability has room for every camper committed to change, no matter who they are, or where they come from. It is a tent of magical proportions that can shelter a beautiful community of revolutionists, filled with love and hope and possibility.

SOCIAL SUSTAINABILITY CORE VALUE 2:

NONVIOLENT ACTION
Responding with compassion

Out beyond ideas of wrongdoing, and right-doing,
there is a field. I will meet you there.
—**Rumi**, thirteenth century Persian poet

Like sustainability, nonviolence is a familiar term that also challenges us to comprehend its true meaning. The practice of nonviolence is also just as challenging as the practice of sustainability. At its roots, nonviolence is the opposite of aggression and conflict, a state of peace. The idea of peace cannot be separated from the concept of sustainability, according to the United Nations. Its sustainable development goals state, "There can be no sustainable development without peace, and no peace without sustainable development."[200]

The forms violence takes will vary. Personal violence shows up as highly visible acts including physical force, intimidation, and abuse. Structural violence is a subtler form, wherein institutional and power systems dominate and subvert fundamental rights of the less powerful.[201]

Gandhi developed a personal philosophy of nonviolence, coining his own term for it—*satyagraha*. The word is forged from several Sanskrit words: *Satya*, the word for truth, and ā*graha*, the word for persistence. Gandhi defined it as "pressure for social and political reform through friendly passive resistance." His thinking was influenced by Henry David Thoreau's *Civil Disobedience*, written after the naturalist spent a night in jail for refusal to pay a poll tax to which he was philosophically opposed. Thoreau's tax resistance was a form of peaceful protest. Gandhi also drew heavily from one of the cardinal virtues of the ancient Indian religion of Jainism, one which he learned as a child. This virtue is described as do no harm, or *ahisma*.

Gandhi recognized the universality of love as a guiding principle in his own and other major religions of the world. Gandhi, through Jainism, saw all life as one sacred cosmic family. He wrote about respect for the sacredness of life centered around love as "the law of our being."[202] For him, the practice of nonviolence was "the supreme law." This focus on love leads us to a fundamental ability required for practicing nonviolence, known as empathy.

According to Daniel Pink in his foundational book *A Whole New Mind: Why Right-Brainers Will Rule the Future*, "Empathy is the ability to imagine yourself in someone else's position and to intuit what that person is feeling. It is the ability to stand in others' shoes, to see with their eyes, and to feel with their hearts."[203] Without a generalized attitude of love, there can be no empathy. With some effort, empathy can be learned.

A statement from the nonprofit Charter for Compassion explains that empathy teaches us to 1) see the world as others see it, 2) practice non-judgment, 3) understand another person's feelings, and 4) communicate understanding. Practicing empathy requires active listening skills without advising, fixing, correcting, explaining, or scripting. Empathy is considered one of the five key components of emotional intelligence, as defined by Daniel Goleman in his wildly popular books on leadership. Goleman suggests that by teaching people to tune into their emotions with intelligence, and to expand their circles of caring, "we can transform organizations from the inside out and make a positive difference in our world."

For the sustainability practitioner today, one of the most basic tools for practicing nonviolence is nonviolent communication. Nonviolent communication requires the release of moralistic judgments. We avoid attaching labels such as bad or wrong to others and their actions. Judging others blocks our compassion for them. Instead, observing others without evaluating them is the foundation of nonviolence.

The tendency to quickly classify and size up others in snap judgements is difficult to overcome. One of the reasons this occurs is that defining our own identities often happens in social groups, through identifying those who are not like us. Thus, others can be conveniently defined as outsiders or, in extreme cases, our enemies. Human beings often use otherness, conflict, and war to help define personal or group identity. Rising levels of migration, the emergence of a global economy, and rapid interconnectedness of communication systems all force nations to grapple with crises of identity.[204]

Gandhi noted that "Fear of the foreigner is what gives rise to hatred." People across the globe are agonizing over whether identity is defined by location, history, culture, wealth, or political systems. The shift toward a European Union is illustrative of the healthy broadening, rather than the narrowing, of national identity, although that transition has not been without notable bumps.

In the previous section, we saw that nonviolence offers practices we must take up if we are to achieve peace. The idea of practicing nonviolence indicates there is something that must be done. We can't simply sit back and watch violence occur around us, even if we are not directly participating in it. Retreating into a nonviolent but introverted existence is not enough.

We have a responsibility to engage with the world around us, to work to make it better. Revolutionists don't sit around waiting for change to happen. They are by definition activists; they act in order to create the change they want to see. Georgia-based Congressman and humanitarian John Lewis began his career in the civil rights movement leading one of three Selma-to-Montgomery nonviolent marches. In the essay he penned, published upon his death, he stated that "Democracy is not a state. It is an act." He often referred to the activism which defined his life as "necessary trouble."[205]

Violence is a fundamental threat to sustainability. One revolutionist taking action against nonviolence is Bandy Lee, MD, internationally recognized expert on violence and member of the Yale medical faculty. Lee, who contributed to the United Nations 2030 Agenda addressing violence, co-authored a book called *The Dangerous Case of Donald Trump*. The book takes up a medical professional's "duty to warn," a law in many states that requires a doctor to break confidentiality if a patient is in imminent danger of physically hurting someone. The doctor has a moral duty to take action against violence, requiring that potential victims and the police be contacted.[206] Lee and her fellow authors posited that Trump's position in office posed danger precisely because past violence is the best predictor of future violence.[207]

Acting in the service of nonviolence can take many forms: careful communication with stakeholders using nonviolent expression; raising children to be empathetic adults; banding together to reform political injustice; working to dismantle institutionalized structural violence; stopping bullying in our streets and schools. Every act of nonviolence is important, because violence tends to be contagious. Cycles of violence tend to repeat themselves during lives and across multiple generations.

"When children grow up in safe, stable, and nurturing relationships and environments," said Dr. Lee, "they learn empathy, impulse control, anger management, and problem-solving—all skills that protect against interpersonal, self-directed, and collective violence and allow for learning, play, and healthy development."[208] She says that violence prevention helps generate viable ecologies that lead to economic growth and general well-being. Human ecologies informed by all of sustainability's Core Values can yield satisfying, healthy, and vibrant experiences across our wondrous planet.

MODERN-DAY REVOLUTIONISTS: THE ART OF NONVIOLENCE

In the previous section, we vicariously enjoyed a theater performance tied to the sustainability goals the union was attempting to achieve. Arts and media-based projects continue to serve as a fascinating tool in the non-violent action toolkit. Here, we'll take a quick look at the continuing legacy of several of these that were born during the early UFW days. The Teatro Campesino troupe has evolved to a permanent home in the Los Angeles area. Luis Valdez, who had befriended Chávez, has been a continuous presence and serves at the helm of the troupe today. Not only did he stay the course performing alongside Chávez throughout his political career, but he also eventually came to be widely acknowledged as the founder of modern Chicano theater and film.[209]

Valdez more recently wrote and directed the play *Valley of the Heart*, a story of star-crossed love between the Mexican and Japanese American children of two sharecropper families. The lives of the Montaños and Yamaguchis are disrupted following the Japanese internment in the aftermath of Pearl Harbor. The *Los Angeles Times* reviewed the production, saying "Bridging differences has always been difficult and hobbled by injustice, as the experiences of the Montaños and Yamaguchis remind us. But at a time when refugees are being scapegoated for partisan political ends, *Valley of the Heart* celebrates diversity as the true ingredient of America's enduring greatness."[210]

The nonprofit organization Valdez founded stages many performances and ongoing programs, including an annual youth-focused educational theater workshop. The youth program's mission is to "preserve the legacy and history of El Teatro Campesino and to promote social and environmental justice by exposing young audiences to various current and historical social issues . . . dedicated to the use of art as a tool for social change and . . . to inspire community involvement, social consciousness, and political action through our theatrical performances, costumed lectures and workshops."[211]

Another legacy of Chávez's nonviolent Campesino movement is a Spanish-language radio network. Radio Campesina started in 1983 with a single underground station in rural Tulare County, California.[212] The network now broadcasts across three states and eight cities from Yuma to Phoenix, Las Vegas to Salinas.

Anthony Chávez, son of César, serves as president of the network, whose focus is newly-arrived immigrants from rural areas of Mexico and Central America between the ages of 25 and 49. The network uses "a culturally vibrant format with Mexican regional music, along with educational and public service programming quality . . . [Presenting] forums and debates on key issues such as health, safety, education, political and consumer issues . . ."[213]

Here's Hope: Community radio is a widely recognized tool around the world for empowering people with politically, geographically, and linguistically relevant information. Such freely accessible information is the lingua franca of sustainability. Information is power. In the world of sustainability, community radio is a tool of empowerment. Mobile phones also aid in streaming community radio programming that can enable individuals to "become agents of their own transformation" by providing a platform to respond to disasters, raise issues, and share grievances.

Here's a great example. In 2012, Sesame Workshop India's Radiophone project utilized community radio combined with mobile technology to reach 1.4 million children and caregivers in remote areas of Northern India. Content development, capacity building, and technology deployment relied on a community participatory approach to explore issues and solutions. The highly successful effort gained traction on topics ranging from tobacco cessation, childhood inoculation, waste management, and flood disaster recovery.[214]

Race, class, immigration, and political revolution have inspired a diverse array of creative visual and performance artists, from Diego Rivera's political murals to Ai Wei Wei's revolutionary installations and social media stream. Turkish producer Recep Tuna worked on a performance art piece focused on immigration issues, entitled *Tamra*. He said of the piece "When people have a hard time understanding each other, culture and art have always been a very important unifying method."[215] One of the more recent rising stars in this movement is an anonymous French guerilla artist who goes solely by the moniker "JR."

JR seems to thrive on visiting conflict zones, where he uses temporary installations to uplift people using the human instinct for curiosity. His portrait-focused photographic installations have been staged at locales including the Sudan, Sierra Leone, Syria, Cuba, India, and Brazilian favelas. He has staged clandestine temporary art works centered around issues of immigration and racial tension at Ellis Island, as well as after the unprecedented 2005 riots in the working-class, heavily immigrant Paris suburb Les Bosquets.[216]

Walls that separate us are the symbolic antithesis of inclusion and empowerment. They are often designed to separate the haves from the have-nots, the unfamiliar from the familiar, "them" from "us." We build walls thinking they will make us safe, but in fact they can result in the opposite becoming true. Walls divide us versus joining us together. They foster division versus understanding. In a sustainable world without walls, everyone has the same rights. All are accepted, celebrated, and empowered to be their best expression of themselves. In a world without imaginary borders or physical fences, it's easier to see that in reality, we are all in this together. In the political world, criminalizing immigration stands in opposition to the realization of sustainable communities based on freedom, equality, and agency for all.

Next, let's visit the days surrounding the unveiling of one of JR's installations at the Mexico border, intended to draw attention to immigration and border policies. His installation is *Kikito*, drawn from the name of a young Mexican boy whose photo portrait was an integral part of the piece. The basic facts are all based on video accounts, photographs, and published reports. Some of the story details are imagined.

BUILDING BRIDGES, NOT WALLS

In spite of the October calendar date, the sun is blazing down with its usual fury, regardless of which side of the border you happen to be standing on. The lives of countless migrants have been taken by this desert, a cruel punishment for trying to cross into the United States from Mexico. Some couldn't survive the forced cross-country marches, while others perished inside trucks without air conditioning where their "coyotes" left them to die. These days, there are fewer and fewer people willing to take the risk. Contrary to popular belief, lots of people like young Kikito's family have no desire to come to the States, other than to take a vacation to Disneyland or Hawaii. Lizy Higareda, Kikito's mother, prefers to stay safe in her hometown of Tecate in Baja, Mexico. Here she has family roots, a career, and access to good schools for her son. She is studying criminology and has plans to become a jail therapist. She is clear about her goals. "I don't want to fight the drug war. I want to help end it."[217]

The town of Tecate, 40 miles east of San Diego, is a magical place, she says, drawing air quotes she explains her community, which is best known for its massive beer brewery. The *Pueblo Mágico* program was created by the Mexican government in 2001 to promote tourism to some of its lesser known and infinitely charming towns, whether esteemed for their natural beauty, cultural delights, folklore, or rich history. The *Visit Mexico* tourist guide describes Tecate as "under an extensive blue sky, combining the sea and the desert, surrounded by beautiful mountains and stone cliffs . . . accompanied by Cerro Cuchuma, a mountain sacred to the Kumiai people . . . The incredible scenery of La Rumorosa with its giant rocks . . . is one of the most striking landscapes in the country."

Mexican officials are quick to point out their country is consistently in the top ten tourist destinations in the world.[218] Since the great recession, more Mexicans have been departing from the US than seeking to enter it.[219] In spite of the fact that the number of undocumented border crossings reached a historic low in 2016, President Trump announced in

2017 his administration would be rescinding DACA and moving forward with building his campaign-promised border wall to keep out the "bad hombres." Since that time the courts have moved to restore DACA, a situation that is still in play. Such hyperbole is catnip to someone like the lanky, perpetually restless JR.

The artist's wheat-pasted giant portrait murals give unrecognized people a chance to be seen. "They are a way to say, 'I exist,'" he explains, but they also remind us of the "inherent dignity of every individual and can safeguard against the instinct to distance and dehumanize."[220] When working in Palestine, he displayed giant portraits of Israeli and Palestinian people, side by side, doing the same jobs. When he asked local residents if they could tell which side the people were on, just by looking at the images, he cleverly made his point: Conflicts based on differences are an illusion—we are all one. Most political, ethnic, and cultural dividing lines seem patently absurd to him, so he has decided to explore how his particular brand of community artistic engagement might find expression along the Mexico border.

As he arrives in Tecate, JR is afraid his thick French accent might put the residents off. Instead, he finds friendly, warm people, curious about what he is up to. JR meets the Higareda family, whose home overlooks the huge border fence. Here, they are able to reach right through the bars to touch US soil if they are so inclined.

Sustainability recognizes the boundless nature of the world. Borders are political constructs unrecognized by nature. Migrating jaguars at the Texas-Mexico border don't understand why a wall cuts across their natural territory. In addition, climate change knows no political boundaries. Catastrophic floods, hurricanes, heat waves, fires, and rising sea levels destroy homes, structures, and property, regardless of anyone's political affiliations or country of residence. However, we also see that the "have-nots" are bearing the brunt of these devastating impacts.

Humanizing political issues by putting a face on them is JR's most reliable tactic. Kikiko's wide-eyed gaze riveted JR from the first moment he met the 14-month-old. Could those dark eyes be the window into an old soul? Immediately, he knew. The boy's innocent face could draw attention to the fallacy of the wall, the mistreatment of children being separated from their families. Springing into action, he photographs the toddler, then prints out a massive 65-foot-high panel with his visage. He installs the panel on scaffolding next to the Tecate side of the wall. The resulting illusion is of a child appearing to grip the top of the wall with his fingers, as he peers curiously into the United States from over the rusting steel barrier.[221] The gargantuan portrait height plays visual tricks with the wall's scale, making it appear miniscule and insignificant.

To JR's delight, the border wall installation attracts droves of tourists, prompting a host of photo ops, Facebook posts, and media attention. In October, JR's vision culminates with the staging of an enormous community potluck using a 100-foot-long picnic table he built, with each half on opposing sides of the wall. The tabletop is adorned with a giant pair of feminine eyes, a photo of a Dreamer's eyes, making for stunning aerial imagery.

When asked why he does what he does, JR responds with a question. "Can art change the world?" In a TED talk, he goes on to answer his own question. "My work is about connecting people, the power of bringing people together. It all starts with believing. If you don't believe that you can make change, change can never happen. Even if it's a small change in one person, that's positive change."

Kikiko and his mother are the celebrities of the moment, posing for selfies and enjoying the celebration among the crowd of 50 or so people on each side of the wall. JR worries that their unpermitted event is going to be shut down by the authorities, but instead the authorities actually seem to be enjoying themselves. One border guard, equally as anonymous as JR behind his dark glasses, appears unfazed by the situation. Suited up in his long-sleeved olive-green uniform, covered in badges, American flag patches and various pieces of strap-on equipment, this federal agent seems more prepared for a raid than a picnic.

JR strikes up a conversation with the agent through the eight-inch gaps between the rusted steel bars of the wall. "Can you share tea with me now?" A volunteer offers up the refreshment in simple earthenware bowls the size of a hand. The two men smile a bit shyly at one another, clink cups, and drink deeply. The agent's serious face dissolves into a broad smile as he savors the drink. "Nice," he announces, repeating the word a second time to make sure his response has registered.

A group of musicians are pumping out a cheerful conjunto song with an accordion and a snare drum. Half the band is on each side of the wall, but it doesn't seem to interfere with the integrity of the tune. JR seems content. "At the border today in Tecate," he says on Instagram, "people eating the same food, sharing the same water, enjoying the same music around the eyes of a Dreamer. We forgot the wall for a minute. Together we are stronger." For Kikito's proud grandpa, the biggest outcome is more love to go around. "The whole world wants to hug him."[222]

JR's compelling piece of guerilla border theater took advantage of the nonviolent tools in the sustainability revolutionist's toolkit. These tried and tested tools include picket lines, boycotts, marches, banners, pilgrimages, community radio, and theater. Creative arts give expression to sustainability in new ways, speaking to people in a variety of different modalities. The nimble change agent can become adept at a variety of different tools to get their messages across. Just as there are four different learning styles—visual, auditory, kinesthetic, and reading—we can try different communication tools to reach the broadest audience.

CHAPTER FOUR

Collective Impact

Remember that no one succeeds alone.
Never walk alone in your future paths.

—**Sonia Sotomayor**, Associate Justice of the US Supreme
Court, the first Hispanic and Latina to serve

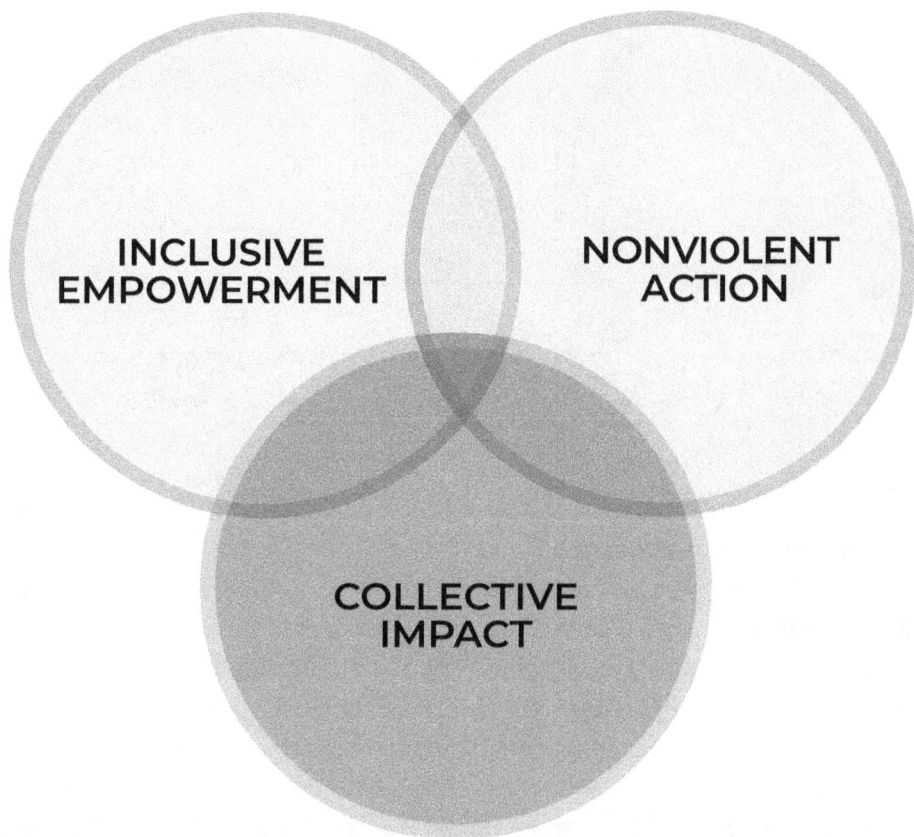

INCLUSIVE EMPOWERMENT

NONVIOLENT ACTION

COLLECTIVE IMPACT

Social Sustainability Core Value Three: Collective Impact

NINTH COURSE: A COURSE IN COLLECTIVE IMPACT

Back at my imaginary dinner party, it's time for the ninth course to be served: a course in Collective Impact.

Considering how many acts there have been in this evening's proceedings, it was a natural choice to serve a cheese course. I have selected a local Texas Hill Country goat cheese, a Humboldt Fog bleu cheese from California, and one of my all-time favorite French cheeses. Brillat Savarin is a soft-ripened triple cream cow milk cheese, hard to find, but well worth the search.

"Humor your host for a moment, if you will," I say. "Let me tell you about the first time I ever enjoyed this particular cheese. I was visiting the Cote d'Azur with my mother. We ordered a dessert that was deceptive in the simplicity of its three ingredients: A slice of warmed Brillat Savarin, swimming in a bowl of warm red wine sweetened with honey. Such a simple preparation, but the results were simply brilliant! It was one of the most amazing desserts I have ever eaten in my life. I still remember it well over twenty years later."

Anita clearly gets it. "Ah, so you are talking about three ingredients, with three entirely different characteristics. But put together creatively, the end result is magnificent. That sounds similar to the melding together of sustainability's Three Pillars."

"What I find even more interesting," César adds, "is all the unseen players who had to be involved somehow in order to achieve the end goal. There were the dairy farmers, cheese makers, grape pickers, the vintners, the beekeepers. Let's not forget the cows, the bees, and the grapevines. Each had to be skilled at what they were doing individually. Collectively the result is greater than any could have achieved alone."

"And of course," says Cousteau, "we must celebrate the chef. Perhaps we are all the sustainability chefs, working to amplify the intelligence of the collective." He proffers a bit of the dessert on his spoon. "We offer the best and brightest mix of ingredients, to serve what the world needs now."

I can feel poetry rise in me. "The right combination creates more than a series of individual solo performances. It creates a beautiful planetary symphony."

César leans in. "Such beautiful words. Perhaps we can achieve more than we have dared to dream thus far. We must combine all our unique gifts and talents for a unified cause."

"Anita," Cousteau adds, "with your business acumen and César's political skill, what would happen if we combine that with my ability to tell a great story. Grounded in scientific facts, bien sur! And of course, we must throw in Lucia's apparent flair for getting the right people together around a table and guiding the conversation."

Words are bubbling up again for Anita. "It doesn't matter who you are, where you come from, your gender, your race, or what neighborhood you grew up in."

I cut another slice of the Savarin. "What we are talking about here is the power of the collective. I'm from the South, where the term y'all is in heavy rotation. I find it to be a useful, inclusive turn of phrase that embraces everyone. Y'all means *all*."

YES WE CAN / SI SE PUEDE

For revolutionaries focused on shifting the status quo, creating collective impact is crucial to success. Collective impact is how we scale up change, from individual actions toward a groundswell, setting in motion massive and powerful movements. As we saw in Chapter Three, the labor strike was one of César Chávez's key strategies in the toolbox for nonviolent action. The coordinated action by many individual workers, organized around a common purpose, provides a concrete example of how collective action can create impact if everyone is working with a mutually agreed-upon strategy. If we aggregate many such actions over time, the collective results can galvanize a movement.

Even when the odds seem stacked against the agents of change, collective action requires the scattered participants to believe that change is possible. The slogan *Si Se Puede* (Yes It Can Be Done) captures this spirit. Dolores Huerta coined the phrase as a comeback to opponents during a recall campaign against Arizona's Republican conservative Governor Jack Williams, who had signed legislation to criminalize boycotts, make union elections impossible, and keep the UFW out of the state. The dispirited progressives in the state were commonly heard to say *"No se puede,"* or "It can't be done" in reference to the recall. Huerta hurled back her rebuttal, which became the rallying cry of the countermovement.[223] The phrase has been adopted broadly by many labor unions and civil rights organizations. An English version, "Yes We Can," was adopted by President Obama for his 2008 campaign.

By 1967, the UFW realized that its activities centered mostly in California were not going to be enough to gain the widespread awareness and sympathy needed to achieve the massive labor reforms they sought. They needed to expand their activities across the country to build broader support for their cause. As momentum began building, Chávez asked dock and warehouse workers to join in their cause by refusing to load or unload grapes. Many of them listened. Ultimately thousands of tons of the fruit were rejected and left to rot on loading docks across the country.

Emboldened by this success, Chávez began to consider whether consumer boycotts might be the ticket to broaden the movement's reach and create a tidal wave of collective impact that could tip the political scales in their favor. He had studied the boycotts that had been staged by his nonviolent heroes.

In 1930, Gandhi led thousands of followers in the famous Salt March to the Arabian sea. This was part of a British salt boycott, a response to the British Salt Act, which forced Indian subjects to buy expensive and heavily-taxed salt from the British overlords. Indians were not even allowed to collect their own salt. The Salt March was an act of defiance wherein marchers made a show of harvesting salt from the sea at the end of their journey.

Lunch counter sit-ins were a series of civil rights protests that spread rapidly throughout a single year, 1960. Inspired by Gandhi, the movement began with four young Black college students, Ezell Blair Jr., David Richmond, Franklin McCain, and Joseph McNeil, who refused to give up their seats at a Woolworth's segregated lunch counter. Within a few short months, sit-in actions spread to fifty-five cities in thirteen states throughout the South and into the North, with protests at restaurants, hotels, beaches and libraries. By the summer, many Southern dining facilities decided to integrate, a turning point in the civil rights journey.

Chávez decided to launch a North American campaign requesting that consumers boycott all table grapes. (It would have been challenging to differentiate only non-union grapes for a consumer boycott.). Later the boycott would also include wines made with non-union grapes from Christian Brothers, Almaden, and Gallo. Later a lettuce boycott was undertaken.

In Cleveland, the popular Fisher-Fazio's grocery stores were picketed as one of the largest retail food outlets in the area.[224] The hope was that if they stopped selling the grapes and lettuce, other local grocery stores would follow. Let's imagine some of the boycott events in Cleveland unfolding. This is a fictional account inspired by real events and the personal files of a current-day Cleveland resident who was part of the local union organizing activities. The character named Faith is a composite. I have used literary license to enliven the details.

Collective Impact in Practice

"Thank You HAVE A NICE DAY" is printed in cheery red on brown paper grocery bags at the Fisher-Fazio supermarket. The stores feel like a modern grocery paradise to Clevelanders. Most astonishing of all are the new-fangled electric doors that open automatically to welcome shoppers. Some patrons are eager to cash in on specials like the thirty-nine cent per pound chicken quarters. Others come for the fancy imports like artichokes in glass jars.

The volunteers selected the store in the Great Northern Shopping Center to stage a series of protests. Lots of shoppers visit Sears or Woolworth's nearby. On their way home, they might stop at Fazio's to pick up TV dinners or pot roasts.

Most grocery stores close at 6 p.m. and aren't open Sundays, so Saturdays are the best day to reach large numbers of 9-5 workers who needed to get their shopping done. Boycott volunteers usually work in teams. The largest group stands on the sidewalk in front of the parking lot leading up to the grocery store. Their signs read "PLEASE HELP FARMWORKERS—BOYCOTT GRAPES & LETTUCE."

A volunteer named Faith approaches people as they get out of their cars. She hopes her freckles and fresh-scrubbed appearance will be unintimidating, inviting shoppers to open up their minds and maybe even their pocketbooks to support farmers. She knows almost nothing about farm work. Faith has graduated from Oberlin College. She learned about the boycott at a house meeting hosted by the aunt of one of her dorm mates. The farmworkers' cause fits easily into the values of her Catholic upbringing, where Proverbs preaches to "uphold the rights of the poor." Faith cut her activist teeth on the Oberlin campus, protesting in demonstrations against the war in Cambodia and the Kent State shootings.

Like a lot of other volunteers, Faith has agreed to serve as a boycott worker. In return, the union provides her room and board plus five dollars a week. On Cleveland's West Side, just a few blocks from the office donated to the UFW by the Meat Cutters Union,[225] Faith is sharing an apartment with three women. Two are recent college grads who share her sense of idealism. The last housemate is Valentina, a Hispanic farmworker who had traveled all the way from Delano. She speaks English beautifully and has taught the other volunteers pitch-perfect traditional union songs such as "De Colores."

The crispness of September has brought a chill to the air coming off Lake Erie, causing many of the volunteers to don fuzzy sweaters or frayed denim jackets. Faith loves the picket sign that says "For Love . . . And for Justice." Two other boycott workers at the automatic entrance are handing out purple-tinged flyers printed off the mimeograph machine at the union office. One has a photo of a mother and child in squalid conditions, above large bold letters that read: "Your Salad, or Their Future? Please Boycott Lettuce!"[226]

The person who's behind the wheel of the AMC Gremlin pulling in looks like she might be a good prospect. Faith waits patiently, moving into position exactly where they'd be walking by. The UFW guidebook script of openers was going to come in handy.[227]

"Excuse me miss, have you heard about the plight of the farmworkers and how we are trying to stop the grapes?" The woman shakes her head. "Well, if you can spare a minute, I'd like to tell you about it." Faith plunges on since the mother doesn't seem to be in a rush. "Children not much older than your son here are forced to work in the fields for extremely low wages. They don't have rest breaks, toilets, decent housing, food or water. We're here on behalf of the United Farmworkers Union to ask this store not to sell non-union grapes and iceberg lettuce. Can you help us?"

The woman nods. The pledge cards are attached to Faith's union-issue clipboard. She wished she had a better writing surface. Some volunteers are using ironing boards at their events. Cheap and easy to transport, they provide the perfect height for signing petitions and pledge cards. Such groups are often called Ironing Board Brigades.[228]

The woman takes the pen and fills out the form. *"Dear farm workers, I _____ pledge not to eat or buy iceberg (head) lettuce for the duration of the boycott. I pledge to tell all my friends about the lettuce and grape boycott."* There was also a place on the form to volunteer to host a house meeting.[229] House meetings were how Chávez first built grassroots support that blossomed into a movement. These kitchen table gatherings provide an unintimidating venue for enrolling others. Kitchens provided a safe place to build personal connections, to listen to people's questions and concerns one-on-one.

When shoppers were asked how they felt about the boycott, they'd say things like "I'd never thought about my buying meaning anything," or "Once you realized there was something horrible going on, it made you feel good because you realized there was something concrete you could do."

Not only did the UFW have the AFL-CIO, the International Union of Electricians, the Retail Clerks International Union, plus unionized bakery workers, plumbers and pipe fitters on their side, they also had the church. The National Conference of Catholic Bishops unanimously adopted a resolution endorsing the grape and lettuce boycotts. In Cleveland, letters of support were received from the bishops of the Episcopal diocese, rabbis at the local temple, and ministers of the United Church of Christ. During Farm Worker Week in May, many churches were holding special services devoted to farmworkers, paired with information tables and pledge cards.[230]

Faith was inspired by how the Cleveland clergy had rallied behind the boycott. The church was a key component of the boycott strategy. The union's instructions directed each city to pursue collective support including a four-pronged operation requiring organization of the community, church, schools, and labor.[231]

Support from the local church is about to take a dramatic turn on the day when several nuns appear at Fisher-Fazio's. Sister Judith Maloney and Sister Renee Krisko show up at the store with the intention of blessing the grapes. The Sisters are members of the Order of the Congregation of Saint Joseph, working on a wide variety of social justice issues including immigration, anti-racism, human trafficking, and environmental sustainability.[232]

John Fazio has gotten wind of what is about to happen, and he is waiting for them, his collar crisp and his tie straight. His family has been in the grocery trade since the 1920s. As Sicilian immigrants, his ancestors started a produce stand in the Cleveland Heights neighborhood, eventually owning six supermarkets and later merging with the failing Fisher grocery chain in the 1960s.[233] If there was one thing John and his brother Carl know, it's fruits and vegetables. How dare these women try to tell them their business? He knows he had to keep a lid on his temper since they are Catholic Sisters. Quietly, he asks the nuns to leave his store. But they can't seem to hear him.

His usual friendly neighborhood grin begins to evaporate. He begins to address the women more overtly, annunciating each word. "LADIES," he tells the nuns and protesters, "you are obviously not here to shop. You have no business here. If you don't leave now, I WILL HAVE YOU ALL ARRESTED—for trespassing!"

But there seems to be no quieting these revolutionists working on behalf of the humble farmworkers and their families. The nuns know their church is behind them. They form a semicircle around the fruit as they begin to join in prayer. Fazio begins backing away, trying to put the mounds of grapes between him and a retailer's worst enemy: bad publicity. But there is no escaping this headline fodder. Shoppers are staring. A small crowd lugging half-empty grocery carts has begun to gather.

Sister Judith chants her blessing for the tainted grapes. Sister Renee joins in. "We pray that Thou would bless and forgive Mr. Fazio and all his shoppers who might buy these grapes. Lead us not into temptation, but deliver us from evil." The usual bustle of the store has evaporated into a huddled shopper's hush.

A short while later, the six women are arrested. The nuns in their habits are loaded into the police cars outside the store. Supporters are chanting "Don't buy lettuce, don't buy grapes, don't buy wine that Gallo makes." The judge rules against arguments that the nuns' actions were justifiable on moral grounds, and the six women are all found guilty of trespassing.[234]

Across the country, the "creative peskiness" of boycott organizers blossomed as did their organizing skills. The decentralized nature of the boycott allowed organizers to make many of their own decisions on-the-fly, creating a training ground for grassroots community organization. If one thing failed, they experimented with another.

New leaders emerged from such ranks. Sustainability's victories often show up in a dispersed and widespread manner. But no matter how small the victory may seem, a rising tide lifts all boats. In this story, the breadth and geographic spread of the boycott activities meant that every individual boycott did not have to succeed as long as many of them did. In some cities, boycotters held candlelight vigils outside the homes of grocery store owners. They staged sit-ins at corporate offices. They wrote telegrams to elected officials. They stalled their cars at the entrances to grocery store parking lots. They bought shares in Safeway and Jewel supermarkets and then disrupted annual shareholder meetings. The less confrontational boycott participants would create store inconvenience by loading up grocery carts with frozen foods and canned goods, abandoning them at the checkout line after asking if the store carried non-union grapes.[235] Their well-organized, peaceful tactics proved impossible to ignore.

Groundswell and Victory

While the boycott actions on the ground in Cleveland never did change Fazio's mind, the collective impact of all the boycotts across the country finally created the groundswell of support the UFW was looking for. Tiring of the bad publicity and the costs of dealing with protests, executives began pressuring growers to resolve their labor disputes. Some supermarkets and chains folded, refusing to stock grapes on their shelves (even though some put them back as soon as the protesters left).[236] By late 1974, the market for table grapes was crashing. An estimated 7.2 million boxes of unsold grapes were piling up in cold storage warehouses.[237] According to one poll, between 1973 and 1975, 17 million Americans were boycotting grapes, with many of these also boycotting lettuce and Gallo wine.[238]

When progressive Democrat Jerry Brown became California's governor in 1974, the tables would decisively turn in the UFW's favor. Brown was the youngest Golden State governor in 111 years. He favored the underdog. "The farmworkers do not have the power the growers have. The growers have the lawyers, they have the allies, they belong to golf clubs, they talk to editors of newspapers . . . This is power."[239] He sent a clear signal about his political intentions from day one: two of the fifteen paragraphs of his inaugural speech were devoted to the needs of farmworkers.[240]

Over the ensuing months, Brown would begin collecting ideas for a Farm Labor Bill. He invited Chávez, who showed up wearing his usual plaid work shirt, to spend a Saturday with him at Brown's Los Angeles home. The meeting wasn't quite the private audience Chávez was expecting. They were joined by a crowd of aides and various manila folder-toting officials. The tension was palpable amid the coffee cups and the mile-high piles of draft bill language. They didn't seem to be getting anywhere. Brown invited Chávez to step outside for a walk. Freed by the ability to connect one-on-one during their private stroll, the two began forging a closer, more personal bond. After the trust walk, the group of aides and officials, along with Brown and Chávez, started to make progress negotiating terms the UFW would later embrace.

Within months, the two would be at the Governor's Office at the California State Capitol building, finalizing negotiations that would lead to Brown's first bill as Governor. This was a dramatic contrast to the behavior of Jerry's father, Governor Pat Brown, ten years earlier. He had left Chávez standing on the Capitol steps at the end of the march from Delano, snubbing his requests to talk farmworker rights. This time, the younger Brown committed himself to brokering the end to the long-standing feud between the Teamsters Union and the UFW.

A round-robin of talks in May 1975 took place with the UFW in one room and Teamsters in another. Brown led the delicate negotiations, dancing back and forth between the two rooms and each group's demands until he successfully brokered an agreement. Thirty days later, the landmark Agricultural Labor Relations Act was signed into law, the first law to establish collective bargaining rights of farmworkers in California. The new requirements established the right to join unions without retribution, to vote in secret ballot elections, and to strike. Further empowering the workers, growers could face severe penalties, including back pay to strikers, if they failed to negotiate in good faith.[241]

As Brown took up his pen to sign the sweeping legislation into law, over 10,000 farmworkers became guaranteed these rights. He would later say, "Many problems depend on an intangible . . . on a principle, on an idea. And an idea is more powerful than anything else. If that idea is grounded within the structure of a people, there is no stopping it if it fits with the time."[242] In the months following the law's adoption, almost 50,000 farmworkers voted for the first time.[243] They were a collective force to be reckoned with.

The Chávez story abounds with examples of collective organization. He led labor strikes and sparked the union's collective bargaining on behalf of members. With the experience of the grape boycott, the UFW went beyond the impact of its union members. It learned to amplify its success by engaging a broad coalition including non-labor community members, schools, and churches.

SOCIAL SUSTAINABILITY CORE VALUE 3:

COLLECTIVE IMPACT
Gathering together to scale up

I have seen that in any great undertaking it is not enough
for a man to depend simply upon himself.
— **Lone Man (Isna-la-wica), Teton Sioux**

Relying on the collective power of a group is essential to advancing the cause of sustainability. A *collective* is a group of people, animals, or things. English is rich with collective nouns that elegantly describe gathering together—a caravan of travelers, a choir of singers, a swarm of bees, a pride of lions, a loaf of bread, a quiver of arrows. Such organized groups have huge potential energy compared to an isolated individual.

The term collective impact was introduced in 2011 as an approach to a common problem-solving agenda by actors from different sectors.[244] The definition has been refined to be centered on equity, as "a network of community members, organizations, and institutions that advance equity by learning together, aligning, and integrating their actions to achieve population and systems-level change."[245] While the idea of collaboration is obviously not new, the complexity of large-scale social change requires broad cross-sector collaboration in order to be successful. The norm has tended to fall back on many individual organizations trying to tackle big problems with uncoordinated isolated interventions, sometimes competing for the same scarce resources. This tends to be particularly true within the nonprofit sector.

There are two categories of problems: technical problems, which are well-defined problems with easily envisioned answers; and adaptive problems, which are complex problems with unknown answers, in which no single entity encompasses the authority or resources to deliver a solution.[246] Technical problems such as building a bridge, or establishing inventory controls at a food bank, are better suited to simple, more hierarchical forms of problem-solving.

Most sustainability challenges are adaptive. They encompass vast interconnected systems necessitating a Long View. To move the needle, complex problems—with so many convoluted, scattered aspects—require the action of many individuals and organizations, equally dispersed.[247]

Sharing Leadership

The Grammy-winning Orpheus Chamber Orchestra has recorded over seventy albums on major classical labels, having toured forty-six countries across four continents. What is most remarkable is that they do this without a conductor. Music is fundamentally a creative endeavor, rendering traditional orchestra models of top-down conductor leadership a bit of a mismatch with musicians who aspire toward self-expression. The democratic Orpheus model relies on constantly rotating formal leadership roles, combined with many spontaneous ad hoc leadership moments. The orchestra's thirty-four members "work together in a collective, and rotate leadership roles for all works performed, giving flight to unconventional interpretations."[248] This unique egalitarian structure is based on non-hierarchical collaboration in pursuit of excellence.

For collective impact to function effectively, cross-sector entities must feel empowered and act together. The entities spread leadership in a polycentric system. There is no one-size-fits-all approach; each process must be defined by its context. Most importantly, the players must share a common vision or agenda for the impact they seek.

When there's a clearly articulated shared purpose, a variety of players can take part in different ways. We describe such a distributed system of change as cascading levels of linked collaboration within a strategic action framework.[249]

For example, the Children's Health System of Dallas gathered a range of partners to coalesce fresh perspectives on children's health.

The focus was asthma. Based on deep listening to elicit new insights, they successfully forged a broad-based coalition of health professionals, families, school officials, and public housing administrators. Each was able to understand their role in decreasing childhood asthma. The health system has now linked partners across all these sectors. Programs based on social, environmental, and clinical outcomes are now connected, too. Measuring progress over three years, they have made significant progress toward reducing childhood asthma. The program cut the number of unique patient visits with a primary diagnosis of asthma by nearly 50 percent.[250]

Sustainability thrives on a shared sense of optimism. A shared belief that change is possible is necessary for collective impact to succeed. For example, ending apartheid in South Africa required a collective sense of optimism that change was possible. Nelson Mandela never gave up hope that a peaceful end to apartheid could be achieved; his sense of optimism proved to be contagious. Outside political pressure and ongoing local protests sealed the deal.

Another precursor to success is a wide array of participants who share a belief that change can be achieved through the accretion of many small efforts. This way of looking at the world assigns importance and validity to each individual player in the collective. It also acknowledges that there is no single answer, but rather thousands upon thousands of unique answers, all contributing to pool their influence in order to collectively aggregate change within a "thousand points of light" model.

In his powerful book *Blessed Unrest*, author Paul Hawken describes sustainability as "the largest movement in the world." He compiles a massive global catalogue of sustainability-focused organizations working toward environmental activism, social justice, and indigenous rights. For Hawken, these are all interrelated actions under the single banner of sustainability.

According to Hawken, the sustainability movement represents "a reimagination of public governance emerging from place, culture and people." It comprises hundreds of thousands of organizations. "The movement can't be divided because it is so atomized—a collection of small pieces, loosely joined. It forms, dissipates, and then regathers quickly, without central leadership, command, or control. This movement strives to disperse concentrations of power through witnessing, informing, and massing."

The growing success of collective impact provides a useful antidote to a widespread sense of apathy that nothing can be done in the face of seemingly intractable problems. Combatting climate change requires a collective impact model. It will require people on every corner of the planet to collectively curb greenhouse gas emissions. Leveraging collective impact puts the power in the hands of the many, instead of the few. We share a sense of responsibility for reversing the messes we have gotten ourselves into. This invites everyone to take action, instead of waiting for someone else to do something.

The collective mindset is the lifeblood of revolutionary thinking. Increasingly, citizens are realizing that government alone is unable to solve our complex sustainability conundrums. The sustainability revolution will require everyone, from every sector, every walk of life, every lived experience, to collectively take up the reins of change.

Yes, we can.

THE EVOLUTION OF AGRICULTURE WORKER RIGHTS

Through the collective impact efforts of many individuals, from many walks of life, the Agricultural Labor Relations Act of 1975 was passed. Adopted at the height of the United Farmworkers' movement, it served as a vehicle to empower tens of thousands of workers who realized the potentiality of organizing for the first time. Unfortunately, the promise of the law has never been fully realized and progress since then has largely been a mixed bag. Over the years, Union activity in the fields would dissipate and the Union would never again appear so powerful and well-organized as it did in the time surrounding the grape strike.

The wages and conditions of the largely undocumented farmworkers of California are not necessarily significantly better than they were decades ago.[251] However, some progress continues to be made, indicating gradual evolution toward better protections for the workforce who grows the food we rely on. The New York Farm Laborers Fair Labor Practices Act, signed into law by former Governor Andrew Cuomo, took effect in January 2021. It requires permits for migrant farm worker housing, overtime pay, at least one day of rest per work week, workers' compensation, paid family leave, and the right to organize.[252]

Elsewhere, increasing climate, change-related heat waves and fires in the Pacific Northwest have wreaked havoc on a farming way of life and the lives of farm owners and migrant field workers, spawning the need for new health protections. Brutal triple-digit heat for days on end caused deaths of day laborers, resulting in Oregon and Washington establishing new worker safety regulations starting in August 2021. These include mandatory access to shade, cool drinking water, rest breaks, and wellness checks. The rules also require temporary housing to be maintained at a maximum temperature of 78 degrees.

The states of Washington, Minnesota, and California have similar rules. Hazardous air quality caused by wildfires also threatens the health of outdoor workers, particularly those with asthma or other health conditions. The Oregon mandate requires employers to provide filtration masks to workers if the air quality index reaches unsafe levels. Continuing droughts and fires also ruin crops or make it impossible to continue growing food at all. In 2021, Meyer Orchards of Medford Oregon, a four-generation family farm in operation for 111 years, was forced to throw in the towel. They chopped down their entire 115-acre orchard of pear trees—the drought made it too costly to irrigate any longer.[253]

Today, many organizations have taken up the causes of food justice and farmworker rights. In 2011, Mily Treviño-Sauceda and Mónica Ramirez, working from Oxnard, California, formed the National Farmworkers Women's Alliance to champion the nation's 700,000-plus vulnerable women working in the agricultural industry.[254] These women suffer from unequal pay, exploitation, violence and sexual abuse, and reproductive health problems stemming from pesticides. In 2017, they helped launch the Time's Up legal defense fund, to support women working low-wage jobs. This is a story of the power of love and solidarity to empower disparate people to join forces.

Mily and Mónica were planning to contact women in the entertainment industry in conjunction with sexual harassment allegations against Harvey Weinstein and others. Some supporters urged that the letter should criticize the Hollywood movement for leaving out female farmworkers in a broader discussion of women's right to freedom from sexual harassment. Instead, the letter took a tone of empathy and allyship on behalf of many underrepresented workers including janitors, hotel and domestic workers.

"Dear sisters," the letter read, "even though we work in very different environments, we share a common experience of being preyed upon by individuals who have the power to hire, fire, blacklist and otherwise threaten our economic, physical and emotional security." The letter went on to say "We understand the hurt, confusion, isolation and betrayal that you might feel . . . Please know that you're not alone. We believe and stand with you." The letter was later shared by one of Hollywood's biggest influencers, Reese Witherspoon, with nearly four million followers on Facebook. The collective voice of #MeToo had expanded exponentially to include women, according to NBC News, "from opposite ends of the country's economic and class divides: actresses and farmworkers." In addition, the women of Hollywood realized that their voices were powerful enough to influence change for others beyond their small group.

Here's Hope: Perhaps the most inspiring and promising recent example of transformational change for farmworkers is occurring in Florida. The Coalition of Immokalee Workers have successfully organized against abysmal living and working conditions within the tomato industry. Immokalee is an unincorporated community in Southwest Florida, on land once occupied by the Seminole and Miccosukee peoples. The word Immokalee means "your home." The coalition describes the social conditions they are working to reform as a little-known form of American apartheid.[255]

The Coalition works to end slavery and human trafficking in the agricultural industry and to establish supply chain standards to eliminate forced labor. *Harvard Business Review* named the coalition's Fair Food program as one of the 15 most important social impact success stories of the past century. Their labor standards program leverages the collective impact of farmworkers, Florida tomato growers, a national consumer network, and retail buyers including Subway, Whole Foods, and Walmart. The organization staged a national boycott of Taco Bell, protesting the use of Florida tomatoes tied to unfair wages and working conditions. The coalition gained broad student, religious, and community support, including many campus-wide boycotts of Taco Bell. National news attention ensued, causing Taco Bell to eventually agree to the Coalition's demands to purchase only Fair Food tomatoes at slightly higher prices, with the price increase guaranteed to go directly to tomato pickers.[256]

Food can be both a unifying and divisive issue—the way we grow it, harvest it, source it, prepare it, and dispose of it when we are done.

This next section picks up the thread of how toxics can impact human health, related to our food sources as well as how we power our homes and businesses.

COLLECTIVE ACTION
MOTHERS AGAINST TOXICS

Eight years after Rachel Carson published her seminal work *Silent Spring*, identifying DDT as a killer with both ecological and human health consequences, Chávez took up the cause of eliminating harmful agricultural pesticides. Carson's book is widely seen as a tipping point for the environmental movement. The title refers to the risk of a spring devoid of birdsong that would ensue if the massive bird deaths that were already being caused by DDT were allowed to continue. She accused the government of blindly accepting chemical industry propaganda. Animals exposed to DDT in laboratory studies developed tumors, and after decades of its widespread use, it was classified as a probable human carcinogen. Today, the World Health Organization bans DDT for all uses except for control of malaria-bearing mosquitoes, with the benefits to human health seen as outweighing the risks.[257]

The UFW integrated a DDT ban into their contracts before the EPA enacted its 1972 DDT cancellation order. In the San Joaquin Valley of 1983, high incidences of childhood cancers, referred to as cancer clusters, were beginning to alarm parents. The UFW produced a controversial short film called *The Wrath of Grapes*. It featured a five-year-old child named Felipe Franco, born without legs and arms. Chávez held press conferences with affected families. "Farmworkers and their children are society's canaries,"[258] he said, comparing them to the canary in the coal mine whose death would serves as an early indicator that the air was unsafe to miners.

Grapes continue to show up today on the consumer "dirty dozen" list of produce containing high levels of pesticide residues, in addition to strawberries, spinach, tomatoes, and potatoes.[259] Public information tools like the dirty dozen help busy consumers with quick reference guides to assist them in making the best sustainability choices to protect the environment and their family's health.

MODERN-DAY REVOLUTIONISTS: MOMS UNITED AGAINST TOXICS

While Chávez was unable to gain the leverage against pesticides that he had achieved with his other labor causes, many Latinx are working today to halt the environmental toxins and climate change they see to be impacting the health of their children and communities.

Gabriela Rivera, a former undocumented immigrant from Chihuahua, Mexico, is the field manager of a powerful nonprofit called the Moms Clean Air Force. This organization of over one million moms and dads brandishes a mission "to protect children from air pollution and climate change. We envision a safe, stable future where all children breathe clean air."[260] Their members believe that protecting children is a non-partisan issue. They function as an educational and political advocacy organization fighting for clean renewable energy, clean vehicle emission standards, as well as mercury and air toxin standards. They describe themselves as an unbeatable combination of passion and power.

Moms Clean Air Force joined up with another group, called GreenLatinos, to launch an initiative called EcoMadres. Their EcoMadres Cafecitos program hosts "intimate coffee break-style conversations" about environmental impacts on Latinx family health, similar to the house meetings that were the backbone of UFW organizing.[261] Their actions are motivated by the fact that climate change has disproportionately impacted low-income neighborhoods. People of color, and in particular Latinx, disproportionately bear the burden of toxic environments. Poverty and a lack of access to adequate healthcare and health insurance, combined with proximity to environmental threats, put Latinx at greater risk. Such a confluence of factors is often referred to as the social determinants of health.

The statistics make it undeniable. Latino children are 60 percent more at risk than white children of having asthma attacks exacerbated by air pollution, while 68 percent of US Latinos live in areas that do not meet Federal Air Quality Standards. Air pollution is linked to heart disease, stroke, and even some forms of dementia. Air pollutants can enter the bloodstreams of pregnant mothers, impacting their children even before they are born. Air pollution is also a problem that knows no borders.

The profile of Moms Clean Air Force has been raised by members including movie stars such as Julianne Moore and Maya Rudolph. Dolores Huerta, at age 91, is also a part of the movement. In December of 2019, Gabriela Rivera interviewed Huerta on behalf of EcoMadres.

Here's Hope: Huerta offered this advice to all the women listening on a Facebook Live broadcast, which was delivered in both Spanish and English. "To all the abuelitas, tias, grandmothers, all the women in our society: We have to get involved, and work on environmental injustice, for all of us."[262] Another woman of color joining the organization is Heather Mcteer Toney, the first African-American, first female, and youngest mayor ever to serve Greenville, Mississippi. As the national field director for Moms Clean Air Force, Toney is on a personal crusade to change perceptions that Black people are not environmentalists.

The ranks of the Clean Air Force also include thousands of people the world has probably never heard of. Phoenix mother Columba Sainz discovered that her child's asthma was linked to the county where she resides, which received an "F" grade for air quality from the American Lung Association. Yarita Perez is a mother and veteran who is proud to serve her country through her environmental activism. Make no mistake, these are sustainability revolutionists. They exist on every street corner, in every country, every city, and every rural community. They look like you, they look like me. The next vignette features one of these local heroes.

The story is based on newspaper reports, video accounts, and published photographs. Some details are imagined in my literary retelling.

Something Rotten in Paradise

One of the world's sustainability revolutionists is a woman named Michelle Irizarry. She and her children live in a Florida community that is the epitome of an idealized American suburb. Located not far from Orlando, here one can find a master-planned community surrounding a championship golf course.

The street layout is a developer's dream, with its perfectly landscaped winding streets and cul-de-sacs. Many of the nice homes have swimming pools and clipped lawns that would be perfect for a game of croquet.

Residents enjoy 271 days of Florida sunshine per year, along with a snow-free winter. There's an IHOP, Dunkin Donuts, both Walmart and Target superstores, and top-ranking schools nearby. When family members come to visit, they can choose from four different theme parks including Disney World and Lego Land. But there's something wrong. The residents' lives are darkened by the shadows of two looming towers of a coal-fired power plant.

Emissions from such power plants can include ash particles, sulfur dioxide, nitrogen dioxide, heavy metals, and radioactive material in coal ash, a waste byproduct of the coal-burning process. Burning coal releases radioactive contaminants including uranium, thorium, ruthenium, and radioactive isotopes. Studies demonstrate that people living near coal plants have higher death rates and die at an earlier age. Toxic air pollution from the burning of coal is linked to a myriad of human health impacts. For children, it has been linked to infant death, low birth weights, and risks of developmental and behavioral disorders. Higher rates of asthma, cancer, heart and lung ailments, and neurological issues top the list of widespread health impacts. It has been estimated that these toxic effects cause up to 10,000 annual deaths worldwide. However, due to a lack of the necessary data from some countries, the numbers are likely much higher.

In one study, coal plants in India and China which operate without some scrubber controls were associated with the highest death tolls.[263]

The human health toll piles onto other ills including climate change, acid rain, soil contamination, water pollution, and the ecological disruption caused by the mining of coal.[264] Standards in the US requiring clean technology upgrades have become part of a game of political football, fueled by arguments that it is too costly.

Often throughout our racist history, undesirable infrastructure such as coal plants are located in the neighborhoods of people of color. This is environmental racism, a practice repeated over and over, passing the unwanted impacts of climate change and industrial activities disproportionately to Blacks, Hispanics, and the low income. Given language barriers and the fact that many people in such communities are too busy to speak up, working multiple jobs just to make ends meet, the chances of community awareness and backlash can be diminished.

Michelle Irizarry is a water resources engineer, educated at MIT and the University of Puerto Rico. She is able to explain technical topics using simple, unintimidating language. At the same time, she has co-authored numerous scientific articles with abstract titles such as *Probabilistic Projection of Mean Sea Level and Coastal Extremes* or *Climate Links and Variability of Extreme Sea Level Events*.[265] Whether conversing fluently in Spanish or English, Michelle projects a calm, clear perspective on the world around her. She is a master communicator, fluid in many mediums.

Her role as a mother is even more important to Michelle than her role as a scientist. She and her two young daughters live about a mile from the Orlando Utilities Commission's Stanton Energy Center. With the center's 50-story cooling towers looming over the community, it's difficult to forget that they live within the powerplant's viewshed as well as its airshed. Stanton generates power from a blend of natural gas, landfill gas, solar energy, and coal, with a capacity of 1,850 megawatts. According to the powerplant website, their vast cooling towers are "iconic," as part of "one of the most reliable and environmentally responsible power stations in the nation." Interestingly, the site includes a 3,200-acre wildlife refuge.[266] But to quote former Texas Agricultural Secretary and populist columnist Jim Hightower, that refuge might be "like putting earrings on a pig." If the powerplant air emissions are shortening the lives of area residents, no amount of pasted-on green features can erase the sustainability damage being done.

Irizarry's LinkedIn profile lists her interests and causes as children, education, arts, and culture. The latter is not surprising, because in addition to being a scientist, she is also an accomplished artist. Today, she is taking a much-needed break from her day job to work on her latest painting. A vibrant finished canvas depicting a sea turtle rests against the studio wall behind her. She wears a demure pin-tucked blouse in white, scattered with little red and gray dots resembling a field of flowers. Her shoulder-length black hair is simply styled. As a busy mom she doesn't have time for a lot of fuss. At times she appears Madonna-like, with her upright graceful bearing and luminous complexion.

Irizarry's latest work-in-progress is a large, ambitious canvas. The tubes of oil paint she has selected for the piece are scattered about, many in vibrant shades of blue and magenta. But the largest part of the canvas is the drab color of dirt. Dry, cracked, dusty earthen shades of beige and brown. The parched ground in the painting is cracked, like so many broken dinner plates. The canvas depicts her daughters playing in an arid field. The casualness of their play clothes belies the seriousness of the subject. Looming in the background are the unmistakable stacks of the sinister coal-fired powerplant, spewing gray fumes into a blue sky. More clouds of air pollution emanate exponentially from additional sources, ominously cloaked just out of sight beyond the horizon.[267]

"I'm titling it *Where Will the Children Play*?" she explains. "It shows a little flower growing. It shows hope that we can stave off the most catastrophic predictions of climate change. Change is not going to happen in a vacuum. Change can only happen when enough of us protect, march, poll, and demand our elected officials to be accountable for pollution and to put our kids' health and the health of the planet first."[268]

As a scientist, Michelle understands the relationship between burning fossil fuels and the acceleration of climate change. The long-term disruption being created is something she describes in poetic terms. "The climate system has a memory." It's a slow-moving disaster, something that has been difficult to pinpoint and fully grasp. But it's getting harder and harder to ignore. "I want to make sure I leave a livable world for them . . . if we don't act soon, we are going to feel the effects for hundreds of years, so the sooner we act, the better it's going to be for future generations."[269]

Michelle's focus has become distracted. Her brow wrinkles with worry as she looks out the window of her studio at her daughters playing outside. The scene seems innocent enough: a typical suburban yard with grass, lollipop shrubs, and a few trees. Her daughters love to play hide and seek among the thick trunks. On another day they might be collecting pebbles or digging for worms. But their mother doesn't feel comfortable letting them spend a lot of time outside anymore. Soon their play time will be up. She will call them inside the house where she changes the air filters of her HVAC system as frequently as she can. She hardly ever opens a window anymore.

The Stanton Energy Center includes a massive pile of waste produced from burning coal. This 175-foot mountain of un-remediated coal ash is capable of sending dust particles into the wind containing mercury, cadmium, and arsenic.[270] Coal ash management rules are still in question, and the EPA has promised to revisit them.

But there is hope. Luckily, many utilities are taking their own steps to retire coal, driven by climate goals and economics. The Orlando Utilities Commission has committed to retiring the Stanton plant by 2027, at the latest. Their goal is net-zero emissions from power generation by 2050. They will invest in alternative energy options including combined cycle gas turbines, solar photovoltaics, onshore wind, and battery storage.[271]

Michelle leads a group called the Central Florida Climate Artists Group. Her work organizing other environmental artists has given her a meaningful outlet for her concerns. Many of the artists' works were featured at an exhibition she co-curated at the Orlando Science Center, entitled Earth's Voice: An Environmental Art Exhibition. She wants the exhibit to encourage reflection and action. [272] Both of these are essential to building a backbone for the sustainability revolution.

In addition to her environmental art activities, Michelle's work with the Moms Clean Air Force has also given her reason for optimism. "Before I joined the Moms Clean Air Force I was in deep despair over the state of the planet. Thanks to (the) organization . . . now I have some hope. I feel like action is an antidote to despair and depression. Democracy is alive and well; we just have to use it." [273]

Challenges such as cleaning up powerplants, tailpipe emissions, or lead contamination of drinking water only invigorate the Moms Clean Air Force. Their focus is clear. Their group connects the dots between environmental health, climate change, and children's health. As their website explains, "Why Moms? Moms have passion and power. Moms will do everything we can to keep our children safe and sound. That's why we are uniting to ensure that our children have clean air right now, and for their future. Because sometimes, being a good mom means being an active citizen." [274]

The sustainability revolution requires each of us to rise up, in our own way, to become part of the change we seek. No contribution is too large, or too small. Organizing with other sustainability revolutionists helps us to scale up our impact to realize positive changes in the world.

AFTERWORD

If I can't dance, I don't want to
be part of your revolution.

— **Jack Frager**, Anarchist printer

TENTH COURSE: A COURSE IN REVOLUTION

We have come to the final course of our evening's communion. The cheese is in remnants, and the beeswax candles have burnt to stubs. Soon, we will be saying our goodbyes and my guests will be finding their way home. But before that happens, there's still time to top off the party with a nightcap.

Endings can be challenging for many of us, but as one of my favorite poets T.S. Eliot said in *The Four Quartets*, "To make an end is to make a beginning. The end is where we start from."

For my imaginary dinner party, I have decided to finish the night with Calvados apple brandy, served up in petite curved snifters that fit comfortably in the palm. I decide to explain why they are significant to me. "These little glasses are treasured family heirlooms that once belonged to my Greek and Italian grandparents. Their son, my father, was the person who first taught me about sustainability." My guests take a moment to admire the handsome Greek key design on the glasses, taking in this important detail from my personal history. We must all share more of ourselves with our fellow revolutionists. Allowing ourselves to be vulnerable also helps to build our strength.

Once the nightcaps have all been distributed, Cousteau sees fit to share yet more of his expert knowledge about his cultural heritage. "The tradition of drinking fermented apples dates all the way back to the time of Charlemagne." He takes a careful sip, eyes closed as he inhales the fruity perfume. I'm nervous as he pauses. "You have selected an excellent vintage from Normandy, Lucia. My compliments."

Relaxing into his approval, I begin reflecting on what I have learned this night. "One of the most important things from our time together is that it doesn't matter how different our experiences are for us to be able to join together around a common cause."

"So true," Anita chimes in. "I have also learned that I need to take the time to do my homework on all the facts and all the history, before I jump to action. Those closest to a problem are the most likely to know what the solution should be."

Cousteau jumps into the exchange next. "I was beginning to lose my faith in humanity, but tonight I feel it restored. It's as though this gathering has cauterized a wound. I have a new sense of expansiveness and abundance, giving me the chance to heal and hope. That is tonight's gift for me."

I notice that without the candles to light the table, the room has grown rather dark. Yet I don't feel inclined to spoil the mood by turning on the overhead lights. A nearly full moon has risen during our dinner, its moonbeams now streaming down onto the table through the open window.

César is rising out of his seat now, beaming like a schoolboy as he moves toward the window. He points up toward the lunar orb. "One thing that losing our family farm could never take away from us was stargazing. I remember as a kid, the Milky Way was so clear I felt I could reach out and touch it."

Anita jumps out of her chair, performing a nimble pirouette as she crosses the room toward the window. She pulls the curtain wider. "Across the planet, we all stare in awe at the same moon, the same stars. When we connect to such universal elements, it helps us remember we are all one human family."

"Once everyone realizes that fundamental fact," Cousteau says, "the possibilities are endless."

It's well past midnight, but I don't feel tired at all. I could go on all night like this. I am beginning to feel positively buoyant, and I'm pretty certain it isn't just the wine going to my head. I do a little dance in step with the Miles Davis jazz tune now playing in the background. "With each of our brilliant minds working together as one on sustainability, bringing diverse perspectives and experiences and wisdom, I'm beginning to think that there's no problem we can't tackle."

César needs no encouragement. "Perfecta! I have been reminded that I need many more dinner table conversations like this, to discover new friends and unexpected allies. We can roll up our sleeves to do the work, but we can also dance together, in celebration of this amazing planet we are a part of."

Anita agrees by sharing something she learned from César tonight. "We must be sure to include the people we don't understand at first, the people who don't look like us or speak the same language as us."

I join my guests under the gaze of the luminous moon. These ideas feel infectious, undeniable even. I lift my glass, prompting everyone to do this same.

"Let us drink a toast. To a new pact for our planet's future. To a giant banquet table with space for everyone. To dancing at the revolution. To joining all the forces of good for our environmental, our economic, and our social causes."

In unison, we sing out our vision in the form of a toast. "To our planet's bright future—to the Sustainability Revolution!"

OUR FUTURE IS UNWRITTEN

I hold a fantasy scene, folded close within my heart's deepest longing. In my imagination, I pick up on the thread of inspiration provided by the Moms Clean Air Force story. My fantasy envisions the power of over a million moms and growing, joining forces to fight for sustainability. My scene is also inspired by some of my favorite writings from Italo Calvino, Thich Nat Hahn, Robert Macfarlane, and Dan Millman.

I have let my imagination run wild in the following postcard from the future. I hope that this final tale, as well as the stories that have preceded it, will help you feel the idea of sustainability more fully, to breathe sustainability deep into your very cells, to embrace it into the core of your being until it flows naturally through your veins. If I have been successful even in some tiny way, you will hold on to some rays of inspiration and hope, even as we end our journey together. I entrust you to take up, in your own way, the cause of the sustainability revolution. That story is far from over.

It is another perfect gift of a day on Earth. We tend to forget that each 24-hour cycle is a miracle, resulting from the phenomenon created by the orb's rotating axis, always reliably punctuated by a night full of stars. Five billion years previous, a huge explosion produced a vast cloud of gases and dust, forming a massive spinning disc from which was born our life-giving sun. The collision of another planet with Earth later threw debris into space that formed the moon, tilted the axis which forms our seasons, and eventually coalesced the earth's magnetic field which helps to protect us from deadly ultraviolet radiation. "When the cosmic dice was thrown, our planet came out with a double six," says Alistair Fothergill in *Planet Earth As You've Never Seen It Before*. "Consider our planet as a whole and all the living, breathing consequences of plain good luck."[275]

And on this particular day, amidst an all-star cast of earthly wonders as diverse as the aurora borealis, bioluminescence, lava tube caves, and Kevlar-strong spider silk, another wonder is unfolding. A long serpentine line of the human species is coming into our near-Earth view. As we grow closer, we see their arms are linked. As we grow closer still, we begin to see women and mothers of the species. Mothers of all colors and persuasions. There are grandmothers, sisters, daughters—all with their elbows confidently linked together. There are also fathers and parents of every stripe whose nurturing instincts have grown strong. Intuitively, we know they are joined together by their fierce love for their cubs, their young, their descendants.

The linked arms appear so secure, it reminds us of a grand grown-up game of Red Rover that no opponent can hope to crash through. Not a single chink in the armor. Their bodies telegraph a stiff unshakeable defiance, yet many of them are also smiling or laughing. Still others have a mysterious twinkle to their eye. These human creatures are thinking like Mother Earth herself; their wisdom has created a grand sustainability hive-mind. Their neural patterns have become like chains of snow-capped mountains with their cores deeply rooted in the molten center of the earth. Like mountains, Mother power will survive for millennia, embodying a force so powerful that it can create its own weather patterns.

Even more fittingly, we can think of this feminine collective wisdom as an aspen grove, which appears outwardly as many individual trees. Yet we know that they are actually a huge clonal colony of one individual tree, linked by a massive underground root system delivering both nutrients and information, key to the community's wellbeing. Functioning as a single giant organism, the leaves of hundreds of trees tremble together in a grand interconnected symphony. It is as though all of these organisms remember well that once, all the continents of the earth were part of a single land mass called Pangaea. It is time to remember we are all cut from the same cloth, part of one grand tribe comprising the web of life.

From our aerial view, we begin to realize that there are so many mothers in the human grove, it might be possible that they could link arms across entire continents. Already there are enough of them in North America, well over one million, to span 600 miles elbow to elbow. And their numbers are growing by the day. They are linked by sustainability.

We imagine our view on the scene telescoping away, farther and farther, until the women appear like insects below. The rainbow-colored snake line of humanity goes on and on, until the eye can see no farther. Our view pulls so far back, we can begin to see the curvature of the earth's edge. We begin to sense gravity, the wrappings of clouds, the gaseous protective lens of the atmosphere, and a scattering of cosmic dust.

We begin to imagine the long human chain miraculously spanning the landmass we call North America from north to south, across its 5,325 miles of fragile landscapes from Point Barrow, Alaska to the Panama Canal. From the delicate Tuktoyaktuk permafrost of the Northwest territories, to the Sonora desert tinajas that draw thirsty jaguar along the borderlands of the Rio Grande valley. From the boreal carbon sinks of the forests of Terra Nova Newfoundland, to the mysterious Yucatan pyramids of Chichén Itzá. From the shimmering waterfalls of the Cherokee nation's Nantahala River, to Providencia's archipelago of coral atolls.

It's impossible to fully catalogue everything there is to love and protect. But we can try.

These millions of human figures know their fate is linked with that of the Earth, that theirs is a relationship of symbiosis akin to the hermit crab protected within a borrowed mollusk shell. Informed by a vast herd of instinct, these parents have linked their own fates and voices together as a powerful unified force for sustainability. They cry out for us to find balance once again, for the birthrights of clean air, clean water, clean homes and communities. In the name of all the families who came before, for the future of their children, and their children's children. Their force is unstoppable, for theirs is the force of Mother Love. Like the she-bear or the emperor penguin, they are fierce and crafty when it comes to protecting their young. They will sacrifice themselves if necessary, to protect the future of their kind. They are stalwart in the wisdom of knowing that they, better than anyone, understand what is best for their offspring.

Their impulse toward protecting life is as strong as the urge for one cell to divide into two. Their movement is powered by the belief that together, we can do anything. They are eternal optimists, firm in the knowledge that the sun will rise again on a world that they will never stop loving. Pacha Mama is here to receive them all, the earth/time mother, magnificent in the vast fertility of her planetary wisdom. She has no limits, no bounds. She embraces all beings, from the simplest protozoa to the most gargantuan cetacean. Everyone knows that Pacha Mama's ability to nurture and heal is limitless.

As all limitations evaporate, we realize that everything that we thought we knew might not be true. Things that seemed impossible, suddenly appear doable. Every massive environmental, economic, and social challenge we thought was unsolvable, now miraculously seems within our grasp to puzzle out. Everything we ever needed to know is within us. As Dan Millman says, "The secrets of the universe are imprinted on the cells of [our] body."

As we become quiet enough to listen, all our ancestors and their wisdom are suddenly available to us. They are here to contribute guidance to us in this, and every moment. How could we have forgotten them? The spirits of children and creatures and stars yet unborn come into view, as even time dissolves in this vast symphony of imagination. Scientific and technological discoveries yet unknown are suddenly available to us in service to the collective urge toward life.

Our grand dance among the mysteries of the universe has space for everyone to be a part of it. Each voice is important. The idea that we are separate or limited is an illusion that no longer serves us. We are set free in the deep knowing that the future is unwritten. It is ours to write.

NOTES

PART ONE:

CHAPTER ONE

1   Cousteau, Jacques and Susan Schiefelbein. **The Human, the Orchid, and the Octopus: Exploring and Conserving Our Natural World**. Bloomsbury USA, 2007. Page 7. And Matsen, Brad. **Jacques Cousteau: The Sea King**. Vintage Books, Random House USA, 2009.

2   Cousteau, Jean-Michel. **My Father the Captain: My Life with Jacques Cousteau**. National Geographic Society, Washington D.C. 2010. Page 114.

3   Cousteau, Jacques-Yves, with Frédéric Dumas. **The Silent World**, National Geographic Society, Washington D.C., 2004. Page xiv.

4   Cousteau, Jacques and Susan Schiefelbein. **The Human, the Orchid, and the Octopus: Exploring and Conserving Our Natural World**. Bloomsbury USA, 2007. Pages x, xi.

5   Cousteau, Jacques. **The Ocean World**, Abradale Press/Harry N. Abrams, Inc. New York, NY. 1979, republished 1985. PP. 12-13.

6   Matsen, Brad. **Jacques Cousteau: The Sea King**. Vintage Books, Random House. USA, 2009.

7   Cousteau, Jacques and Susan Schiefelbein. **The Human, the Orchid, and the Octopus: Exploring and Conserving Our Natural World**. Bloomsbury USA, 2007. Page 3.

8   Cousteau, Jacques-Yves, with Frédéric Dumas. **The Silent World**, National Geographic Society, Washington D.C., 2004. Page xiv.

9   **The Sea King**. Page 26.

10   Ibid.

11   **The Human, the Orchid, and the Octopus**. Page 8.

CHAPTER TWO

12   Fothergill, Alistair. **Planet Earth As You've Never Seen It Before**. University of California Press, Berkeley, Los Angeles, 2007. Pages 265, 257, 258.

13   Ibid. Page 18.

14   Dizikes, Peter. *The meaning of the butterfly. Boston Globe*, June 8, 2008.

15   Farquhar, Brodie. *Wolf Reintroduction Changes Ecosystem in Yellowstone.* June 30, 2020. https://www.yellowstonepark.com/things-to-do/wildlife/wolf-reintroduction-changes-ecosystem/ Retrieved 6/4/2021.

16   New England Complex Systems Institute. http://necsi.edu/guide/concepts/emergence.html

17   Toomey, Diane. *Exploring How and Why Trees 'Talk' to Each Other.* Yale Environment 360, *Yale School of Forestry & Environmental Studies.* September 1, 2016. https://e360.yale.edu

18   XL Catlin Seaview Survey http://catlinseaviewsurvey.com

19   *Oceans crucial for our climate, food, and nutrition.* Sept. 25, 2014. Food and Agriculture Organization of the United Nations. http://www.fao.org/news/story/en/item/248479/icode

20   Glusac, Elaine. Islands of Resilience. *Hemispheres Magazine.* March 2018. Page 61.

21   Hughes, Terry P. et al. Spatial and temporal patterns of mass bleaching of corals in the Anthropocene. *Science.* Jan. 5, 2018.

22   Holthaus, Eric. Heartbroken scientists lament the likely loss of most of the world's coral reefs. Jan 5, 2018. https://grist.org

23   Adalbjornsson, Tryggvi. A Victory for Coral: UNESCO Removes Belize Reef from Its Endangered List. *New York Times.* June 27, 2018.

24   Root, Tik. How One Country Is Restoring Its Damaged Ocean. *National Geographic.* April 10, 2018. https://www.nationalgeographic.com/science/article/belize-restores-coral-reefs-oil-drilling-ban-environment

25   Many Common Sunscreens May Harm Coral. Here's What to Use Instead. NPR news, July 2, 2018. https://www.npr.org/sections/health-shots/2018/07/02/624379378/many-common-sunscreens-may-harm-coral-heres-what-to-use-instead

26   Boyd, David R. **The Rights of Nature: A Legal Revolution That Could Save the World**. ECW Press, 2017. Page 224.

CHAPTER THREE

27   **Slum Clearance: 1932–1952**, CQ Researcher, CQ Researcher Archives, Retrieved 2/21/22. https://library.cqpress.com/cqresearcher/document. php?id=cqresrre1952112200

28   Don Ritchie, U.S. Senate Historian Emeritus. Interview for C-Span. https://www.c-span.org/video/?327983-1/dirksen-senate-office-building

29   How the United States Looked Before the EPA. *Fortune*. Feb. 28, 2017. Part of an EPA photo documentary project called "Project Docuamerica." http://fortune. com/2017/02/28/how-the-united-states-looked-before-the-epa

30   Angier, Natalie. The Wonders of Blood. *New York Times*. Oct. 20, 2008.

31   Cousteau, Jean-Michel. **My Father, The Captain**. *National Geographic*. Page 220.

32   Becoming Cousteau. National Geographic documentary film; writers Mark Monroe and Pax Wassermann. 2021.

33   Block, Peter. **Stewardship: Choosing Service over Self Interest**. Berrett-Koehler Publishers, San Francisco. 1983. Page xx.

34   Wilson, Edward O. **Half-Earth: Our Planet's Fight for Life**. Liveright Publishing Corporation. New York/London. 2016. Page 44.

35   Velders, Guus. Falling Walls: How Repairing the Ozone Hole Helped the Climate. *Scientific American* blog, Nov. 2, 2017. https://blogs.scientificamerican.com/ observations/falling-walls-how-repairing-the-ozone-hole-helped-the-climate

36   Strahan, Susan E. and Anne R. Douglass. Decline in Antarctic Ozone Depletion and Lower Stratospheric Chlorine Determined from Aura Microwave Limb Sounder Observations. Geophysical Research Letters. Jan. 4. 2018. Research Letter 10.1002/2017GLO74830 https://agupubs.onlinelibrary.wiley.com/doi/ epdf/10.1002/2017GL074830

37   Zhang, Sarah. Half of All Plastic That Has Ever Existed Was Made in the Past 13 Years. *The Atlantic*. July 19, 2017. https://www.theatlantic.com/science/ archive/2017/07/plastic-age/533955/

38   Parker, Laura. The Great Pacific Garbage Patch Isn't What You Think It Is. *National Geographic*. March 22, 2018

39   The Ocean Cleanup. www.theoceancleanup.com

40   Helmore, Edward. Flotsam and fashion: recycler of "ghost" fishing nets makes marine litter trendy. *The Guardian*. Oct. 23, 2016.

41   National Geographic digital encyclopedia on the Great Pacific Garbage Patch.

42   NOAA Podcast. https://oceanservice.noaa.gov/podcast/mar18/ nop14-ocean-garbage-patche

43   Climate Action News http://www.climateactionprogramme.org/news/ June 8, 2018.

44   Falk, Pamela. U.S. joins France in push for global treaty to cut ocean plastic pollution. CBS News. Feb. 11, 2022. https://www.cbsnews.com/news/ us-france-push-global-treaty-reduce-ocean-plastic-pollution

45   Danajon Bank Double Barrier Reef: A Unique and Valuable Resource. Alan White slide deck. U.S. Agency for International Development (AID) and FISH Philippines Project. http://www.oneocean.org/download/db_files/danajon/awhite_pps.pdf Retrieved 2/21/22

46   Ocean Conservancy Report. Stemming the Tide: Land-based strategies for a plastic-free ocean. McKinsey Center for Business and Environment. 2017.f

47   Nipa for Roofs and Nipa House Design Philippines, YouTube how-to videos www.youtube.com/watch?v=wE_8jYwH7wQ and https://www.youtube.com/watch?v=ZTCFwxCbM1k

48   Helmore, Edward. Flotsam and fashion: recycler of "ghost" fishing nets makes marine litter trendy. The Guardian. Oct. 23, 2016.

49   Hill, Dr. Nick. NGO voices: An unlikely alliance that is helping people and oceans. Ethical Corporation. www.ethicalcorp.com. Dec. 16, 2016

50   Great Barrier Reef Aquarium website.

51   Fernbach, Nathalie. Recycled ghost fishing nets furnish floors of Townsville aquarium and turtle hospital. ABC North Queensland. July 5, 2017. http://www.abc.net.au/news/2017-07-06/recycled-ghost-nets-underfoot-at-townsville-aquarium/8681556

52   This scene is drawn from a July 14, 2017 video posted by the Reef HQ Great Barrier Reef Aquarium on their Facebook feed.

53   Results of a study by Dr. Catherine M.F. Lohmann, Dr. Shaun D. Cain and Susan A. Dodge published in *Science Journal*, Oct. 12, 2001.

CHAPTER FOUR

54   *Pioneer of the Sea: Jacques Cousteau: The first 75 years*. Documentary film. Director John Soh. Turner Home Entertainment. 1986.

55   Cousteau, Jean-Michel. **My Father the Captain: My Life with Jacques Cousteau**. National Geographic Society, Washington D.C. 2010. Page 224

56   Antarctica New Zealand government agency website. http://www.antarcticanz.govt.nz

57   European Space Agency

58   AntarcticGlaciers.org, supported by the Scientific Committee for Antarctic Research and the Quaternary Research Association. 2018.

59   International Fund for Animal Welfare

60   National Geographic. https://www.nationalgeographic.com/animals/mammals/group/elephant-seals/

61   A Boy Among Polar Bears. BBC Natural World 2005 documentary.

62   McClintock, James. **Lost Antarctica: Adventures in a Disappearing Land**. Palgrave Macmillan, New York NY. 2012. PP. 43-45.

63   Welcome to the Anthropocene. http://www.anthropocene.info/

64   Professor Will Steffen, research project on the trajectory of the Anthropocene, a joint project between the International Geosphere-Biosphere Programme (IGBP) and the Stockholm Resilience Centre.

65   Potenza, Alessandra. "Doomsday" seed vault meant to survive global disasters breached by climate change. The Verge. May 19, 2017. https://www.theverge.com

66   Novella, Steven. The Marshmallow Test. Neurologica Blog. March 18, 2013. https://theness.com/neurologicablog/index.php/the-marshmallow-test/

67   Mccrory Calarco, Jessica. Why Rich Kids Are So Good at the Marshmallow Test. *The Atlantic*. June 1, 2018., by https://www.theatlantic.com/family/archive/2018/06/marshmallow-test/561779/

68   Jacques Cousteau. Television Interview on the program *Manufacturing Consent*. 1991

69   Primary authors Dr. Gabreil G. Nahas, Dr. E. Allan Farnsworth, both of Columbia University, and Dr. H. Stanley Thayer of the City College of New York. (Source: **The Cousteau Almanac: An Inventory of Life on Our Water Planet**. Jacques-Yves Cousteau and the staff of The Cousteau Society, Dolphin Books, Doubleday, New York. 1980. P. xix.)

70   Cousteau Society Bill of Rights of Future Generations. https://www.cousteau.org

71   UNESCO Declaration on the Responsibilities of the Present Generations Towards Future Generations. Adopted November 12, 1997. www.unesco.org

72   Developing Priorities for the Future Generations Commissioner. 2017. https://future-generations.wales/

73   Organic Trade Association. Get the facts about Organic Cotton. https://ota.com/advocacy/organic-standards/fiber-and-textiles/get-facts-about-organic-cotton

74   Oceans 2050 website. Oct. 22, 2020. Retrieved 9/13/2021. https://www.oceans2050.com/news/mbfy606l4v7c5neqc9r9p9p4ic59ii

75   Duarte, Carlos M., with Susana Agusti, Edward Barbier, Gregory L. Britten, Juan Carlos Castilla, Jean-Pierre Gattuso, Robinson W. Fulweiler, Terry P. Hughes, Nancy Knowlton, Catherine E. Lovelock, Heike K. Lotze, Milica Predragovic, Elvira Poloczanska, Callum Roberts & Boris Worm . Rebuilding Marine Life. Nature. inter-https://doi.org/10.1038/s41586-020-2146-7. Received: 24 May 2019. Page 1.

76   Landis, Emily. Why Blue Carbon is REDD Hot. The Nature Conservancy. https://oceanwealth.org/why-blue-carbon-is-redd-hot/. Retrieved 9/14/2021.

77   Cousteau, Alexandra. Remarks to The Nature Conservancy at the 51st Annual Earth Day Summit. April 21, 2021.

PART TWO

CHAPTER ONE

78   Anita Roddick and various authors. **The Body Shop Book**. Macdonald & Co Publishers Ltd. Great Britain. 1985. Page 7

79   Roddick, Anita. **Body and Soul: Profits with Principles, The Amazing Success Story of Anita Roddick and The Body Shop.** The Body Shop International and Crown Publishing. 1991. Pages 31-58.

80   **Body and Soul**. Pages 72, 73, 159.

81   Butler, Sarah. L'Oreal to sell Body Shop to Brazil's Nature in 1billion Euro deal. *The Guardian*. June 9, 2017. Retrieved 1/28/2021.

CHAPTER TWO

82   www.conservation.org. Retrieved 4/22/2021.

83   Politi, Daniel. 'Everything is Dry': In Argentina, a Vanishing Life. *New York Times*. September 5, 2021. Page A4.

84   Every Culture digital resource. https://www.everyculture.com/wc/Brazil-to-Congo-Republic-of/Kayapos.html#ixzz6SNeu3gL1

85   Astor, Michael. Paulinho Paiakan, Indigenous Defender of Rainforest, Dies at 67. *New York Times*. June 23, 2020.

86   Every Culture digital resource. https://www.everyculture.com/wc/Brazil-to-Congo-Republic-of/Kayapos.html#ixzz6SNeu3gL1

87   Roddick, Anita. **Business as Usual: The Triumph of Anita Roddick**. Thorsons, London. Harper Collins. 2000. Page 24.

88   Global Impact Investing Network (GIIN) IRIS System. iris.thegiin.org/core-characteristics-of-impact-investing/

89   Klinger-Vidra, Robyn. **Social Impact: Origins and Evolution of the Term**. Global Policy Journal. Dec. 19. 2019.

90   Chang, Ann Mei. **Lean Impact: How to Innovate for Radically Greater Social Good**. John Wiley and Sons, Inc. Hoboken, NJ. 2019. Page 247.

91   Morgan Stanley 2020 Sustainability Report. Page 10.

92   India's Mandatory CRS Law Inspires Innovation. Triple Pundit. Oct. 8, 2014.

93   Bertolini, Mark. **Mission-Driven Leadership: My Journey as a Radical Capitalist**. Crown Publishing Group. New York. 2019. Page 166.

94   **Body and Soul** Pages 200-201.

95   Chemnick, Jean. Amazon Deforestation Falls Where Land is under Indigenous Control. Scientific American E&E News. August 11, 2020

96   Higgins, Tiffany. Belo Monte boondoggle: Brazil's biggest, costliest dam may be unviable. *Mongabay News*. Jan. 17, 2020. https://news.mongabay.com/2020/01/belo-monte-boondoggle-brazils-biggest-costliest-dam-may-be-unviable/

97   Politi, Daniel. 'Everything is Dry': In Argentina, a Vanishing Life. *New York Times*, Sept. 5, 2021. Page A4.

98   Piotrowski, Jan and Miranda X Not in my valley: Dams in the Amazon. *The Economist*, Nov. 5, 2016.

99   Brown, Chip. Photographs by Martin Schoeller. Kayapo Courage, *National Geographic*. January 2014. https://www.nationalgeographic.com/magazine/article/kayapo-courage

100   http://voices.nationalgeographic.com/2015/12/07/kayapo-filmmaker-video-is-our-bow/

CHAPTER THREE

101   Perreault, Abbey. Brazil Nuts Are Brought to You by Rodents. Atlas Obscura. Sept. 14, 2018. Retrieved 4/5/2022.

102   Astor, Michael. Paulinho Paiakan, Indigenous Defender of Rainforest, Dies at 67. *New York Times*. June 23, 2020.

103   Blundell, Sally. **The No-Nonsense Guide to Fair Trade**. New Internationalist Publications, London. 2013. Pages 8-10, 25, 26, 136.

104   Ibid Pages 8, 10, 25, 26, 38, 42, 131.

105   Kukolic, Slobhan. Are You Laying Bricks or Building a Cathedral? Huffington Post. 10/19/2017. Accessed 1/6/2021. https://www.huffpost.com/entry/are-you-laying-bricks-or-_b_12387634

106   Wilhelm, Kevin. **Return on Sustainability: How Business Can Increase Profitability & Address Climate Change in an Uncertain Economy**. 2009. Dog Ear Publishing. P. 139.

107   Comments at National Geographic panel, Exploring Sustainable City Solutions. June 1, 2017. Washington D.C.

108   Candela Annual Sustainability Report 2018. Retrieved 3/9/2021. www.candelaperu.net

109   Thunderbird School of Global Management, Arizona State University. thunderbird.asu.edu/global-impact/programs/strengthening-women-entrepreneurs-peru Retrieved 1/17/2021.

110   **Body and Soul**. Page 73.

CHAPTER FOUR

111   **The Body Shop Book**. Macdonald & Co Publishers Ltd. Great Britain, 1985. Page 7.

112   Note: L'Oreal would in eventually sell The Body Shop to Brazilian cosmetics company Natura & Co in 2017.

113   Pitman, Simon. Body Shop owner defends selling to L'Oreal. Nov. 3, 2006. *Cosmetic Design*. Cosmeticdesign.com. Retrieved 1/28/2021.

114   L'Oreal 2015 Progress Report: Sharing Beauty with All, The Loreal Sustainability Commitment, www.sharingbeautywithall.com

115   Meadows, Donella H and Dennis L, Jorgen Randers and William W. Behrens III. The Limits to Growth: A Report for the Club of Rome's Project on the Predicament of Mankind. Universe Books, New York, NY. 1972. P.9.

116   Tyson Backs Chicken Fat-to-Fuel project. November 18, 2007. GreenBiz. https://www.greenbiz.com

117   Dr. Niccolo Athens, Professor of Composition at Tianjin Juilliard School, personal communication.

118   http://www.quotationspage.com/quote/27413.html

119   Phil Hansen. Embrace the Shake. TED talk 2013. http://blog.ted.com/embrace-the-shake-phil-hansen-at-ted2013

120 Paprocki, Sherry Beck. **Anita Roddick: Entrepreneur. Women of Achievement Series**. Chelsea House Publishing. New York NY. 2010. Page 76

121 European Commission website. https://ec.europa.eu/food/animals/welfare_en Retrieved 5/1/2021

122 Practice Greenhealth. Practicegreenhealth.org/waste. Retrieved 2/6/2021.

123 Booth, Sara. Reducing Waste in the Operating Room. Sustainable City Network. July 1, 2015. http://www.sustainablecitynetwork.com/topic_channels/community/article_ 4f75089a-2023-11e5-845d-77ea3aaa4065.html

124 Medical Waste Management Market to Reach USD 17.89 Billion by 2026/Reports and Data. Globe Newswire. Nov.26, 2019. New York. Retrieved 2/6/2021. https://www.glo-benewswire.com/news-release/2019/11/26/1952758/0/en/Medical-Waste-Management-Market-To-Reach-USD-17-89-Billion-by-2026-Reports-And-Data.html

125 Gotkine, Elliot, Bloomberg, Loreal Makes Fake Skin as Animal Testing Ban Looms. July 15, 2011. Loreal data is for 2010.

126 Zhang, Sarah. Inside the Lab that Grows Human Skin to Test Your Cosmetics. *Wired*. 12.3 0.16. https://www.wired.com/2016/12/inside-lab-grows-human-skin-test-cosmetics/

127 New England Anti-Vivisection Society. http://www.neavs.org/alternatives/in-testing

128 Testing cosmetics on animals: MEPs call for worldwide ban. *European Parliament News*. March 5, 2018. Retrieved 5/9/2021. https://www.europarl.europa.eu/news

129 Organovo Press Release. New York, May 5, 2015 /PRNewswire/ www.organovo.com

PART THREE

CHAPTER ONE

130 Smithsonian National Portrait Gallery. Exhibition label accompanying portrait of César Chávez.

131 Del Castillo, Richard Griswold, and Richard A. Garcia. **César Chávez: A Triumph of Spirit**. University of Oklahoma Press. Norman, Oklahoma. 1995. Page 4.

132 Dunbar-Ortiz, Roxanne. **An Indigenous People's History of the United States**. Beacon Press, Boston, Massachusetts. 2014. Pages 20-22.

CHAPTER TWO

133 Ferriss, Susan and Ricardo Sandoval. **The Fight in the Fields: César Chavez and the Farmworkers Movement**. Harcourt Brace and Company, Orlando, Florida. 1997. Page 15.

134 Pawel, Miriam. **The Crusades of César Chavez**. Bloomsbury Press, New York, NY. 2014. Pages 8, 9.

135 La Botz, Dan. **César Chávez and la Causa.** Pearson Education, 2006. Page 2.

136   González Stuart, Ph.D., Armando. Plants Used in Mexican Traditional Medicine: Their Application and Effects in Traditional Healing Practices. UTEP/UT Austin Cooperative Pharmacy Program.

137   **The Fight in the Fields**. Page 13.

138   **César Chávez and la Causa**. Page 4.

139   **The Fight in the Fields**, Pages 17, 18.

140   The Dust Bowl. Ken Burns documentary mini-series. 2012.

141   **The Fight in the Fields**. Page 16.

142   Taylor, Ronald B. **Chavez and the Farm Workers: A Study in the Acquisition and Use of Power**. Beacon Press. Boston, Massachusetts. 1975. Page 64.

143   **The Fight in the Fields**. Page 20.

144   **Chavez and the Farmworkers**. Pages 65, 66.

145   Fraser Federal Reserve History site. https://fraser.stlouisfed.org/

146   **The Fight in the Fields**. Page 20.

147   **Chavez and the Farm Workers**. Page 61.

148   **The Fight in the Fields**. Page 20.

149   Ibid. Page 26, 27.

150   Holck, Lott. Diversity leads to greater social coherence and well-being. March 22, 2018. Science Nordic. http://sciencenordic.com/diversity-leads-greater-social-coherence-and-well-being

151   Ibid.

152   Benefits of Being Inclusive. The Denver Foundation's Inclusiveness Project. http://www.nonprofitinclusiveness.org/benefits-being-inclusive

153   PolicyLink, www.policylink.org

154   Lange, Martin, Friedhelm Pfeiffer, and Gerard J. van den Berg. Integrating young male refugees: initial evidence from an inclusive soccer project. *Journal for Labour Market Research*. December 2017. 51:6. https://link.springer.com/article/10.1186/s12651-017-0234-4

155   Page, Nanette and Cheryl E. Czuba. Empowerment: What Is It? *The Journal of Extension* Oct. 1999 Vol 37 Number 5.

156   Asante, Shafik. What Is Inclusion? http://www.inclusion.com

157   Dismantling Racism Works. White Supremacy Culture in Organizations. Published by Centre for Community Organizations, Montreal, Quebec. https://coco-net.org/wp-content/uploads/2019/11/Coco-WhiteSupCulture-ENG4.pdf

158   Randel, Becky. How Chef José Andrés Put Aside Partisanship to Provide Disaster Relief: 'This Isn't About Pollitics' *People*, Dec. 18, 2017. https://people.com/food/jose-andres-california-wildfires-puerto-rico-hurricane/

159   World Central Kitchen website. https://www.worldcentralkitchen.org

160   Ibid.

161 El Boricua, a cultural publication for Puerto Ricans. http://www.elboricua.com/sancocho.html

162 Severson, Kim. Jose Andres Fed Puerto Rico, and May Change How Aid Is Given. *New York Times*. Oct. 30, 2017.

163 Brindley, David. Months After Hurricane Maria, Puerto Rico Still Struggling. National Geographic Magazine. July 2018. Corrected online August 2018. https://www.nationalgeographic.com/magazine/2018/03/puerto-rico-after-hurricane-maria-dispatches/

164 Guideposts Interview with Jose Andres. July 26, 2018. https://bit.ly/2MoVmbK

165 Carrión, José B. and Andrew G. Biggs. Don't blame Puerto Rico's poor economy on hurricanes. The Washington Post. Dec. 17, 2018.

166 Facebook Video Sept. 18, 2018. On behalf of WhenWeAllVote.org

CHAPTER THREE

167 Anderson, Carl and Msgr. Eduardo Chavez. Our Lady of Guadalupe: Mother of the Civilization of Love. Doubleday Press. 2009. Page 78.

168 Matthiessen, Peter. **Sal Si Puedes (Escape If You Can): César Chavez and the New American Revolution**. University of California Press, Berkeley. 1969. P. xxvii

169 **The Fight in the Fields**. Pages 185, 187, 188.

170 **The Crusades of César Chavez.** Page 166

171 Ibid. Page 190

172 Marc Grossman Forward to **Sal Si Puedes (Escape If You Can): César Chavez and the New American Revolution**. University of California Press, Berkeley. 1969. Page xliii.

173 Alinsky, Saul. **Rule for Radicals: A Pragmatic Primer for Realistic Radicals**. Vintage Books, Random House, Inc. New York, NY. 1979. Page 3.

174 Sharp, Gene. "198 Methods of Nonviolent Action." Reproduced broadly, originally appeared in **The Politics of Nonviolent Action**. Boston, MA. Porter Sargent. 1973.

175 Dolores Huerta Foundation. Doloreshuerta.org. Retrieved 9/5/2021.

176 Dunne, John Gregory. **Delano: The Story of the California Grape Strike**. Farrar, Straus & Giroux. New York, NY. 1967. Page 15.

177 Ibid. Pages 14, 25

178 **The Crusades of César Chavez.** Pages 121, 123.

179 **The Fight in the Fields**. Page 116.

180 https://youtu.be/MExv2bSnikQ

181 **The Crusades of César Chavez**. P. 123

182 César Chavez Speech: Perigrinacion, Penitencia, Revolution. Chavez Foundation.

183 Ibid.

184 **Sal Si Puedes.** P. 137.

185 Ibid. P. 128.

186   **Sal Si Puedes.** Page134.

187   **The Fight in the Fields.** Page 128.

188   Ibid. Page 112.

189   **The Fight in the Fields**. Page 117.

190   San Jose's Luis Valdez marks 50 years as cultural icon. El Teatro Campesino
       website. Nov. 2, 2015. http://elteatrocampesino.com/uncategorized/
       san-joses-luis-valdez-marks-50-years-as-cultural-icon/

191   Perez, Frank. El Teatro Campesino: Fifty Years and Counting. Benito Link.
       San Benito County online news. November 9, 2015. https://benitolink.com/
       el-teatro-campesino-fifty-years-and-counting/

192   United Farmworkers website.

193   **The Fight in the Fields.** Page 111.

194   Perez, Frank. El Teatro Campesino: Fifty Years and Counting. Benito Link.
       San Benito County online news. November 9, 2015. https://benitolink.com/
       el-teatro-campesino-fifty-years-and-counting/

195   Sinatra House website. https://www.sinatrahouse.com/

196   **Sal Si Puedes**. Page 129.

197   **The Crusades of César Chavez.** Page 130.

198   **The Fight in the Fields.** Page 122.

199   Address to the Commonwealth Club of California. Delivered Nov. 9, 1984.

200   United Nations Foundation. https://unfoundation.org/

201   Galtung, Johan. Violence, Peace, and Peace Research. Journal of Peace Research. Vol.
       6 No. 3. 1969. From the JSTOR archive. Retrieved 9/13/19.

202   **Gandhi on Non-Violence**, Selected Texts from Mohandas K. Gandhi's Non-Violence
       in Peace and War. Edited by Thomas Merton. New York: New Editions. Originally
       published 1965. I-121 and 172

203   Pink, Daniel. H., **A Whole New Mind: Why right-brainers will rule the future**.
       2005 Riverhead Books: Penguin Publishing. P. 159.

204   Huntington, Samuel P. **Who Are We: The Challenges to American's National
       Identity**. Simon and Schuster. New York, NY. 2004. Pages 12-13.

205   Lewis, John. *Together, You Can Redeem the Soul of Our Nation*. New York Times
       Opinion. July 30, 2020.

206   Sheehy, Gail. *This is not normal: At Yale, Psychiatrists Cite Their 'Duty to Warn' About
       an Unfit President*. April 23, 2017. New York Intelligencer.

207   Lee, Bandy. Trump is now dangerous – that makes his mental health a matter of pub-
       lic interest. *The Guardian*. January 6, 2018. Retrieved 9/12/19.

208   Lee, Bandy X, Peter D. Donnelly, Larry Cohen, Shikha Garg. Violence, health and the
       2030 Agenda: Merging evidence and implementation. *Journal of Public Health Policy*.
       Sept. 2016, Volume 37, Supplement 1, pp. 1-12, accessed 9/12/19 from Springer Link.
       https://link.springer.com/article/10.1057/s41271-016-0011-6

209   Internet Movie Database. IMDB. Retrieved 2/21/22.

210   McNulty, Charles. Review: *Luis Valdez's 'Valley of the Heart' shares an immigrant story from California's past*. Los Angeles Times. Nov. 9, 2018. https://www.latimes.com/entertainment/arts/theater/reviews/la-et-cm-valley-of-the-heart-review-20181109-story.html

211   El Teatro Campesino website. http://elteatrocampesino.com

212   **Sal Si Puedes**. Page xxxi.

213   Campesina Radio Network website. http://campesina.com/

214   Banerjee, Sashwati. Managing Director, Sesame Workshop India. *Hello Tomorrow: The Power of Community Radio for Social Change.* Indian Media & Entertainment Industry Report. Posted Feb. 12, 2017 on medium.com. https://medium.com/@SesameinIndia/hello-tomorrow-the-power-of-community-radio-for-social-change-c22e35b0f47e

215   Marshall, Alex, Carlotta Gail and Elisabetta Povoledo. Four Months, 5,000 Miles: A Refugee Puppet Looks for Home. New York Times. Nov. 10, 2021.

216   Rieff, David. Battle over the banlieues. *New York Times Magazine.* April 14, 2007.

217   Carroll, Rory. "Proud to be Mexican": Meet the baby whose huge image gazes over the border. *The Guardian*. Sept. 18, 2017. https://www.theguardian.com/us-news/2017/sep/18/proud-to-be-mexican-meet-the-baby-whose-huge-image-gazes-over-the-border

218   Drillinger, Meagan. A big year pushes Mexico up the tourism ranking. *Travel Weekly*. April 18, 2018. https://www.travelweekly.com/Mexico-Travel/Big-year-pushes-Mexico-up-tourism-ranking

219   Pew Research Center research on Hispanic Trends. https://www.pewresearch.org/hispanic/2015/11/19/more-mexicans-leaving-than-coming-to-the-u-s/

220   May, Kate Torgovnick. Gallery: Portraits of people who've been overlooked. Ideas. TED.Com. Nov. 28, 2017. https://ideas.ted.com/powerful-portraits-of-people-whove-been-overlooked/

221   Stewart, Jessica. Street Artist JR Installs Massive Face of a Child on Mexican Side of US Border Wall. My Modern Met. Sept. 7, 2017. https://mymodernmet.com/jr-street-artist-mexican-border-wall/

222   Carroll, Rory. "Proud to be Mexican": Meet the baby whose huge image gazes over the border. *The Guardian*. Sept. 18, 2017. https://www.theguardian.com/us-news/2017/sep/18/proud-to-be-mexican-meet-the-baby-whose-huge-image-gazes-over-the-border

CHAPTER FOUR

223   **The Crusades of César Chavez**. Page 241.

224   Case Western Reserve Encyclopedia of Cleveland History. https://case.edu/ech/articles/f/fisher-foods-inc

225   Anita Myerson, Cleveland Ohio. Personal communication November 8, 2019

226   Flyer from personal files of Anita Meyerson.

227   "Building the Winning Boycott" handout from personal files of Anita Meyerson.

228   O'Keefe, Ed. Reverend leads ironing board brigade. *Washington Post*. Sept. 6, 2012.

229   Pledge Card from Personal files of Anita Meyerson.

230 El Macriado Archive. Vol. VI # 23, Nov. 30 1973. https://libraries.ucsd.edu/farmworkermovement/archives/

231 "Building the Winning Boycott" handout from Personal files of Anita Meyerson.

232 Congregation of St. Joseph website. https://www.csjoseph.org

233 Riser Foods, Inc. History. http://www.fundinguniverse.com/company-histories/riser-foods-inc-history/

234 Anita Myerson, Cleveland Ohio. Personal communication 11/8/2019 and undated newspaper clipping from her personal files

235 **The Crusades of César Chavez**. Page 186 and personal communication with Judith Corrigan.

236 **The Crusades of César Chavez**. Page 188.

237 El Macriado Archive. Vol VII #11, Nov. 18, 1974. https://libraries.ucsd.edu/farmworkermovement/archives/

238 United Farmworkers chronology. https://ufw.org/research/history/ufw-chronology/

239 **The Fight in the Fields.** Page 191.

240 **The Crusades of César Chavez.** Page 302.

241 Ibid. Pages 305-307.

242 Pawel, Miriam. **The Browns of California: The Family Dynasty that Transformed a State and Shaped a Nation**. Bloomsbury Publishing, New York. 2018. Page 239.

243 Pawel, Miriam. The Sad Lesson from California. NYT Opinion. July 16, 2019.

244 Kania, John and Mark Kramer. Collective Impact. *Stanford Social Innovation Review*. Winter 2011. Copyright 2011 by Leland Stanford Jr. University. Page 36.

245 Kania, John, Junious Williams, Paul Schmitz, Sheri Brady, Mark Kramer and Jennifer Splansky Jester. Centering Equity in Collective Impact. *Stanford Social Innovation Review*. Winter 2022. Page 38.

246 Kania, John and Mark Kramer. Collective Impact. *Stanford Social Innovation Review*. Winter 2011. Copyright 2011 by Leland Stanford Jr. University. Page 39.

247 Ibid. Page 39.

248 Orpheus Chamber Orchestra website. https://orpheusnyc.org/about-orpheus/

249 Channeling Change: Making Collective Impact Work. Hanleybrown, Fay, John Kania and Mark Kramer. *Stanford Social Innovation Review*. Pages 5, 7.

250 American Hospital Association. 2017 Chair Files. Listening, Linking and Leveraging to Improve Community Health. http://www.hpoe.org/resources/chair-files/3022

251 Pawel, Miriam. The Sad Lesson from California. NYT Opinion. July 16, 2019.

252 Arnold, Chad. Farmworkers are getting these new rights in New York. *Democrat & Chronicle*. July 17, 2019. https://www.democratandchronicle.com/story/news/politics/albany/2019/07/17/farmworkers-getting-these-new-rights-new-york/1754407001/

253 Olmos, Sergio. Hard Jobs Turn Perilous on Farms. New York Times. Sept. 5, 2021. Business Section Page 6.

254 Alianza Nacional De Campesinas: Organizing for Equity and Justice. https://www. alianzanacionaldecampesinas.org/

255 Patel, Raj. **The Value of Nothing: How to reshape market society and redefine democracy**. Picador Press, New York. 2009. Page 125.

256 Coalition of Immokalee Workers website. https://ciw-online.org/about/

257 United States Environmental Protection Agency website. DDT – A Brief History and Status.

258 **The Crusades of César Chavez**. Page 458.

259 Environmental Working Group annual "Dirty Dozen" produce list. https://www.ewg. org/foodnews/dirty-dozen.php

260 Mom's Clean Air Force website. https://www.momscleanairforce.org/our-mission/

261 Rémy, Dominique. For These Latina Activists, the Struggle for Climate Justice & Racial Justice Must Be Fought Together. *Remezcla*. November 2019. https://remezcla. com/features/culture/latina-activists-fighting-climate-racial-justice/

262 12/20/2019. Gabriela Rivera y Dolores Huerta. Facebook Live. https://www.facebook. com/watch/?v=769503140183168

263 Environmental Defense Fund. Estimating the Health Impacts of Coal-Fired Power Plants Receiving International Financing. Penney, Sarah, Facob Bell, M. Sc, Johan Balbus, MD, MPH. 2009. https://www.edf.org

264 Union of Concerned Scientists. Coal Power Impacts. Nov. 17, 2017, updated July 9, 2019. https://www.ucsusa.org/resources/coal-power- impacts#:~:text=Coal%20 and%20Air%20Pollution,environmental%20and%20public%20health%20impacts. Retrieved Feb. 10, 2022, and Duke University School of Medicine. Duke Health News. Oct. 12, 2018.
https://surgery.duke.edu/news/
despite-studies-health-effects-coal-burning-power-plants-remain-unknown

265 LinkedIn profile. www.linkedin.com

266 Orlando Utilities Commission. https://www.ouc.com/about-ouc/facts-facilities

267 For more on Michelle Irizarry's artwork, see https://miriza.com/

268 PBS EcoSense for Living Episode: Do We Still Need the Clean Air Act? 4/20/2019 https://www.pbs.org/show/ecosense-living/

269 Mom's Clean Air Force. Michelle Irizarry video clip. Facebook feed Oct. 9, 2018

270 Brugges, James. Coal Powered the Industrial Revolution. It Left Behind an 'Absolutely Massive' Environmental Catastrophe. Inside Climate News. Dec. 12, 2021. https://insideclimatenews.org/news/12122021/coal-powered-the-industrial-revolu-tion-it-left-behind-an-absolutely-massive-environmental-catastrophe/

271 2020 Electric Integrated Resource Plan Report. Orlando Utilities Commission. Nov. 2020. Prepared by Siemens. https://oucroadmap.com/wp-content/uploads/2020/11/ Siemens_OUC-2020-EIRP-Draft-Report_11.09.2020.pdf

272   Orlando Science Center. Exhibition notes. Earth's Voice: An Environmental Art Exhibit shows our planet through artist's eyes. https://www.osc.org/environmental-art-exhibit-earths-voice-opens-at-orlando-science-center/. Retrieved 9/12/2021.

273   PBS EcoSense for Living Episode: Do We Still Need the Clean Air Act? 4/20/2019 https://www.pbs.org/show/ecosense-living/

274   https://www.momscleanairforce.org/

AFTERWORD

275   Fothergill, Alistair. **Planet Earth As You've Never Seen It Before**. University of California Press, Berkeley, Los Angeles, 2007. Pages 13, 14.

Also by Lucia Athens

Building An Emerald City
A Guide to Creating Green Building Policies and Programs